Why? Why? Why?

Why? Why? Why?

Miles Kelly Publishing

First published in 2005 by
Miles Kelly Publishing Ltd
Bardfield Centre, Great Bardfield, Essex, CM7 4SL

2 4 6 8 10 9 7 5 3

Editorial Director
Belinda Gallagher

Art Director
Jo Brewer

Editorial Assistant
Amanda Askew

Authors
Camilla de la Bedoyere, Catherine Chambers,
Chris Oxlade

Designers
Jo Brewer, Venita Kidwai,
Sophie Pelham, Elaine Wilkinson

Jacket Designer
Tom Slemmings

Indexer
Helen Snaith

Production
Estela Boulton, Elizabeth Brunwin

Reprographics
Anthony Cambray, Mike Coupe, Ian Paulyn

Cartoons
Mark Davis, The Maltings Partnership

ISBN 1-84236-597-5

Printed in China

British Library Cataloguing-in-Publication Data
A catalogue record for this book is available
from the British Library

www.mileskelly.net
info@mileskelly.net

Contents

Far-out questions about...

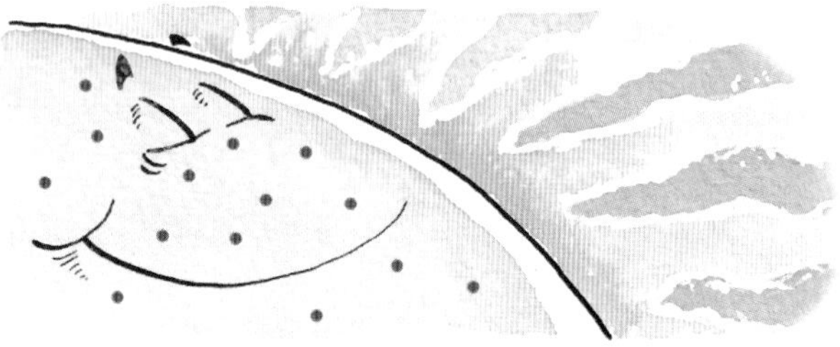

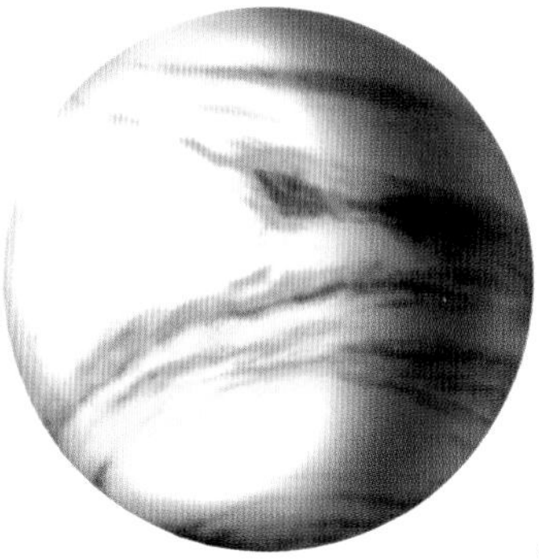

Space

Which star keeps us warm?

The Sun does. It is a star like all the others in the night sky, but it is much closer to Earth. The Sun is a giant ball of hot, glowing gas and it gives off heat that keeps the Earth warm. It also gives us light.

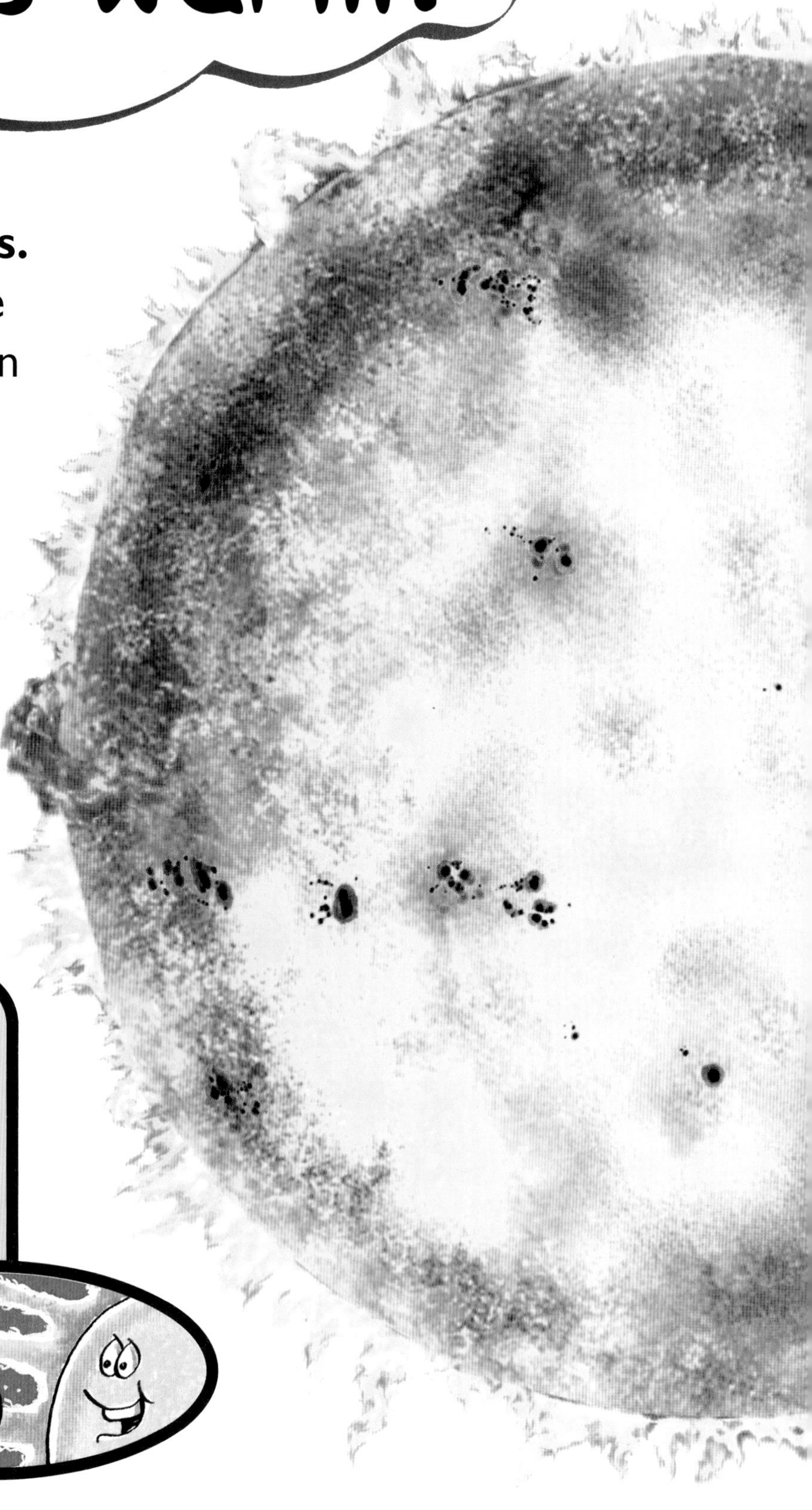

Hot hot hot!

The Sun's surface is so hot that it would melt a metal spacecraft flying near it! It is 15 times hotter than boiling water.

When is it night time during the day?

Sometimes the Sun, the Earth and the Moon all line up in space. When this happens, the Moon's shadow falls on the Earth, making it dark even if it's daytime. This is called an eclipse.

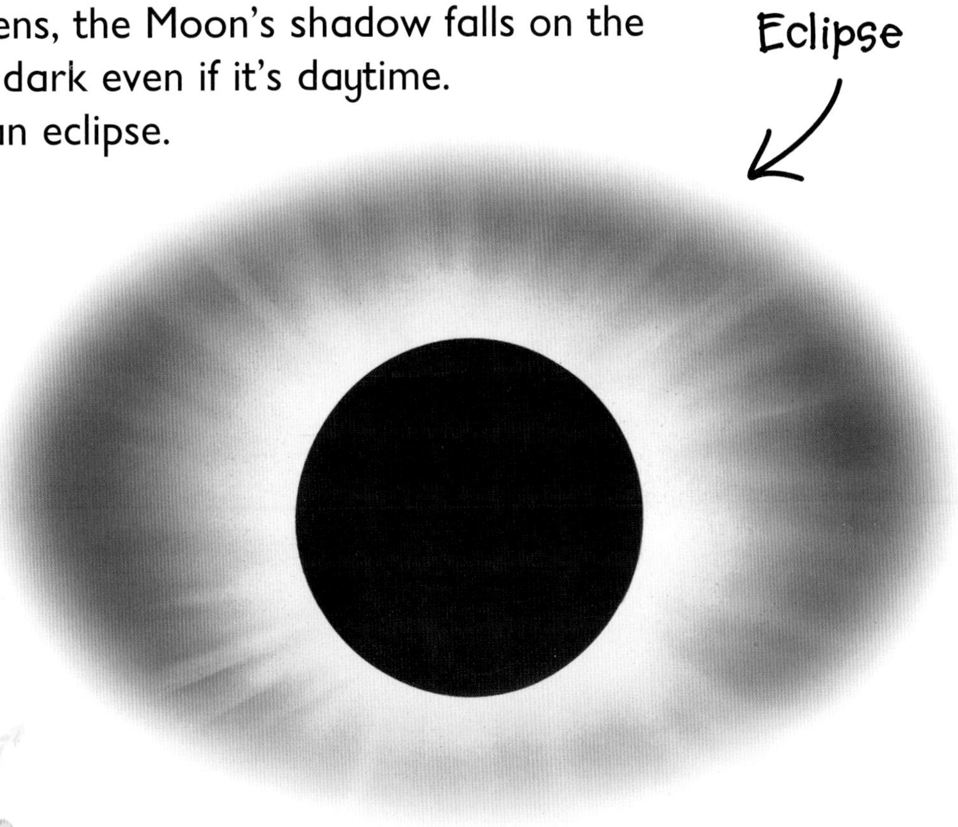

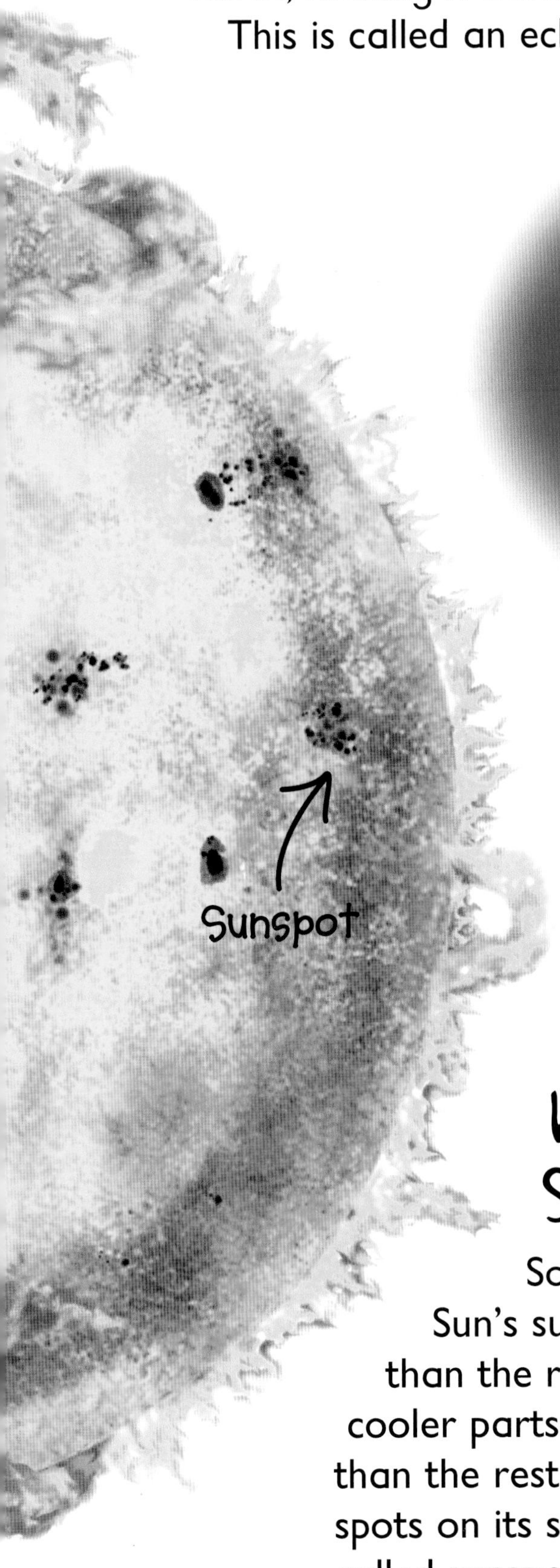

Why is the Sun spotty?

Some parts of the Sun's surface are cooler than the rest of it. These cooler parts appear darker than the rest of the Sun, like spots on its surface. They are called sunspots.

Remember

Never look straight at the Sun. Your eyes could be badly damaged.

Is Earth the only planet near the Sun?

There are eight other planets near the Sun. Mercury and Venus are nearer to the Sun than the Earth is. The other planets are further away. All the planets move around the Sun in huge circles. The Sun and its family of planets is called the Solar System.

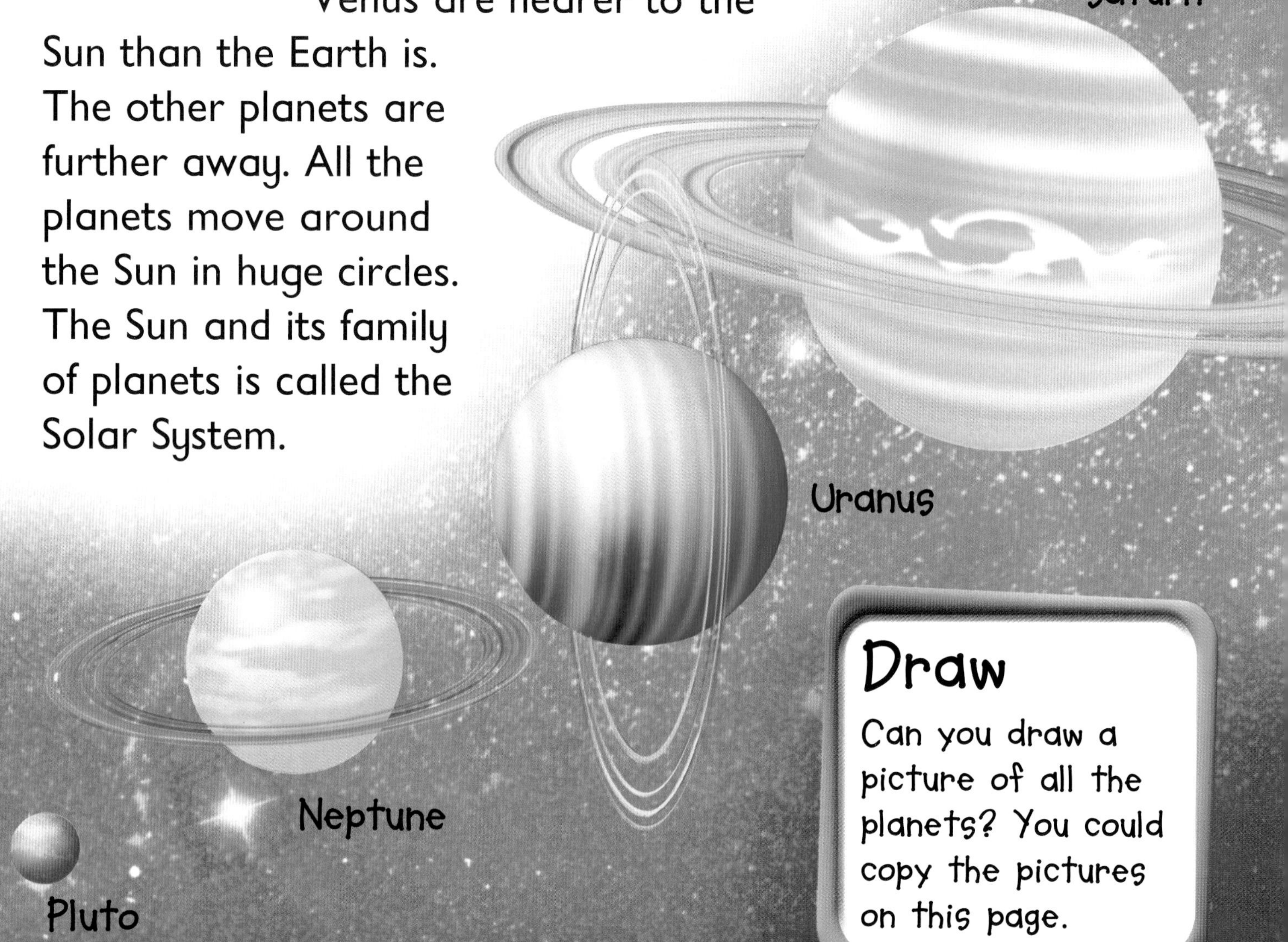

Draw

Can you draw a picture of all the planets? You could copy the pictures on this page.

Do other planets have moons?

Earth is not the only planet with a moon. Mars has two moons. Jupiter and Saturn have more than 30 moons each. Venus and Mercury are the only planets with no moons.

What are the other planets like?

Mercury, Venus and Mars are rocky planets, like the Earth. They have solid surfaces. Jupiter, Saturn, Uranus and Neptune are balls of gas and liquid. They are much bigger than the rocky planets. The last planet, Pluto, is solid and icy.

One big, happy family!

There are millions of smaller members in the Sun's family. Tiny specks of dust speed between the planets along with chunks of rock called asteroids.

What is inside the Earth?

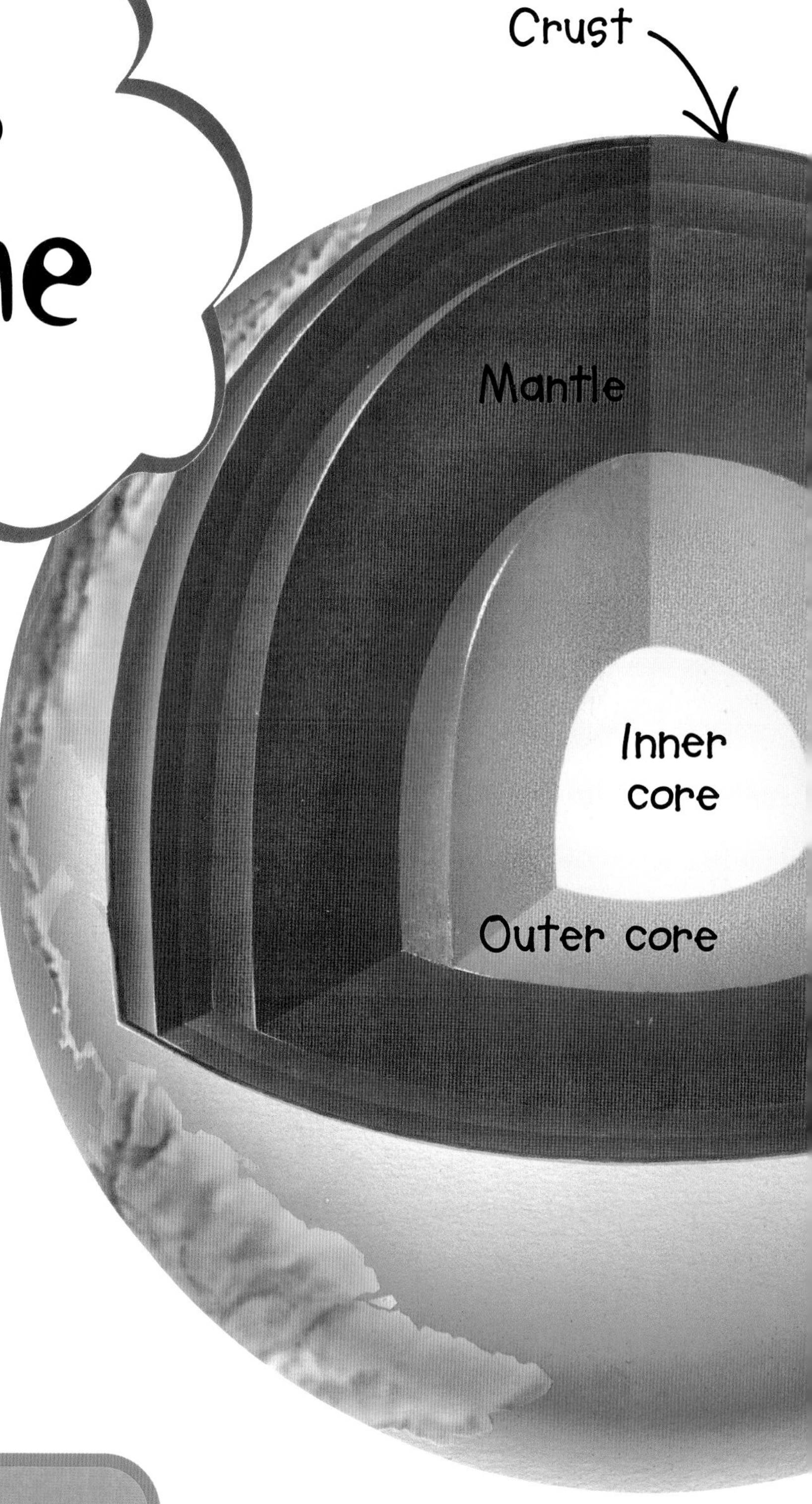

There are layers of hot rock inside the Earth. We live on the Earth's surface where the rock is solid. Beneath the surface, the rock is hot. In some places, it has melted. This melted rock may leak from a volcano.

Living it up!

Earth is the only planet with water on its surface. This means that people, plants and animals can live here. No life has yet been found on other planets.

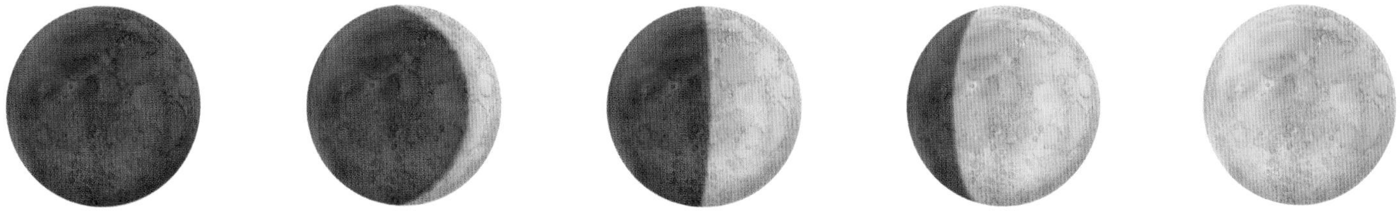

New Moon | Crescent Moon | First quarter Moon | Gibbous Moon | Full Moon

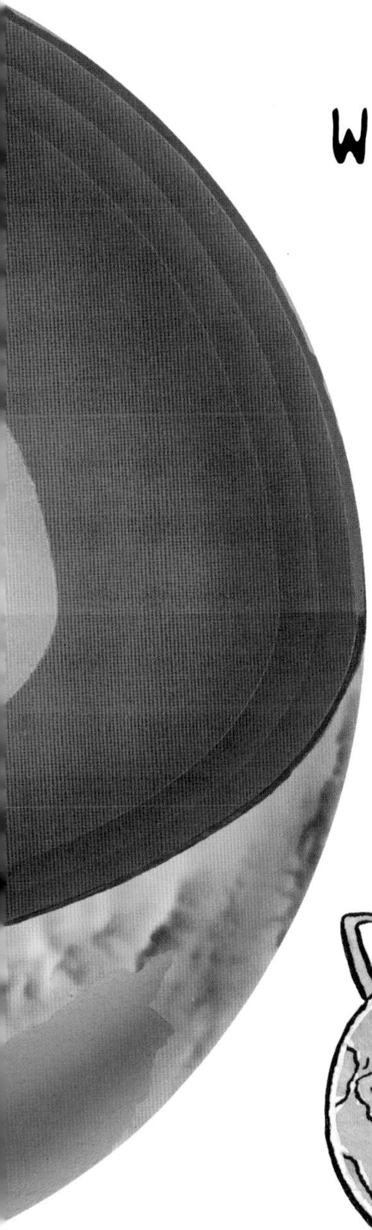

Why does the Moon change shape?

The Sun lights up one side of the Moon. The other side is dark. As the Moon circles the Earth, we see different parts of the lit side. This is why the Moon seems to change shape.

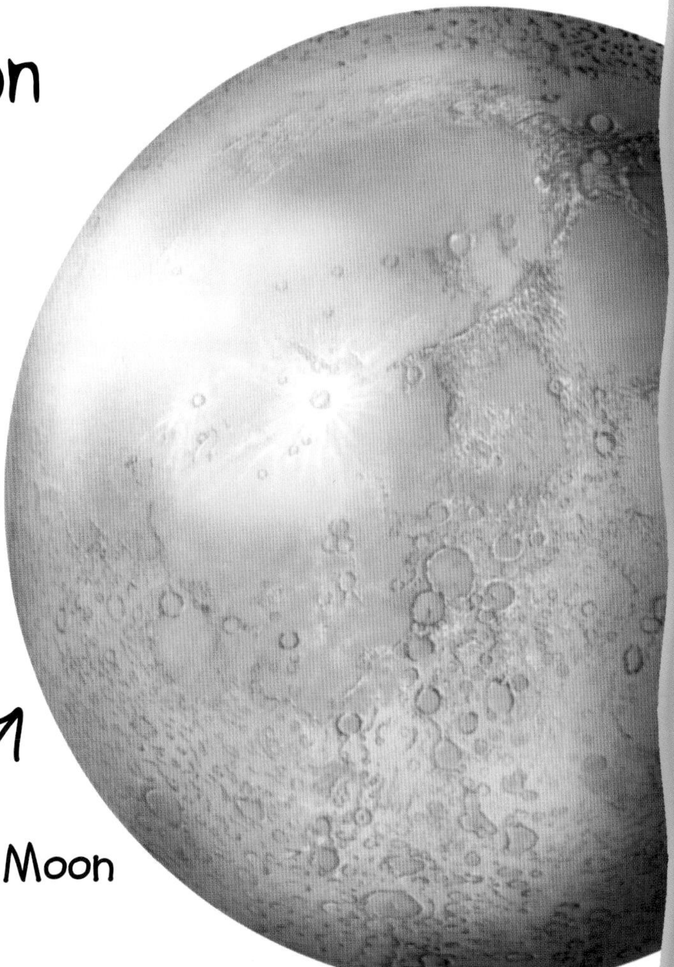

The Moon

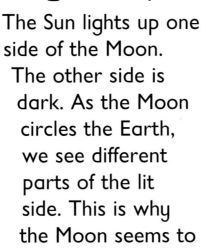

Why do we have day and night?

The Earth spins round once every day. When the part you live on faces the Sun, it is daytime. When this part faces away from the Sun, the sunlight can't reach you. Then it is night time.

Look

Look at the picture of the Moon. The circles are called craters. They were made by lumps of rock smashing into the Moon's surface.

What is the hottest planet?

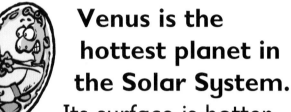

Venus is the hottest planet in the Solar System. Its surface is hotter than the inside of an oven. Venus is covered in a blanket of thick, yellow gas. The gases trap heat from the Sun but don't let it escape. This means that Venus can't cool down.

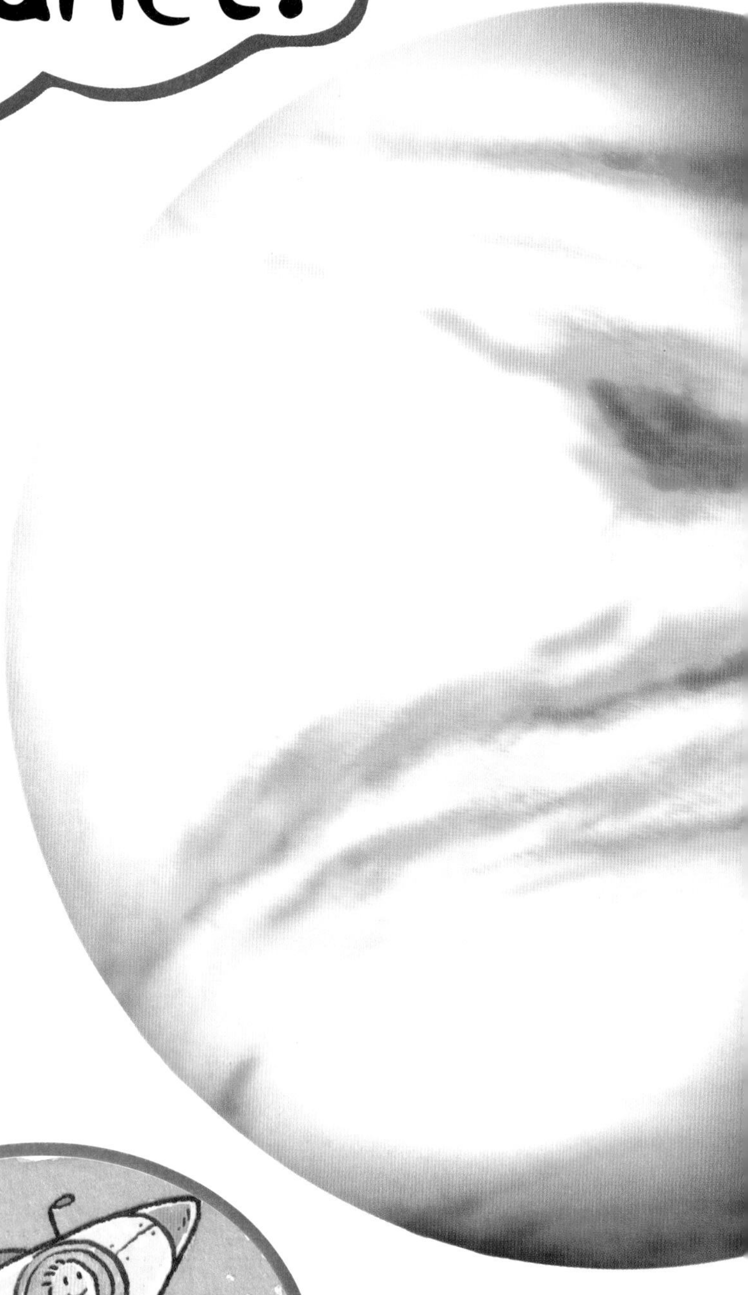

Venus

Back in a year!

Nobody has ever been to Mars. It is so far away that it would take a spacecraft six months to get there. It would take another six months to get home again!

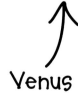

Why is Mars called the red planet?

Mars looks red because it is covered with red rocks and red dust, the colour of rust. Sometimes, winds pick up the dust and make swirling dust storms. In 1971 dust storms covered the whole planet. The surface completely disappeared from view!

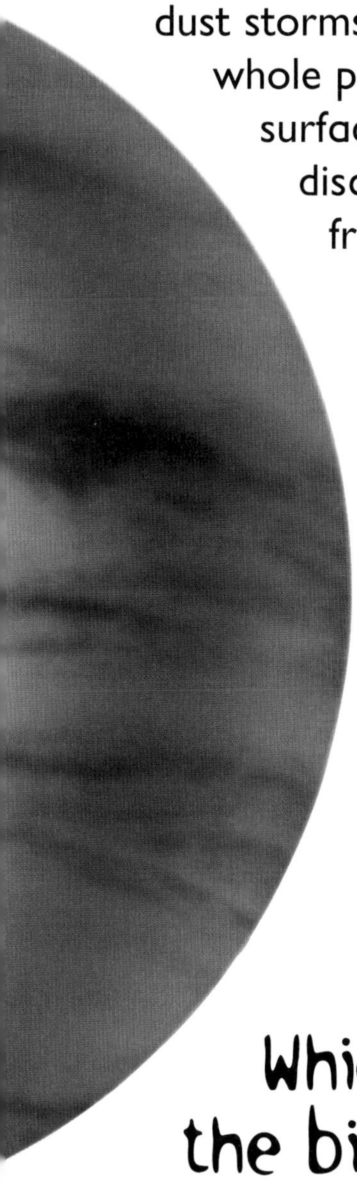

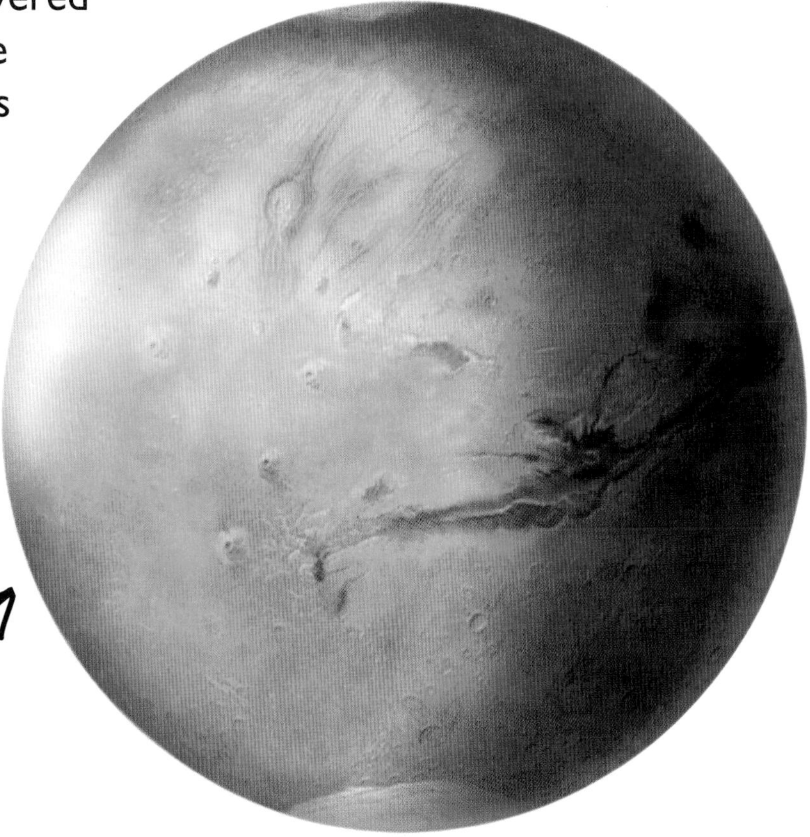

Mars

Which planet has the biggest volcano?

Mars has the biggest volcano. It is called Olympus Mons and it is three times higher than Mount Everest, the highest mountain on Earth. Olympus Mons has gently sloping sides, like an upside-down plate. Mars has many other volcanoes, too. There are also giant canyons and craters.

Discover

Try looking for Venus in the night sky. It looks like a bright star in the early morning or evening.

What is the smallest planet?

Pluto is the smallest planet in the Solar System. It is smaller than our Moon. Pluto has one moon, called Charon, which is half the size of Pluto. Because Pluto is a long way away, the Sun is just a tiny speck of light.

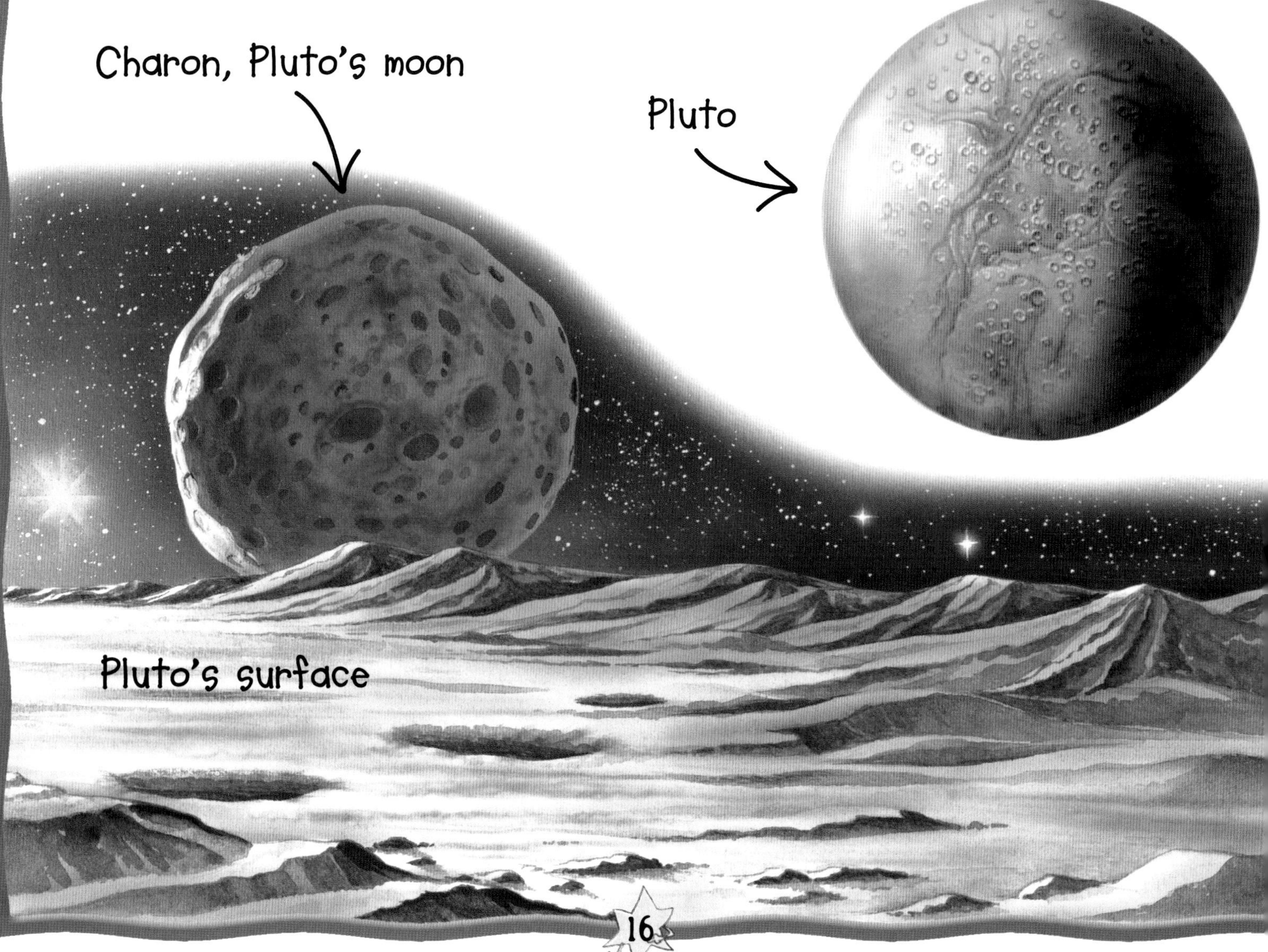

Why does Mercury look like the Moon?

Mercury looks a bit like our Moon. It is covered in dents called craters. These were made when rocks crashed into the surface. There is no wind or rain on Mercury, or the Moon, to wear away the craters.

Sun trap!

Mercury is very close to the Sun. It gets much hotter there than on Earth. If you travelled to Mercury, you would need a special spacesuit and shoes to protect you from the heat.

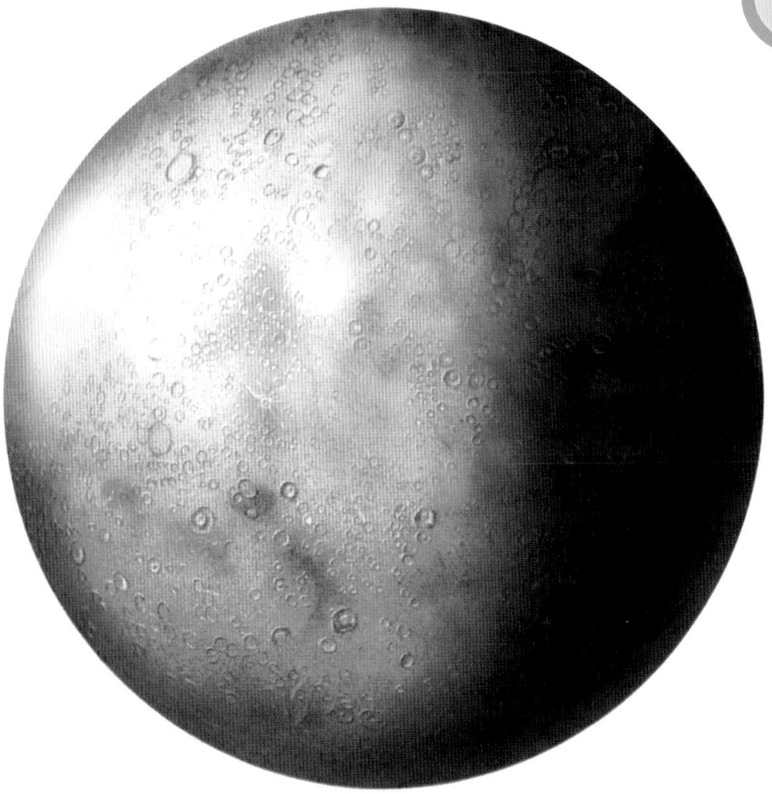

Mercury

Think

Pluto is the coldest planet. Can you think why?

Which planet is baking hot and freezing cold?

Mercury is hot and cold. It spins very slowly. The side that faces the Sun is baked until it is hotter than the inside of an oven. When this side faces away from the Sun, it cools down until it is colder than a freezer.

What is the biggest planet?

Jupiter is the biggest planet. It is 11 times as wide as the Earth. All the other planets in the Solar System would fit inside it! Jupiter is covered in swirls of red and orange gas. These are giant storms.

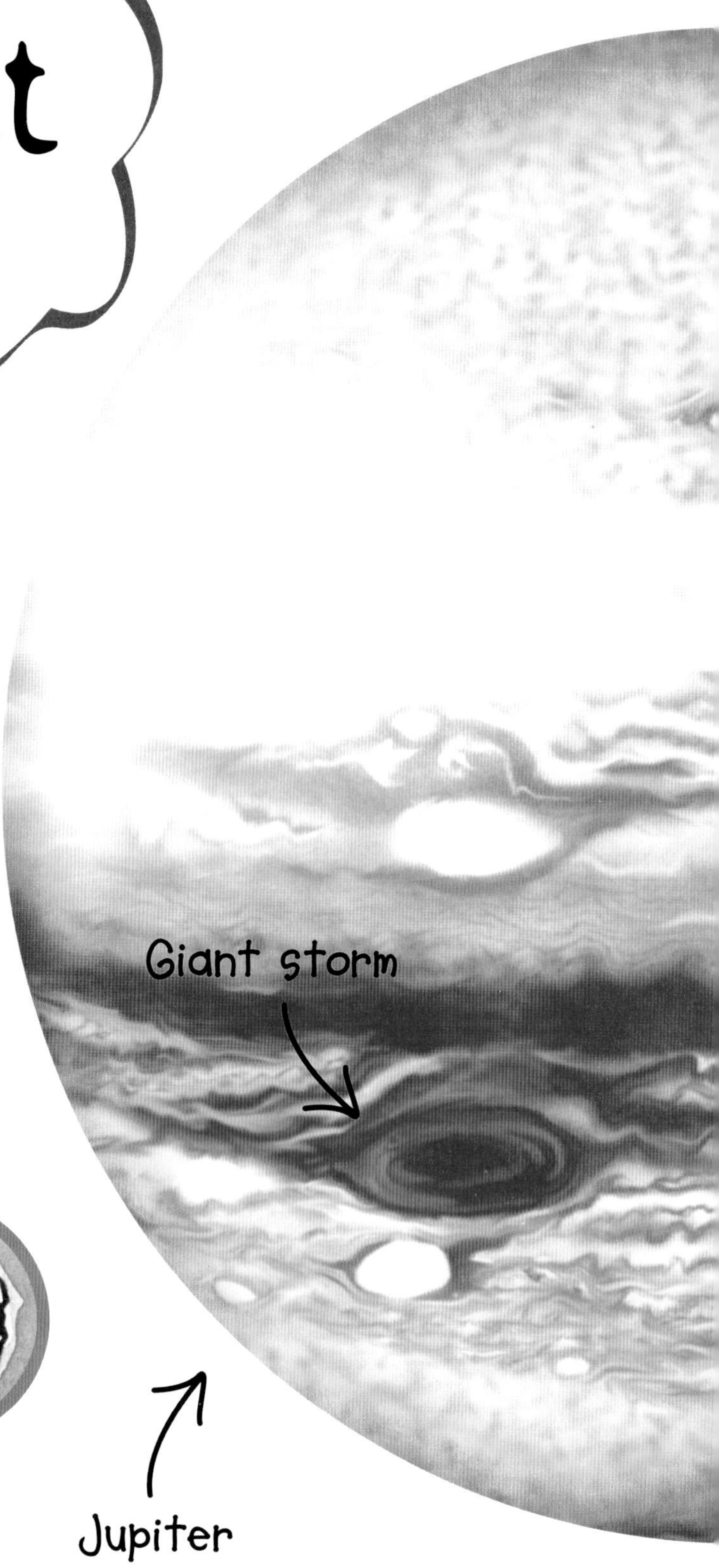

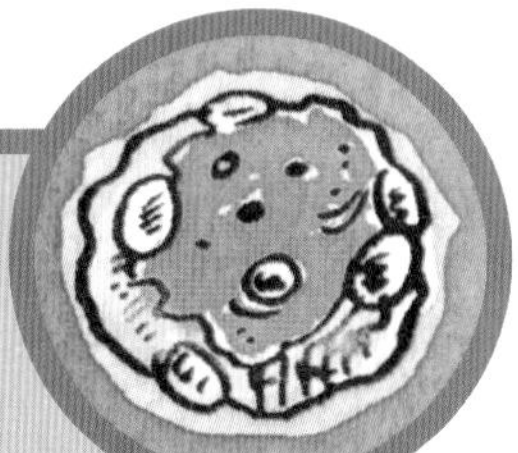

Moon pizza!

Io is one of Jupiter's moons. It is covered in yellow and orange blotches. Io looks like a pizza in space! The blotches are made by hot liquid that comes out of volcanoes.

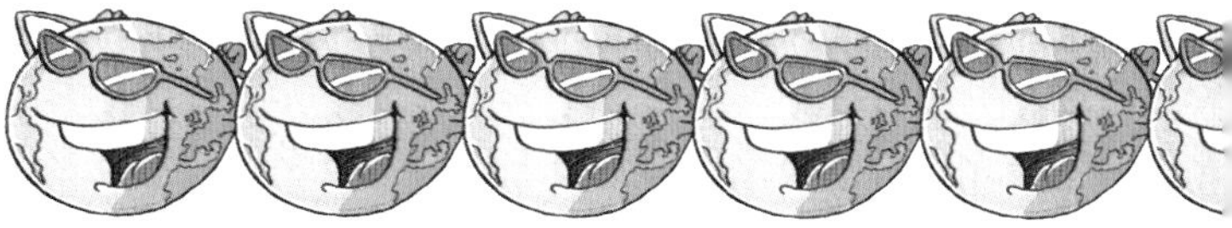

Which planet has rings?

Saturn is surrounded by rings that shine brightly in the sunlight. The rings are made from millions and millions of lumps of ice. Some lumps are the size of ice cubes. Others are as big as cars!

Count

Can you count how many planet Earths there are on these pages?

Is there a giant made of gas?

Not really! However, Jupiter and Saturn are called gas giants. This is because they don't have solid surfaces like the Earth. They have a thick layer of gas and then liquid. You couldn't land on them in a spacecraft.

Which planet rolls around?

Uranus is different to the other planets. Most planets are almost upright. They spin as they move around the Sun. Uranus is tipped right over on its side. This planet spins, too, but it looks as though it is rolling around!

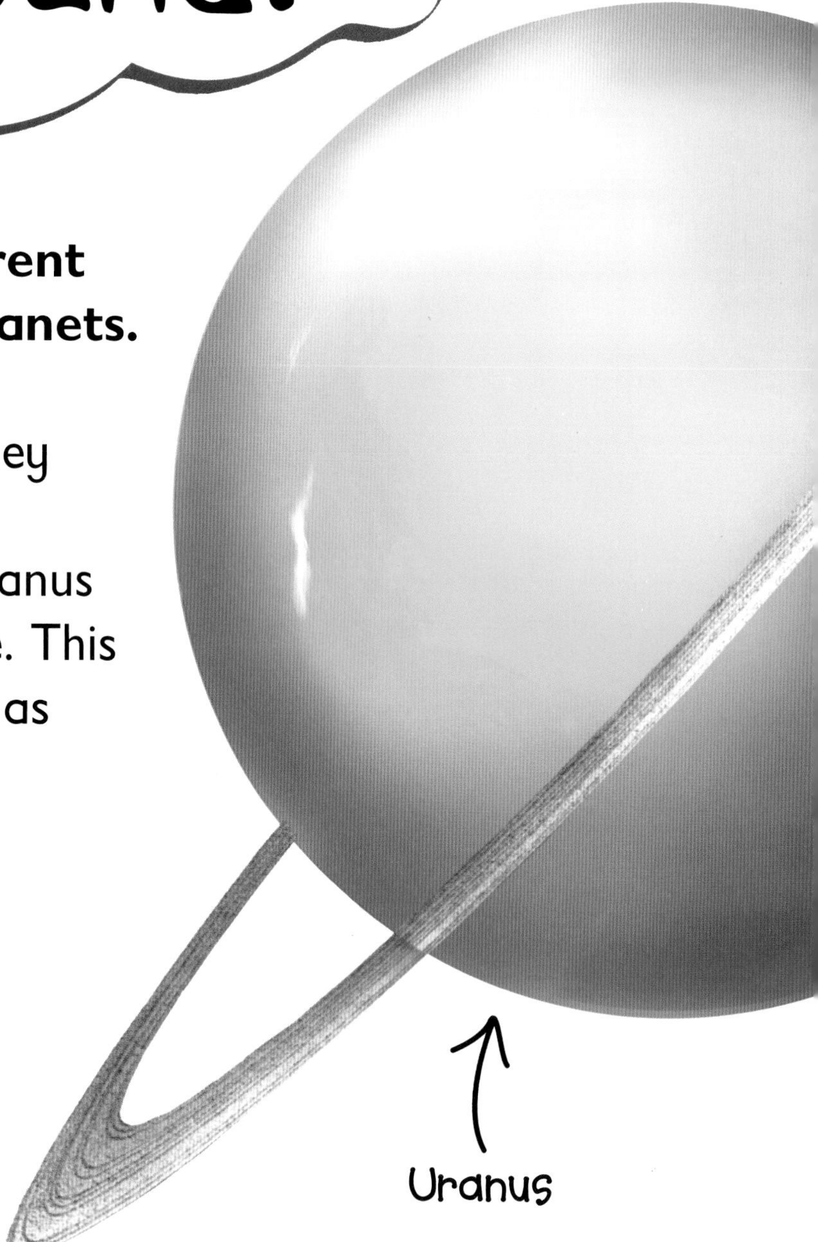

New new moons!

Astronomers (scientists that study space) keep finding new moons around Uranus. They have found 27 so far. There are four big moons and lots of small ones. But there may be more!

Why does Neptune look so blue?

Neptune is covered in bright blue clouds. Sometimes there are streaky, icy white clouds, too. One white cloud is called The Scooter because it scoots around Neptune at high speed. There is also a giant storm called the Great Dark Spot.

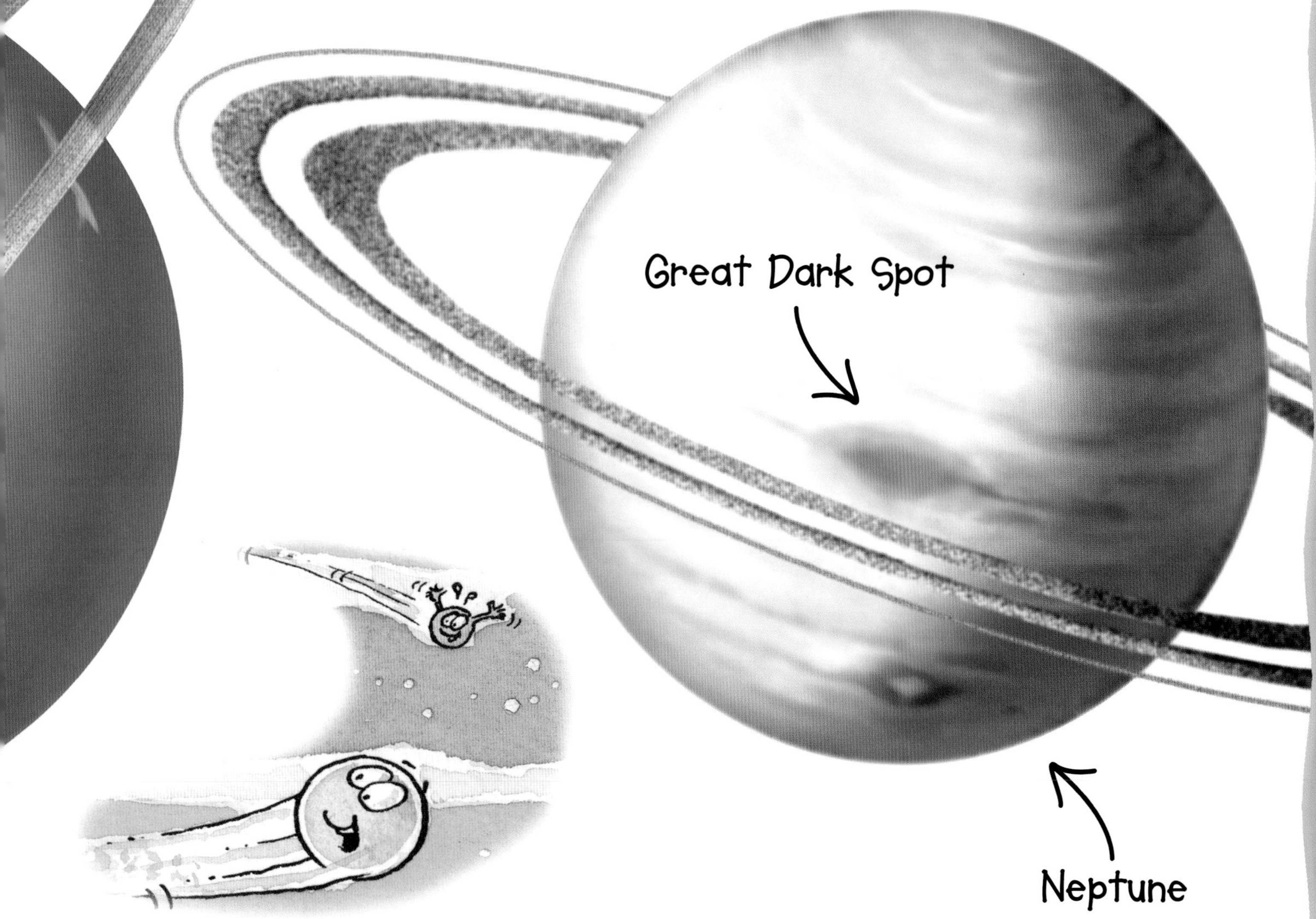

Why do Neptune and Pluto swap places?

Most of the planets move around the Sun in huge circles. Pluto's circle is a bit squashed. This means that it is sometimes closer to the Sun than Neptune. Then it is Neptune's turn to be the planet that is furthest from the Sun!

Remember

Uranus and Neptune have rings. Which other two planets have rings, too?

Are there snowballs in space?

Not really! However, comets are a bit like giant snowballs. They are made up of dust and ice mixed together. When a comet gets close to the Sun, the ice begins to melt. Then dust and gas stream away from the comet. They form a long, bright tail.

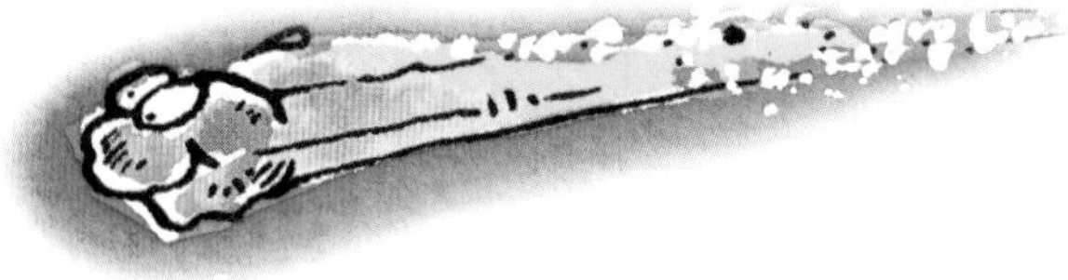

What is a shooting star?

A shooting star is a bright streak across the night sky. It is not really a star. It is made when a small lump of rock shoots into the air above the Earth. Because the rock is going so fast, it burns brightly.

Comet

Rocky road!

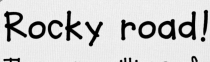

There are millions of asteroids in the Solar System. Some asteroids are tiny, but some are as big as mountains.

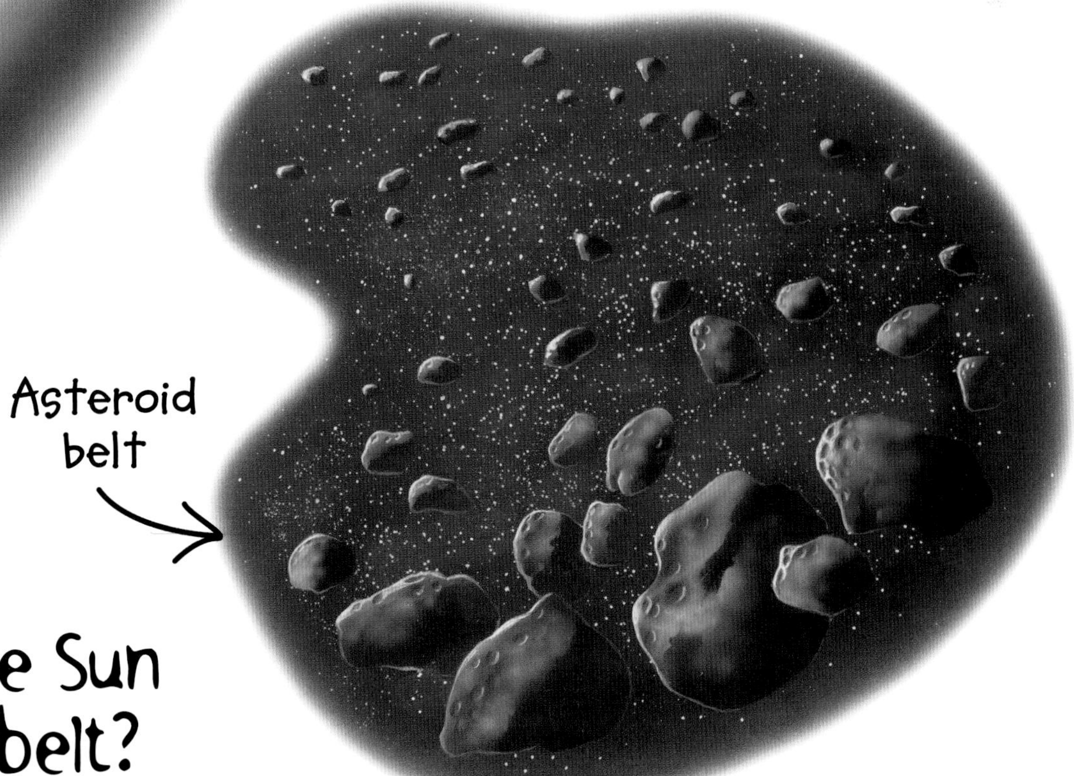

Does the Sun have a belt?

The Sun has a belt made up of lumps of rock called asteroids. We call this the asteroid belt. The asteroids move around the Sun between Mars and Jupiter. The biggest asteroids are round, but most are shaped like giant potatoes.

Discover

Can you find out the name of a famous comet?

How are stars made?

Stars are made from huge clouds of dust and gas. Gradually the cloud shrinks and all the gas and dust clump together. The centre of the cloud gets hotter and hotter and a new star begins to shine. The star gives off heat and light.

Shine on!

Stars can shine for thousands of millions of years! The Sun started shining five thousand million years ago. It will stop shining in another five thousand million years.

What is a group of stars called?

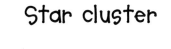

A group of stars is called a star cluster. A star cluster is made from a giant cloud of gas and dust. Some clusters contain just a few stars. Others contain hundreds of stars and they look like a big ball of light.

Star cluster

2. The cloud begins to spin

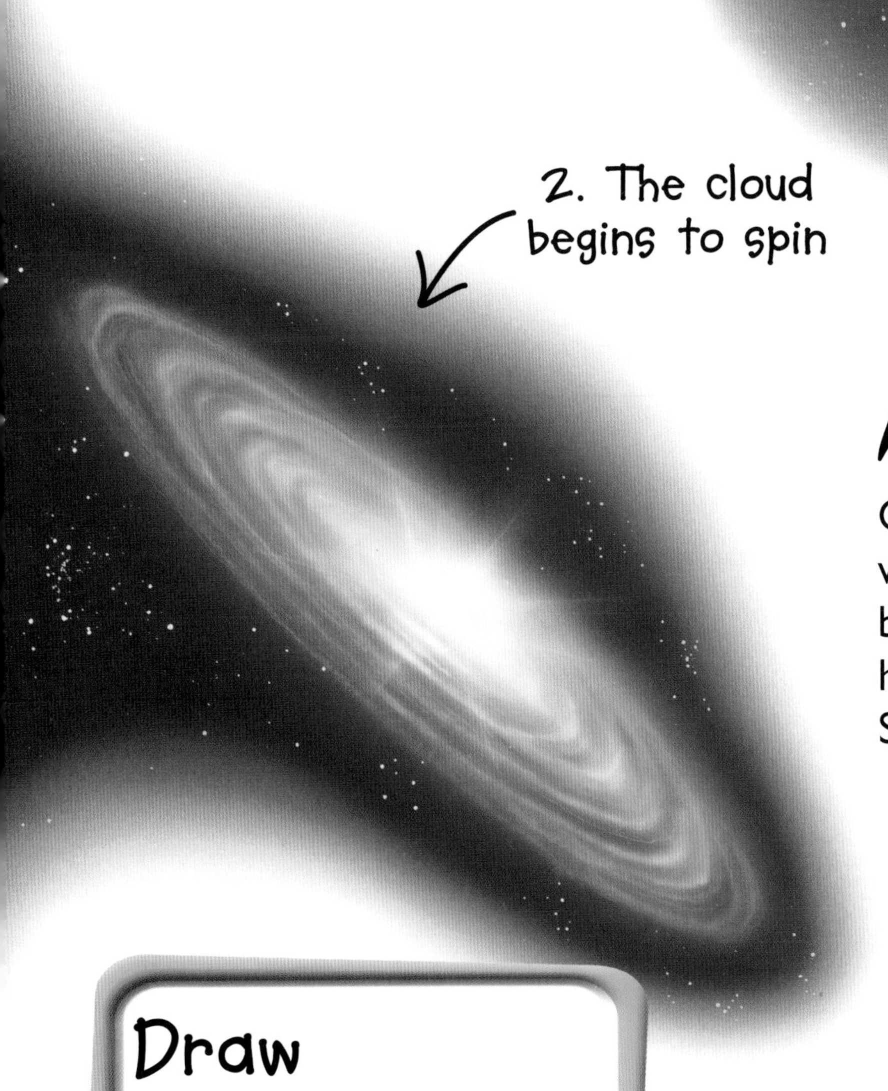

Are all stars white?

Only the most giant stars shine with a bright white light. This is because they are extremely hot. Smaller stars, such as our Sun, are not so hot. They look yellow instead. Very small stars are cooler still. They look red or brown.

Draw

Can you paint white, yellow and red stars on a sheet of black paper?

What is the Milky Way?

The stars in space are in huge groups called galaxies. Our galaxy is called the Milky Way. All the stars in the night sky are in the Milky Way. There are so many that you couldn't count them all in your whole lifetime!

Can galaxies crash?

Sometimes two galaxies crash into each other. But there is no giant bump. This is because galaxies are mostly made of empty space! The stars just go past each other. Galaxies can pull each other out of shape.

Count

Look at the pictures on these pages. How many different shapes of galaxies can you find?

The Milky Way

Elliptical galaxy

Do galaxies have arms?

Some galaxies have arms that curl in a spiral, like the Milky Way. Other galaxies, called elliptical galaxies, have a round, squashed shape. Many galaxies have no shape and are called irregular galaxies.

Irregular galaxy

Spiral galaxy

Great galaxies!

There are thousands of millions of galaxies in space. Some are much smaller than the Milky Way. Others are much larger. They all contain too many stars to count!

How does a shuttle get into space?

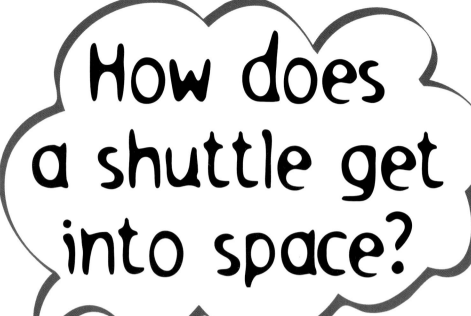

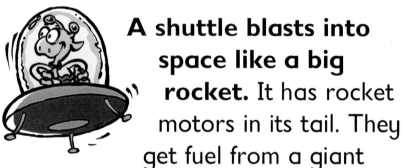

A shuttle blasts into space like a big rocket. It has rocket motors in its tail. They get fuel from a giant fuel tank. There are two booster rockets, too. The fuel tank and the booster rockets fall off before the shuttle reaches space.

Rocket power!

Rockets are filled with fuel. The fuel burns in the rocket motor to make hot gases. The gases rush out of the motor and push the rocket upwards.

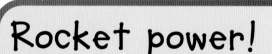

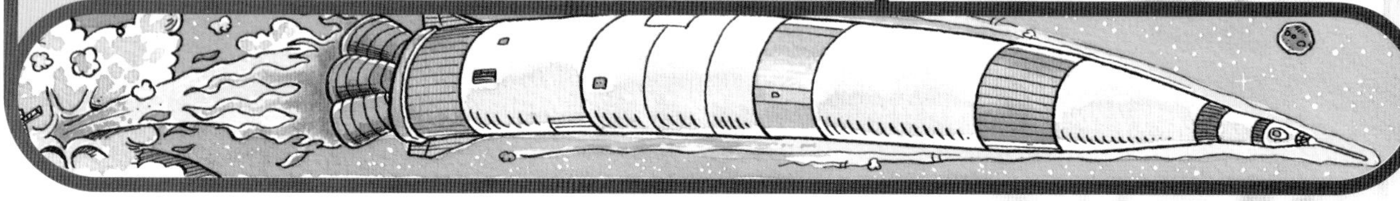

How fast do rockets go?

Very, very fast indeed! After blasting off, a rocket goes faster and faster and higher and higher. When it reaches space, it is going 30 times faster than a jumbo jet. If a rocket went slower than this it would fall back to Earth.

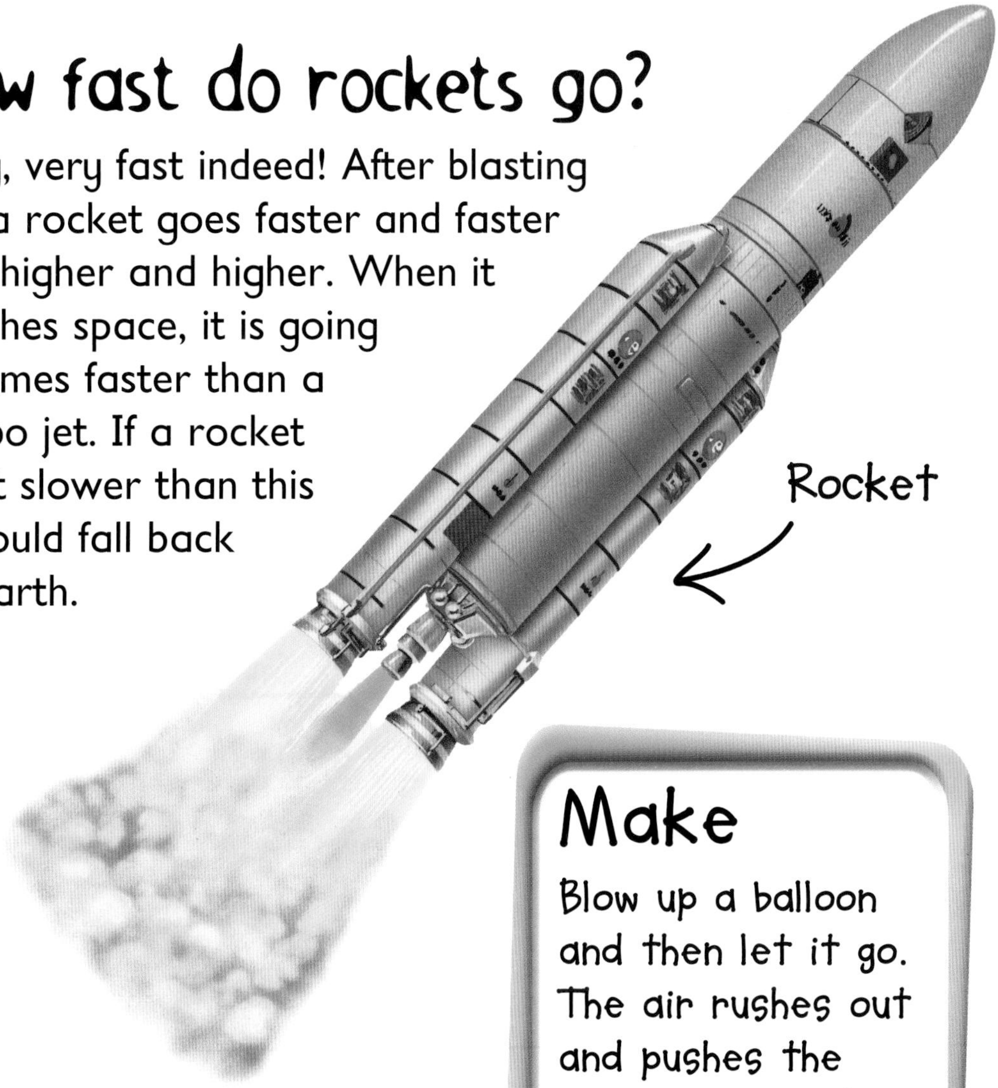

Make

Blow up a balloon and then let it go. The air rushes out and pushes the balloon along, like a simple rocket.

When is a shuttle like a glider?

When a shuttle travels back to Earth it slows down. Then it begins to fall. It does not use its motors to fly down. Instead, it flies like a giant glider. The shuttle lands on a long runway and uses a parachute to slow to a stop.

Why do astronauts float in space?

When things are in space they don't have any weight. This means everything floats. So do astronauts! This makes them feel sick, too. In a spacecraft everything is fixed down to stop it floating away. Astronauts have footholds and handholds to grab onto.

All packed?

Astronauts must take everything they need into space. In space there is no air, water or food. All of these things have to be packed into the spacecraft and taken into space.

Where do astronauts go to sleep?

Astronauts sleep in sleeping bags. The bags are fixed to the wall inside a spacecraft. They keep astronauts warm and stop them floating about while they sleep! A special shower lets the astronauts wash without drops of water floating everywhere.

Why do astronauts wear spacesuits?

Space is a dangerous place. Spacesuits protect astronauts when they go outside their spacecraft. There is no air in space. So a spacesuit has a supply of air for the astronaut to breathe. The suit also stops an astronaut from getting too hot or too cold.

Remember

Can you remember why astronauts have to carry air with them in space?

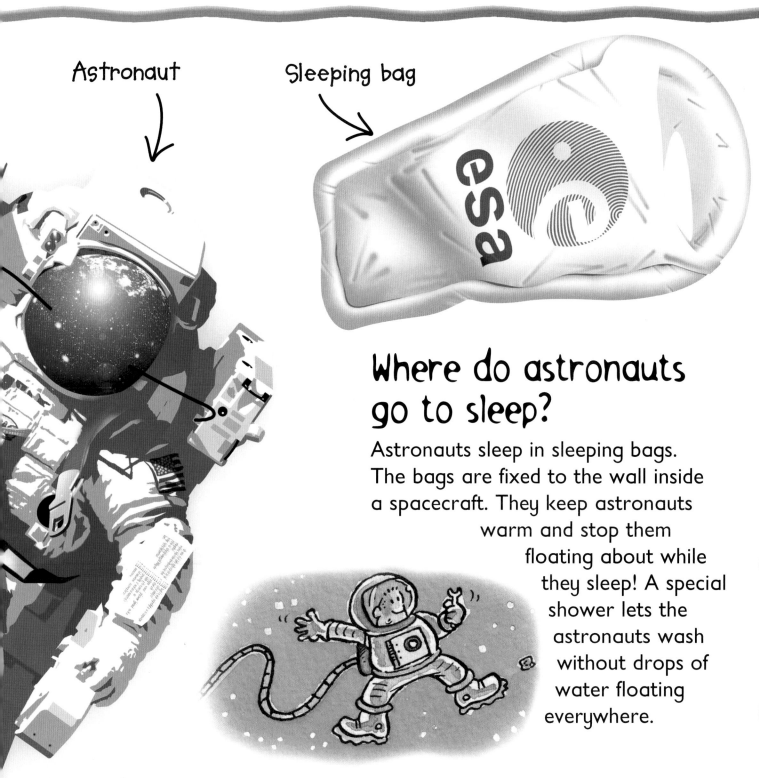

Are there robots in space?

There are robot spacecraft, called probes, in space. They have visited all the planets, except Pluto. Some probes travel around the planets. They send photographs and other information back to Earth. Other probes land on a planet to take a closer look.

Snap happy!

A probe called *Voyager 2* was the first to visit Uranus and Neptune. It took photographs of the planets and sent them back to Earth.

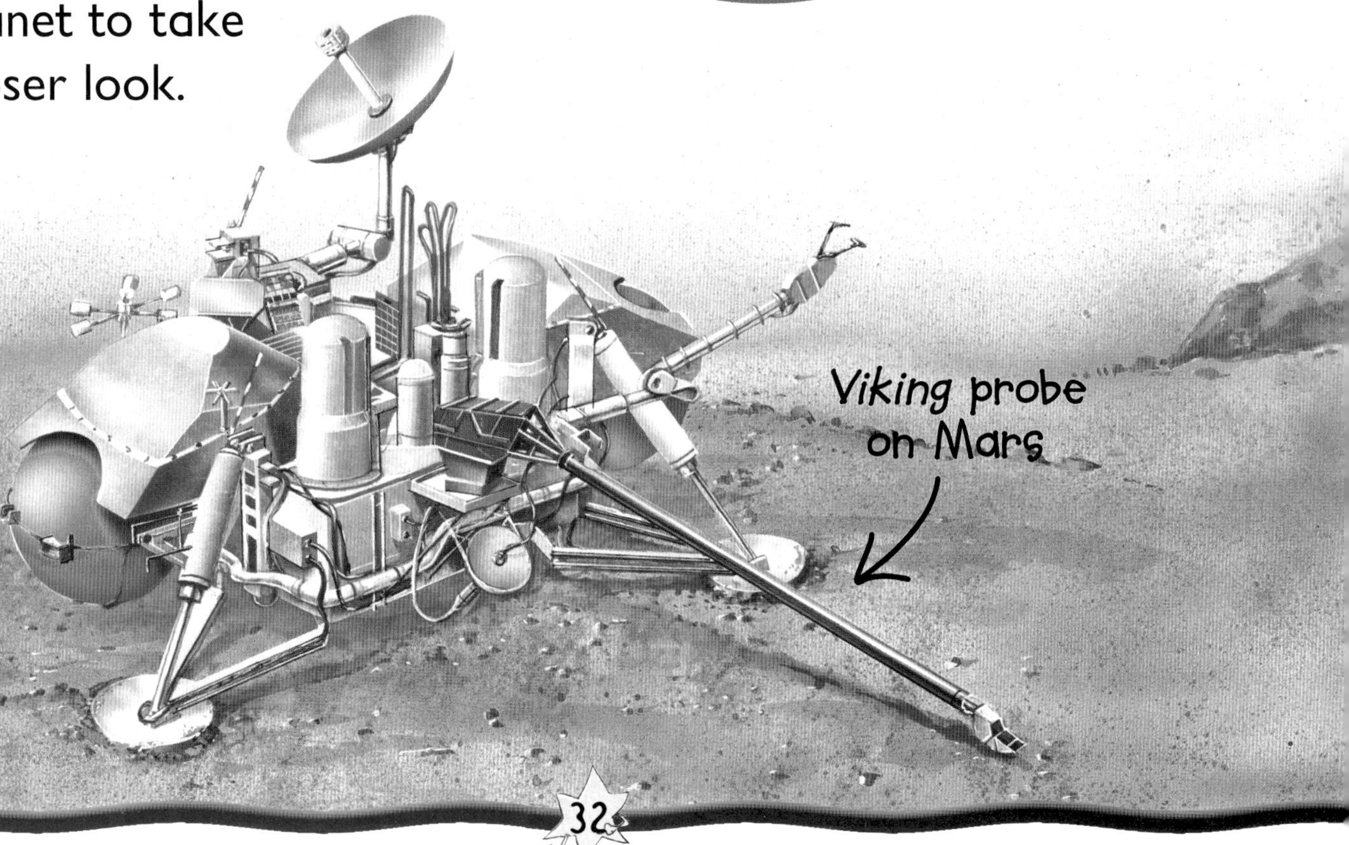

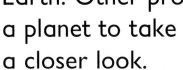

Viking probe on Mars

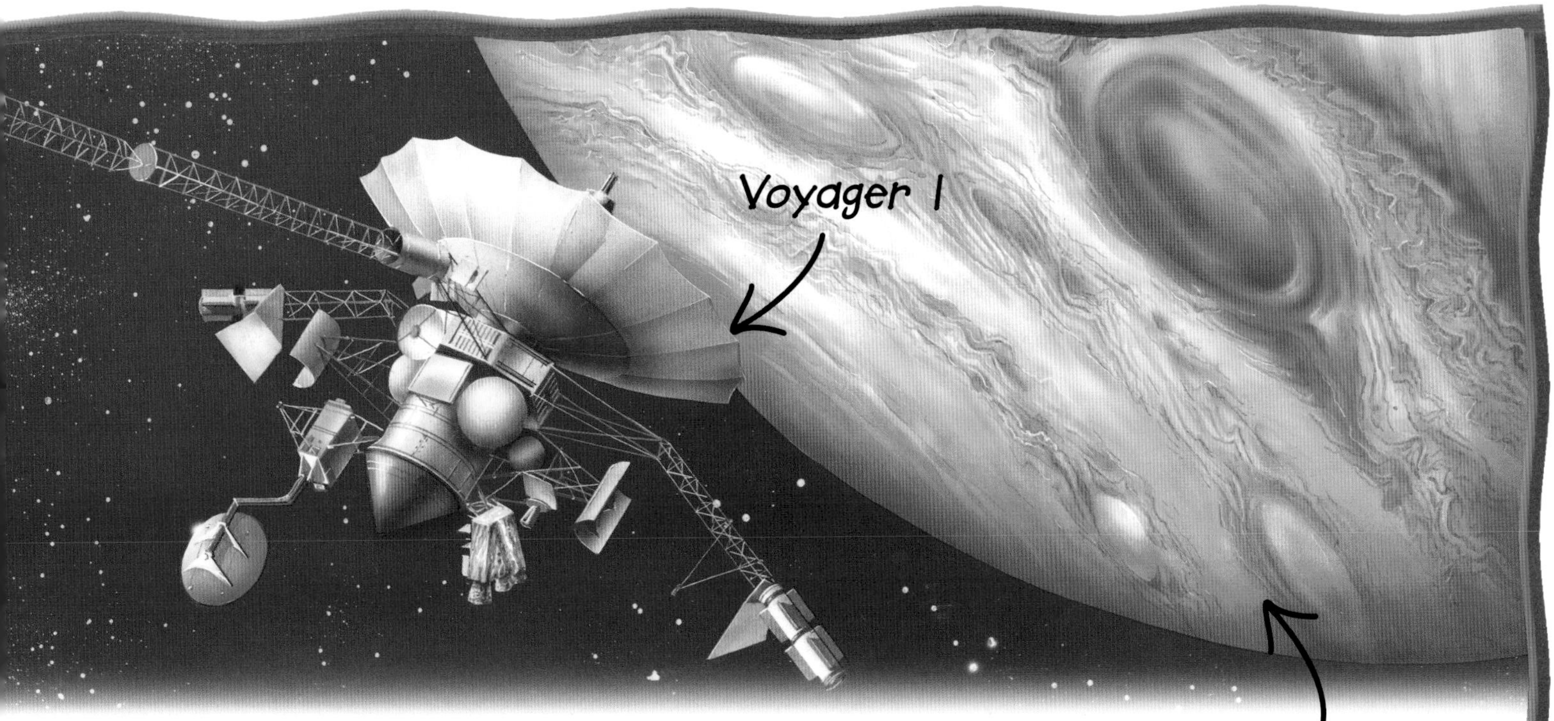

Which probe has travelled the furthest?

A probe called *Voyager 1* was launched from Earth in 1977. It visited Jupiter in 1979 and then Saturn in 1980. Then it kept going, out of the Solar System. *Voyager 1* is now 14 thousand million kilometres from Earth!

Draw

Try designing your own robot explorer. You can take some ideas from these pages.

Have probes been to Mars?

More probes have been to Mars than any other planet. In 1997 a probe called Pathfinder landed on Mars. Inside Pathfinder was a tiny robot vehicle, called *Sojourner*. Scientists steered it using remote control. It investigated the soil and rocks on Mars.

Quiz time

Do you remember what you have read about space?
Here are some questions to test your memory. The pictures will help you. If you get stuck, read the pages again.

1. Which star keeps us warm?

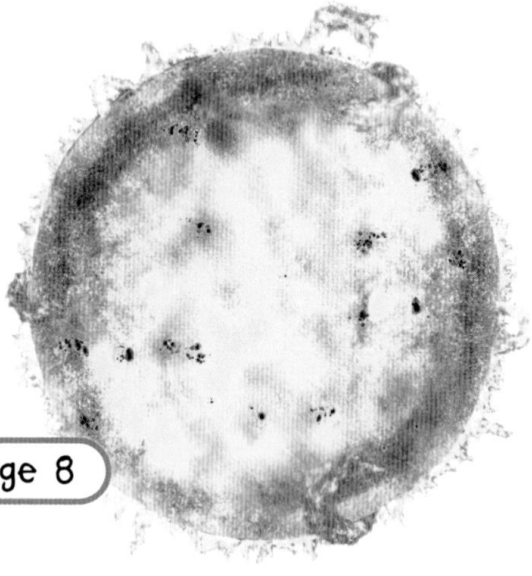

page 8

2. Why is the Sun spotty?

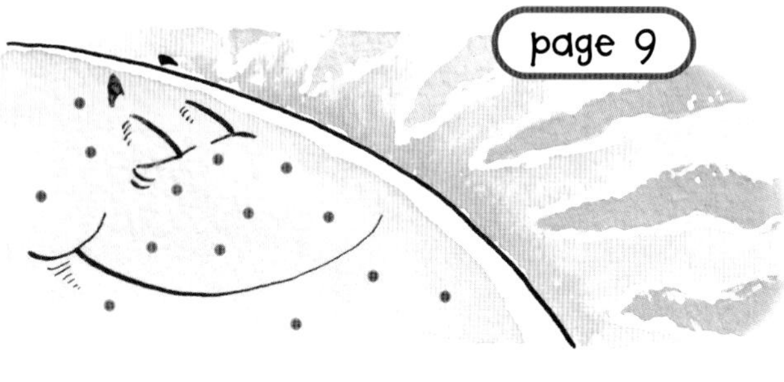

page 9

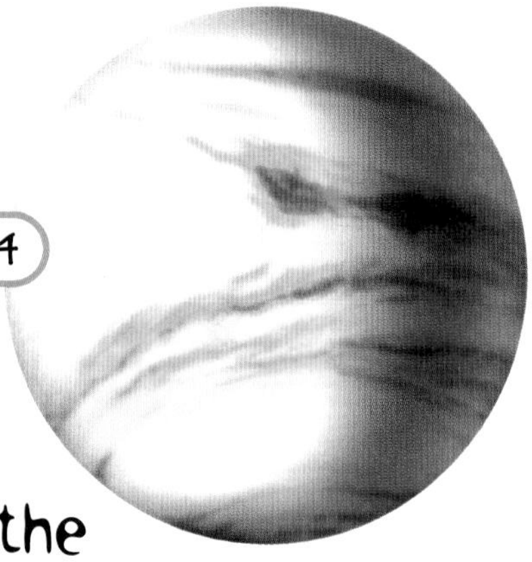

page 14

3. What is the hottest planet?

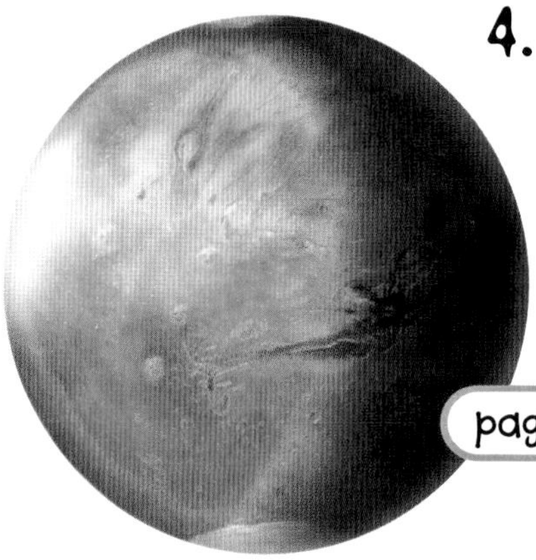

4. Why is Mars called the red planet?

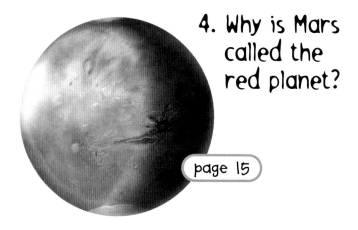

page 15

page 16

5. What is the smallest planet?

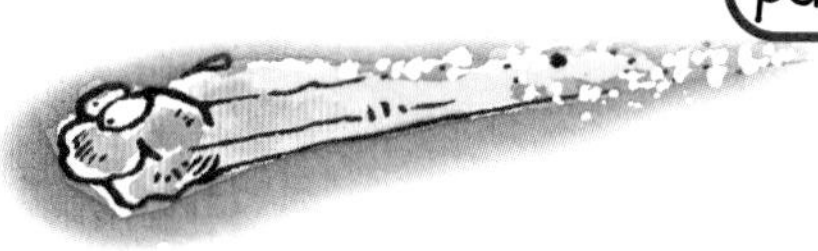

page 22

6. What is a shooting star?

7. Does the Sun have a belt?

page 23

11. How does a shuttle get into space?

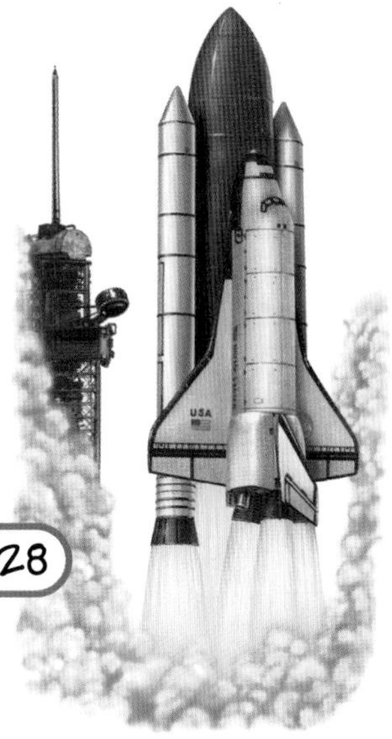

page 28

8. What is a group of stars called?

page 25

12. When is a shuttle like a glider?

page 29

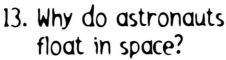

13. Why do astronauts float in space?

page 30

9. What is the Milky Way?

page 26

10. Can galaxies crash?

page 26

Answers

1. The Sun
2. Cooler parts look darker, like spots
3. Venus
4. It is covered with red rocks and dust
5. Pluto
6. A lump of rock burning in the sky
7. Yes, the asteroid belt
8. Star cluster
9. A huge group of stars
10. Yes
11. Like a giant rocket does
12. When it travels back to Earth
13. Because they have no weight in space

Breezy questions about...

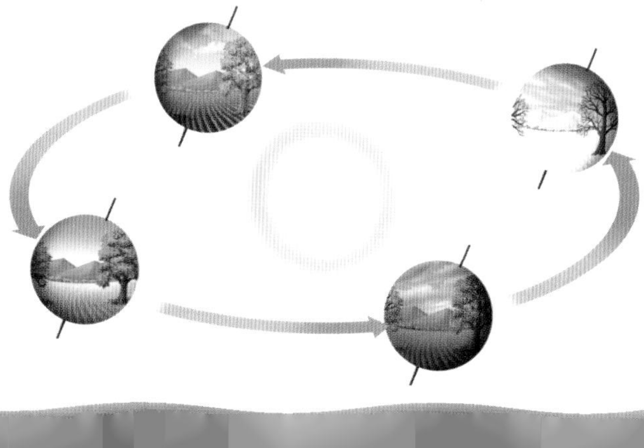

Weather

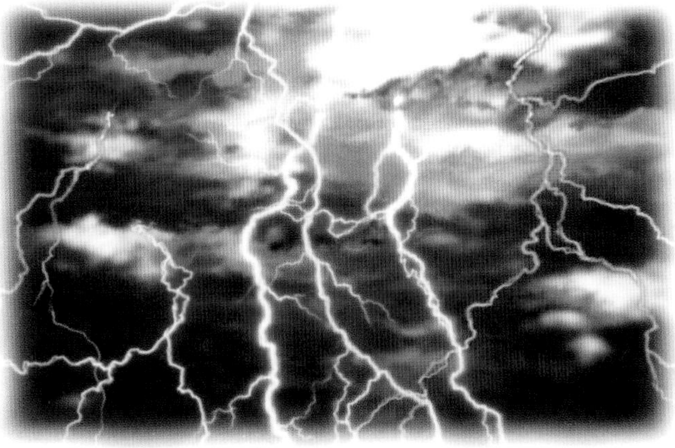

Why is summer warm and sunny?

The Earth is tipped to one side as it moves round the Sun. Some of the year, the north half of the Earth faces the Sun. Then the Sun is higher in the sky, making the weather warm. This is summer. When the southern half of the Earth faces the Sun, it is winter in the north.

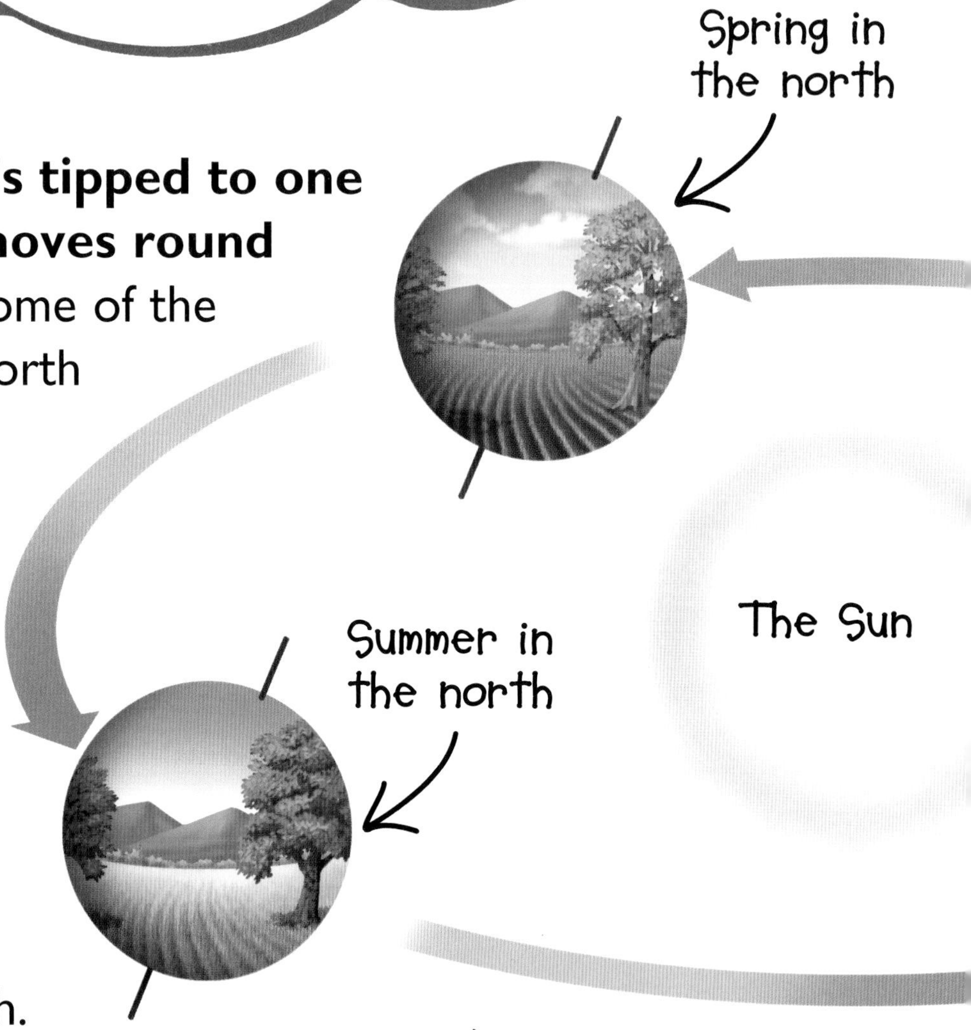

Why are days longer in summer?

Summer days are longer because the Earth is tilted and spins round. In summer, the Sun rises earlier and sets later. This makes daytime last longer than night. In the middle of summer in Sweden it is light for 21 hours!

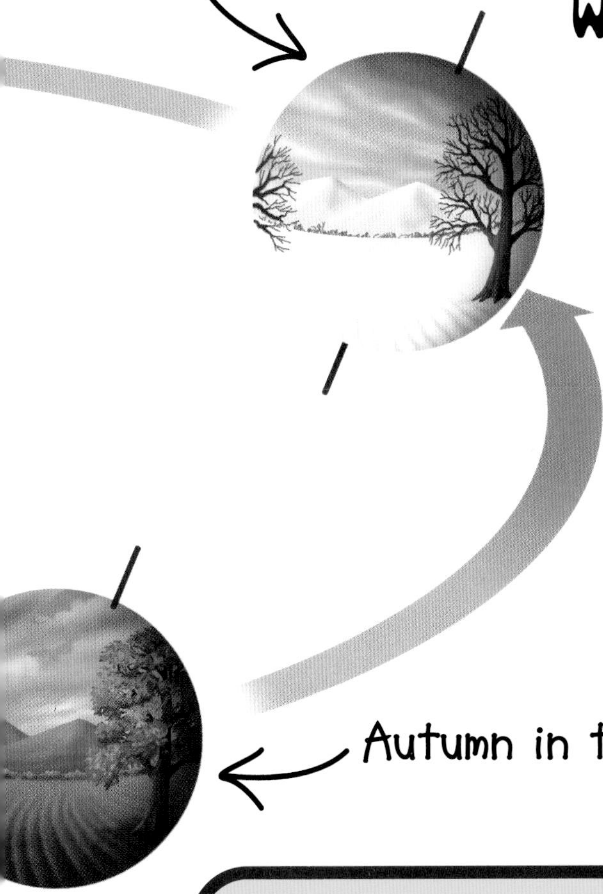

Why do leaves fall in autumn?

Autumn comes between summer and winter. Many trees lose their leaves in autumn because it is hard for them to grow in the dark winter months. The leaves turn from green to red, orange or brown. Then they fall to the ground.

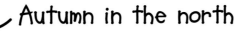

Find

Can you find photographs of red, orange and brown leaves in autumn?

Sunshine at midnight!

At the North and South Poles, the Sun never sets in summer. It is light all day. In winter, the Sun never rises. Then it is dark all day long!

What is the sunniest place?

The Sahara Desert in North Africa is the sunniest place on Earth. It is sunny for nearly 12 hours every day! It hardly rains, which makes it hard for plants and animals to live here. People dress in loose clothes to stop being sunburnt.

Sea makes fire!

Water flowing around the sea can change the weather. El Niño is a warm water current in the Pacific Ocean. Scientists think that this could cause droughts.

When is a lake not a lake?

When it's a mirage! A mirage often happens on a hot day. Hot air near the ground makes light from the bright sky bend upwards. This makes it seem as if there is a lake on the ground in the distance. Really the ground is dry!

People living in the desert

Remember

Can you remember why desert people wear loose clothes, even when it is very hot?

Drought

What happens when it doesn't rain?

Sometimes it is dry for a long time in places where it normally rains a lot. This is called a drought. There was a drought in the United States in the 1930s. Crops didn't grow and fields turned to dust. Many people had to leave their farms.

Does Earth have a blanket?

Yes, it does. The Earth is wrapped in a thick blanket of air. It is called the atmosphere. This is where all the weather happens. The atmosphere also helps to keep the Earth's surface warm at night. In the day it protects us from harmful rays coming from the Sun.

Where does it rain every day?

In a tropical rainforest the weather is always very hot and very wet. The Sun shines every day, and there are downpours of heavy rain, too. Rainforest plants grow very quickly in this steamy weather.

Monsoon downpour!

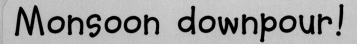

In some countries it pours with rain for a few weeks every year. This is called a monsoon. In India, enough rain falls in one year to cover the ground with water 26 metres deep!

How deep is the atmosphere?

The atmosphere stretches hundreds of kilometres above our heads. If you go up through the atmosphere, the air gets thinner and thinner. High up in mountains, mountaineers find it difficult to breathe so they take breathing equipment with them.

Look

Look at the picture of the Earth above. What do you think the white swirly patterns are?

Where does rain come from?

Most rain comes from the sea! Some seawater turns to gas in the air. If the air rises, the gas becomes water drops. These make clouds. If the drops get big enough, they fall as rain. The water flows back to the sea.

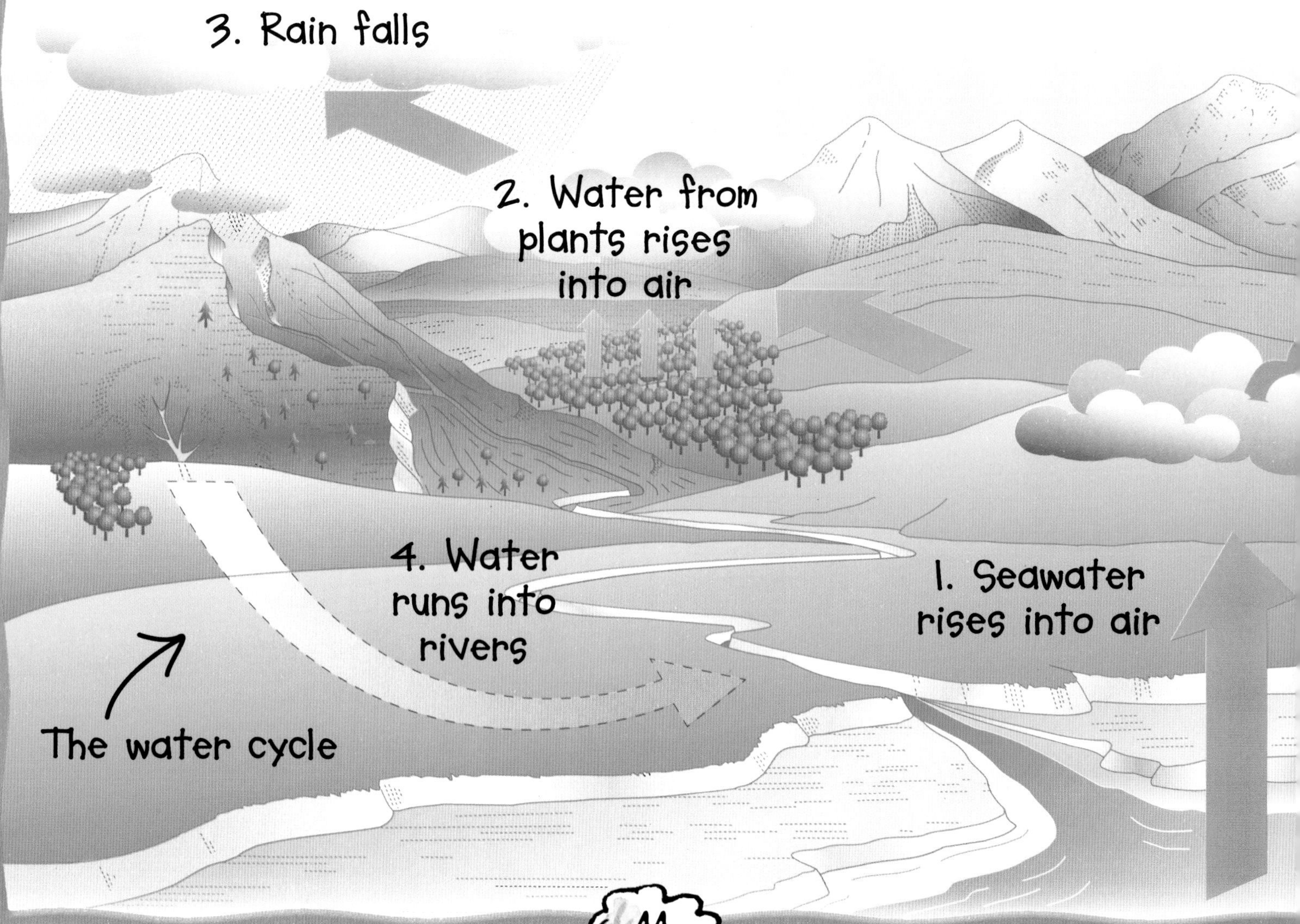
3. Rain falls
2. Water from plants rises into air
4. Water runs into rivers
1. Seawater rises into air
The water cycle

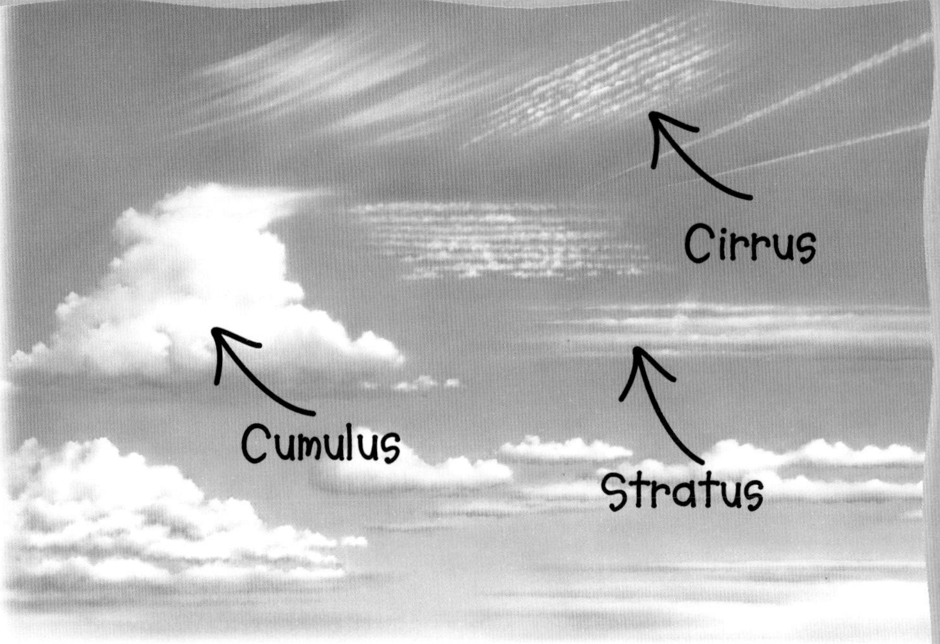

Head in the clouds!

The tops of tall mountains are often in the clouds. At the top it looks misty. Mountaineers sometimes get lost in these clouds!

Are all clouds small and fluffy?

Clouds come in lots of different shapes and sizes. Weather experts give the different clouds names. Fluffy clouds are called cumulus clouds. Some are small and some are giant. Flat clouds are called stratus clouds. Wispy clouds high in the sky are called cirrus clouds.

What rain never lands?

Sometimes rain that falls from a cloud never reaches the ground. If the drops of rain fall into very dry air, the water in them turns into gas. This means that the drops disappear and never reach the ground.

Look

Look at the clouds outside today. Are they fluffy or flat? The picture above will help you.

What happens in a flood?

Sometimes a lot of rain falls in a few hours. So much water flows into rivers that they fill up and burst their banks. The rivers flood the land on each side. Sometimes houses disappear under the flood water.

Floods of tears!

The river Nile in Egypt floods every year. Thousands of years ago, the Egyptians made up a story about the flood. It said that a goddess called Isis cried so much that the river filled up with her tears.

Did Noah build an ark?

The Bible tells the story of a man called Noah. He built a great boat called an ark to escape a flood. We don't know if Noah's ark existed. Scientists have found out that there probably was a huge flood thousands of years ago.

Noah's ark

Flooded house

Find

Can you find the country of Egypt and the river Nile in an atlas?

Can there be a flood in a desert?

Yes there can. Most of the time there is no rain in a desert. The hot Sun bakes the ground hard. Once in a while, it rains heavily. The water flows off the ground instead of soaking in. This can cause a flood.

What is snow made of?

Snow is made of ice, which is water that has frozen. When it is very cold in a cloud, tiny bits of ice (crystals) begin to form, instead of water drops. The pieces clump together to make snowflakes that fall to the ground. The weather must be very cold for snow to fall. If it is too warm, the snowflakes melt and turn to rain.

Shiver!

Antarctica is the coldest place on Earth. The lowest temperature ever recorded there is –89°C. That's much, much colder than inside a freezer!

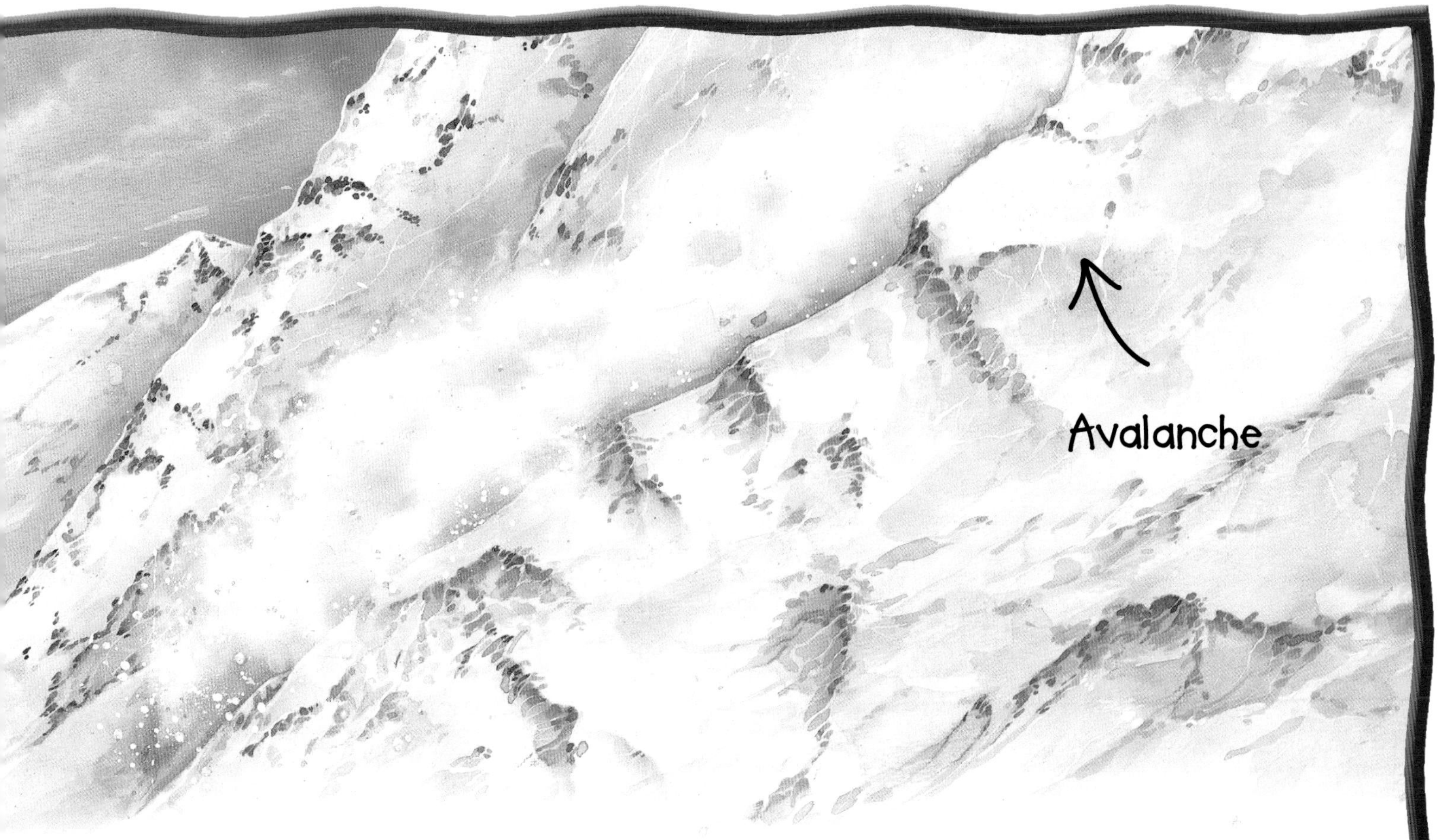

When is snow dangerous?

When lots of snow falls on mountains, deep layers build up on the slopes. The snow may suddenly slide down the mountain. This is an avalanche. A big avalanche can bury a town. A loud noise or even a person walking on the snow can start an avalanche.

Are all snowflakes the same?

It's hard to believe, but all snowflakes are different – even though there are millions and millions of them. This is because every ice crystal in a snowflake has its own shape. No two crystals are the same. Most ice crystals in snowflakes looks like stars with six points.

Think

Can you think why it could be dangerous to ski across a steep hillside covered with snow?

Where are the fastest winds?

Inside a tornado. A tornado is like a spinning funnel made of air. They reach down from giant thunderstorms. The winds can blow at 480 kilometres an hour. That's twice as fast as an express train! Tornadoes can rip trees from the ground and destroy houses.

Which storm has an eye?

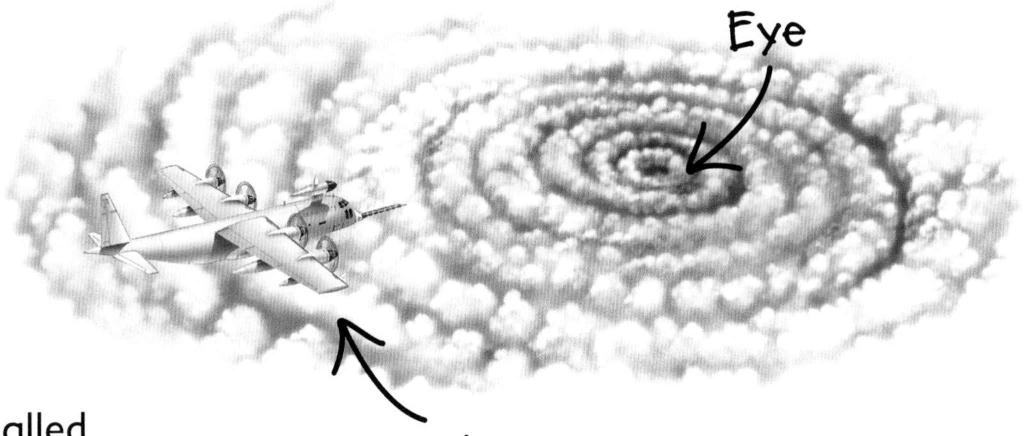

A hurricane is a giant spinning storm made up of super-strong winds. The centre is a hole called the eye. Here it is calm and sunny. If a hurricane reaches land, the winds can damage buildings and heavy rain causes floods. Hurricane hunters are planes that fly into hurricanes to measure the wind speed.

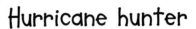

Draw

Look at the pictures on this page. Can you draw a picture of a tornado and a hurricane?

Stormy names!

A tropical storm that starts in the Atlantic Ocean is called a hurricane. In the Pacific Ocean, a tropical storm is called a typhoon. In the Indian Ocean it is called a cyclone.

How do we measure wind?

We measure the wind on a scale called the Beaufort Scale. The slowest wind is Force 1 on the scale. This is called a light breeze. The strongest wind is Force 12. This is called a hurricane. Force zero means there is no wind at all.

What makes the sky clap?

A thunderstorm! Inside a big thundercloud, water drops and bits of ice move up and down, bumping into each other. This makes electricity build up. When the electricity jumps around, we see a spark of lightning and hear a loud clap of thunder.

Huge hail!

Hail is made up of lumps of ice called hailstones. Hail can fall from thunderclouds. The biggest hailstone ever fell in Bangladesh in 1986. It was the size of a grapefruit!

When is lightning like a fork?

When lightning jumps from a thundercloud to the ground, it looks like huge forks in the sky. If lightning jumps from one cloud to another, the clouds light up. This is called sheet lightning. Lightning can be red, blue, yellow or white.

Lightning

Does lightning hit buildings?

Lightning often hits tall buildings. The buildings have a metal spike on top called a lightning conductor. When lightning hits a building, the lightning conductor carries the electricity to the ground. If there was no lightning conductor, the building could be damaged by the lightning.

Thundercloud

Count

Count the seconds between a flash of lightning and a clap of thunder. The bigger the number, the further away the thunderstorm.

What is a rainbow made of?

A rainbow is made of sunlight. The light bounces through raindrops. This splits the light into different colours. The colours of a rainbow are always the same. They are red, orange, yellow, green, blue, indigo and violet.

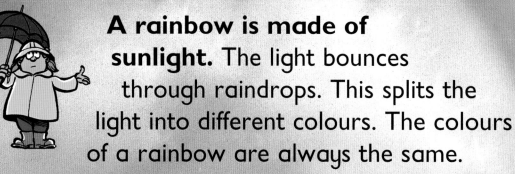

Northern lights

Remember

Can you remember all seven colours of a rainbow?

When does the sky have curtains?

In the far north and the far south of the world, amazing patterns of light sometimes appear in the sky. They look like colourful curtains. The patterns are called auroras (or-roar-rers). They happen when tiny light particles from the Sun smash into the air.

Rainbow with no colour!

A fogbow is a rainbow that is white. You might see a fogbow when the Sun shines through fog. It is white because the water drops in fog are too small to split up the light into rainbow colours.

When can you see three suns?

If there are thin clouds high in the sky, you might see three suns. The clouds are made of bits of ice. These bend light from the Sun. This makes it look as if there are two extra suns in the sky. We call these mock suns, or sun dogs.

What is a rain dance?

In many hot places, such as Africa, it only rains once or twice a year. People may dance traditional rain dances if the rain does not fall. In the past, people believed that rain dances really could bring clouds and rain.

Who first recorded the weather?

Over 3000 years ago in China, people made notes about the weather. They studied how windy it was, or if it rained or snowed. They carved the information onto pieces of tortoiseshell.

Are weather sayings true?

There are many sayings about the weather. Most of them are true. One saying is 'Clear Moon, frost soon'. If there are no clouds in the sky you can see the Moon clearly. It also means it will get cold quickly at night. So the saying is true.

Rain dance

Full Moon

Weather cows!

Some people think that cows lie down when it is going to rain. But this weather saying is not true. Cows lie down on sunny days, too!

Discover

Can you find some more sayings about the weather? You could ask your teacher, or try looking in a book.

Which bird spins in the wind?

A metal cockerel on a weather vane. The cockerel spins so it can point in any direction. When the wind blows, the cockerel spins and points to where the wind is coming from. If the wind is blowing from the north, it is called a north wind. The wind blows from the north, south, east and west.

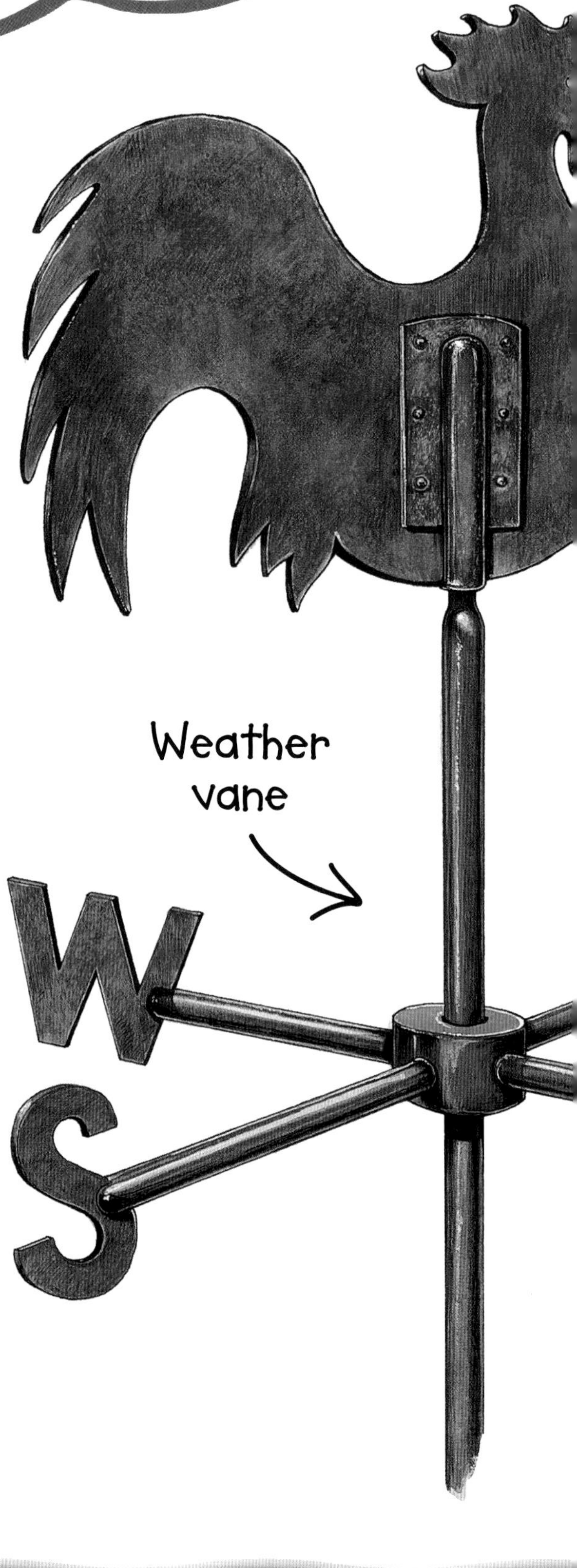

Groundhog Day!

In the USA, February 2 is called Groundhog Day. If people see an animal called a groundhog, they think that it will stay cold for another six weeks!

What is a weather house?

A weather house is a model that can tell how much moisture is in the air. If it is going to be dry, a lady in summer clothes comes out. If it is going to be rainy, a man with an umbrella comes out.

Weather house

How do we know how hot it is?

By reading a thermometer. A thermometer shows the temperature, which is how hot the air around us is. The first thermometer was made in 1714 by Gabriel Daniel Fahrenheit.

Think

From which direction does a southerly wind blow? North or south?

Can planes tell the weather?

Weather planes don't carry any passengers. Instead they fly through the air recording the weather. They measure the temperature of the air, the speed of the wind and how much water is in the air. This information helps weather forecasters tell us what the weather is going to be like.

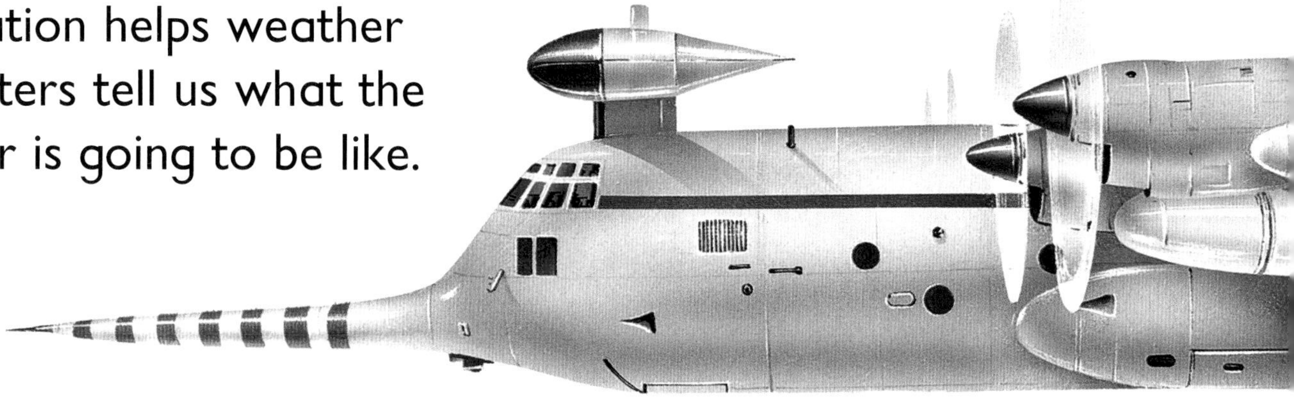

Weather plane

Astronaut snaps!

Astronauts who travel on the space shuttle and live on space stations take cameras with them. They often take amazing photographs of clouds and thunderstorms from space.

Why do scientists fly balloons?

Scientists fly balloons to find out about the weather. The balloons are filled with a gas called helium. They float up through the air and carry instruments that measure the weather. The information is sent back to the ground by radio.

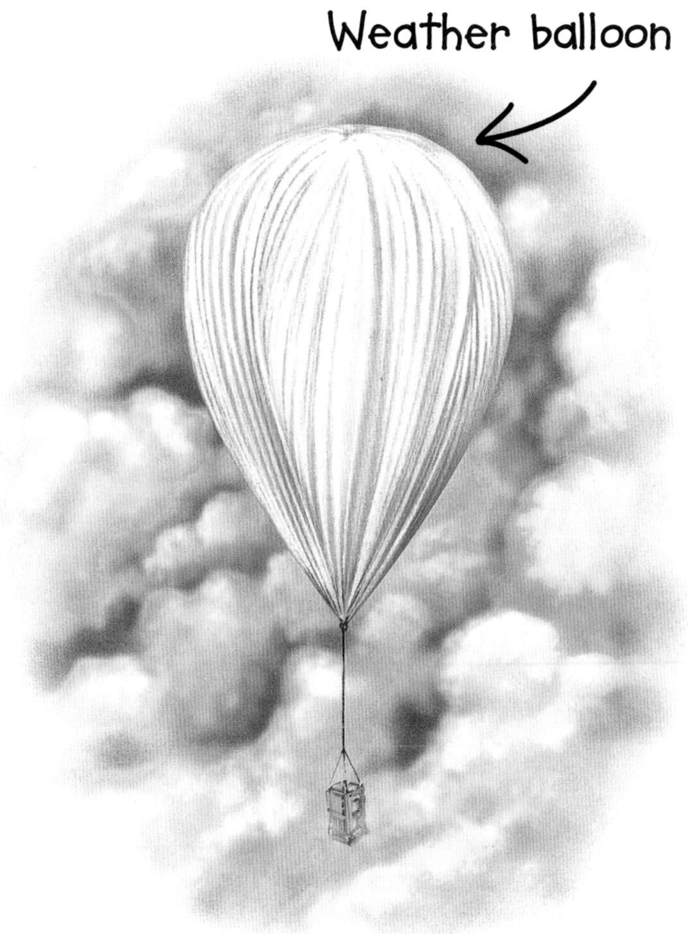

How do we watch weather from space?

With weather satellites. A satellite moves around the Earth in space. It takes photographs of the clouds below and sends them back to Earth. Satellite photographs show which way hurricanes are moving. They help forecasters to warn people if a hurricane is heading their way.

Remember

Can you remember how information gets from a weather balloon down to the ground?

Did weather kill the dinosaurs?

Dinosaurs lived millions of years ago. Scientists think that they may have died because the weather all over the world got colder. They think this happened when a giant rock (meteorite) from space hit the Earth. This threw lots of dust into the air, which blocked out the Sun.

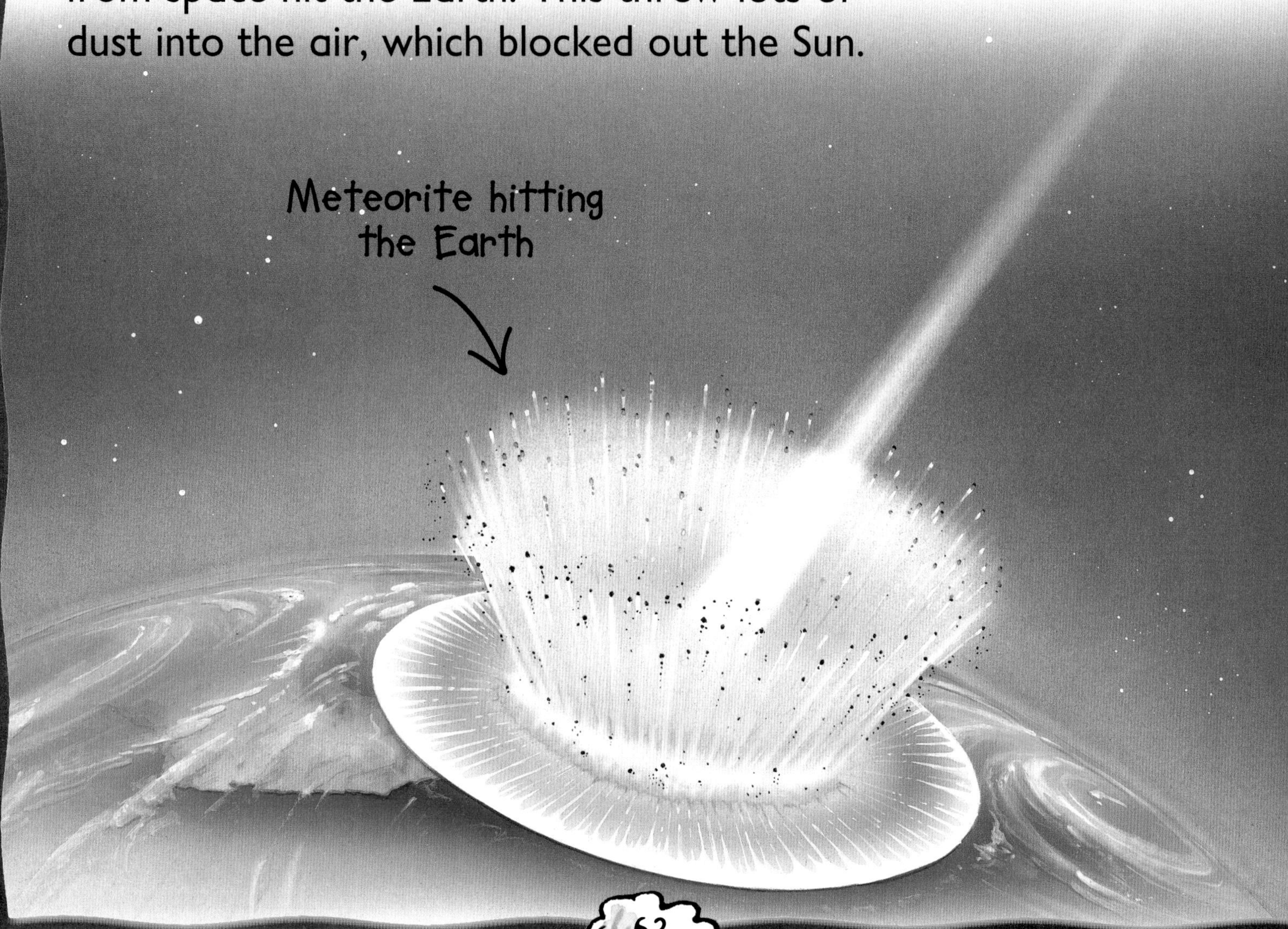

Is Greenland green?

Greenland is a big island in the Atlantic Ocean. It is covered with a thick sheet of ice. Hundreds of years ago, Greenland was green because it was not so cold and icy. People from northern Europe called Vikings farmed there. They moved away when the weather got colder.

Vikings in Greenland

Windy tower!

The Tower of Winds is a tower in Athens, Greece. It was built 2000 years ago. It had a giant wind vane on top to measure the direction of the wind.

Find

Can you find Greenland on a map of the world?

Is our weather changing?

Weather experts think the weather is getting warmer. This might be happening because we are cutting down forests. When trees are burned, they release a gas called carbon dioxide. This traps heat from the Sun in the atmosphere.

Quiz time

Do you remember what you have read about weather? These questions will test your memory. The pictures will help you. If you get stuck, read the pages again.

1. Why do leaves fall in autumn?

page 39

2. When is a lake not a lake?

page 41

3. Where does it rain every day?

page 42

4. How deep is the atmosphere?

page 43

5. Are all clouds small and fluffy?

page 45

6. What rain never lands?

page 45

7. What happens in a flood?

page 46

8. Did Noah build an ark?

page 47

9. When is snow dangerous?

page 49

10. Which storm has an eye?

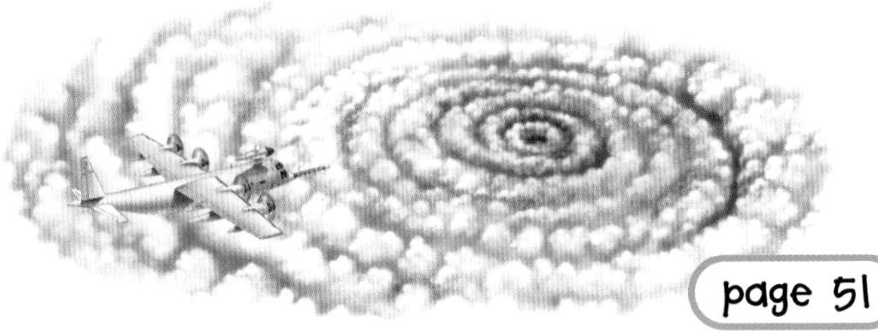

page 51

11. What makes the sky clap?

page 52

12. Who first recorded the weather?

page 56

13. What is a rain dance?

page 56

Answers

1. Because it is hard for them to grow in the dark winter months
2. When it's a mirage
3. In a tropical rainforest
4. Hundreds of kilometres
5. No, they come in different shapes and sizes
6. Drops that fall into very dry air
7. A lot of rain falls and floods the land
8. We don't know if Noah's ark existed
9. In an avalanche
10. A hurricane
11. A thunderstorm
12. The Chinese
13. A traditional dance to bring on clouds and rain

Electrifying questions about...

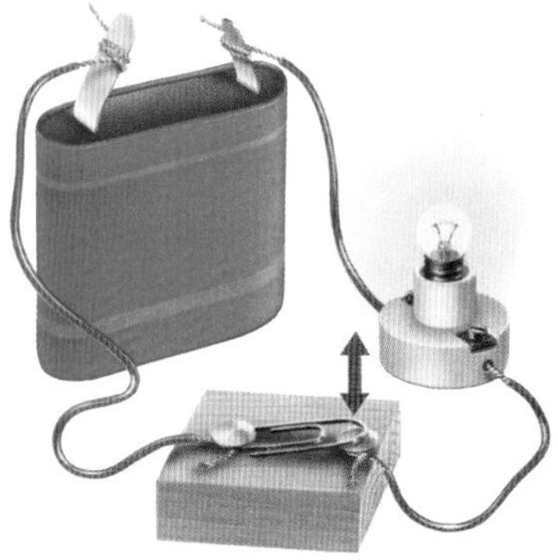

Science

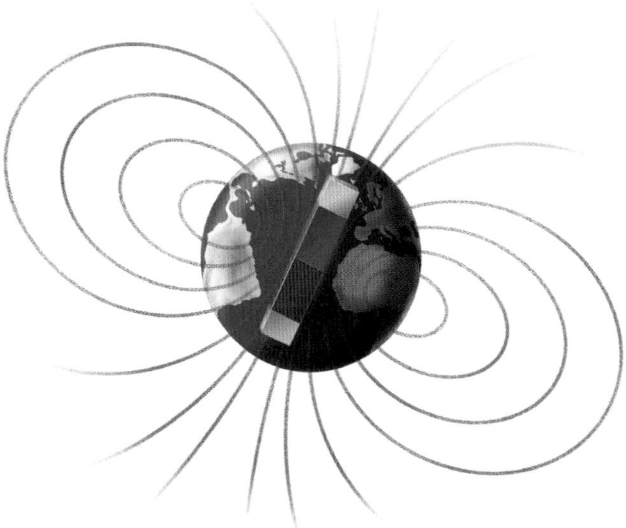

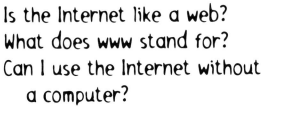

Is science in the playground?

Yes, it is! Lots of science happens in a playground. The playground rides could not work without science. A see-saw is a simple machine called a lever. It has a long arm and a point in the middle called a pivot. As you ride on the see-saw, the lever tips up and down on the pivot.

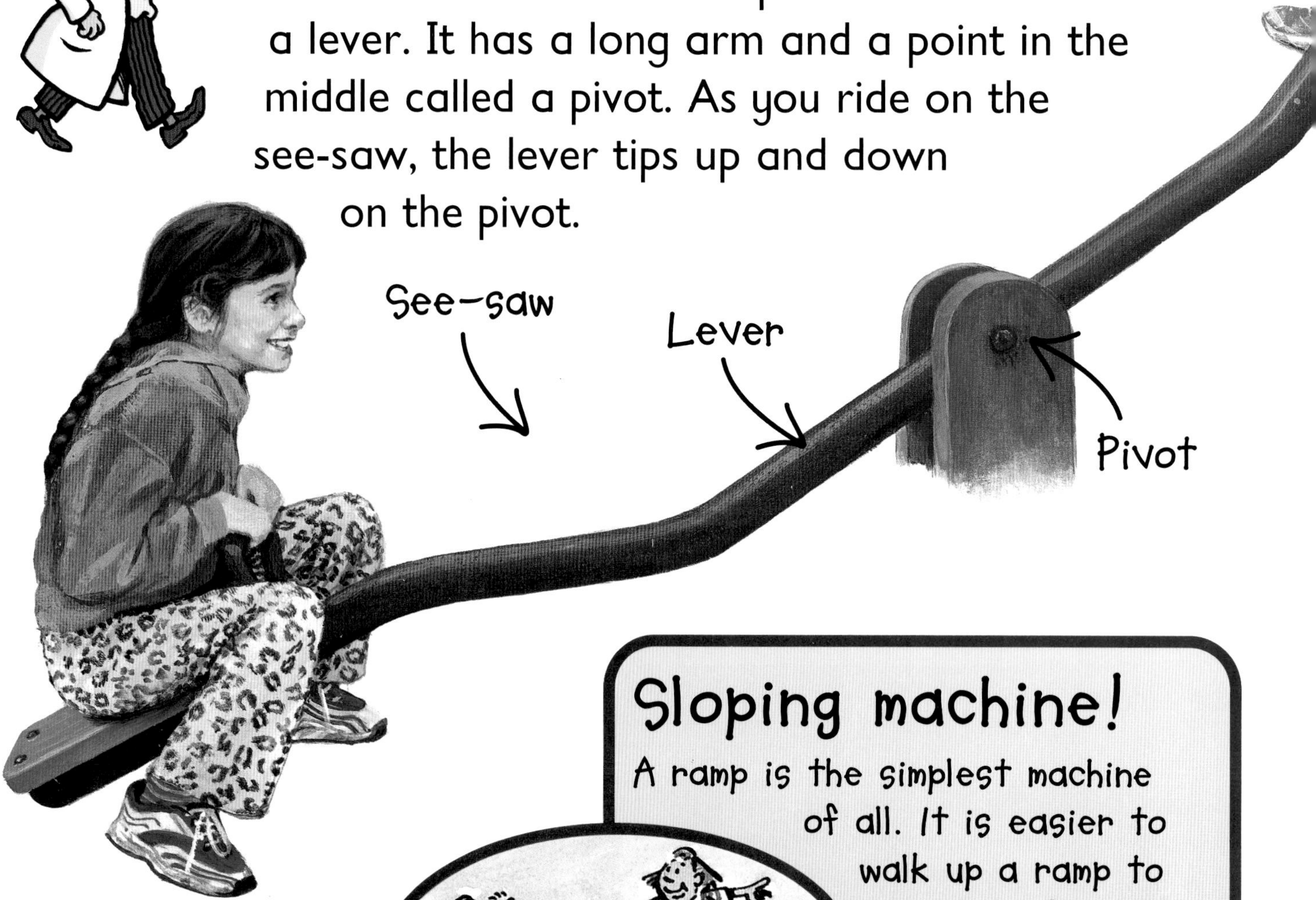

Sloping machine!

A ramp is the simplest machine of all. It is easier to walk up a ramp to the top of a hill than it is to climb a steep hillside.

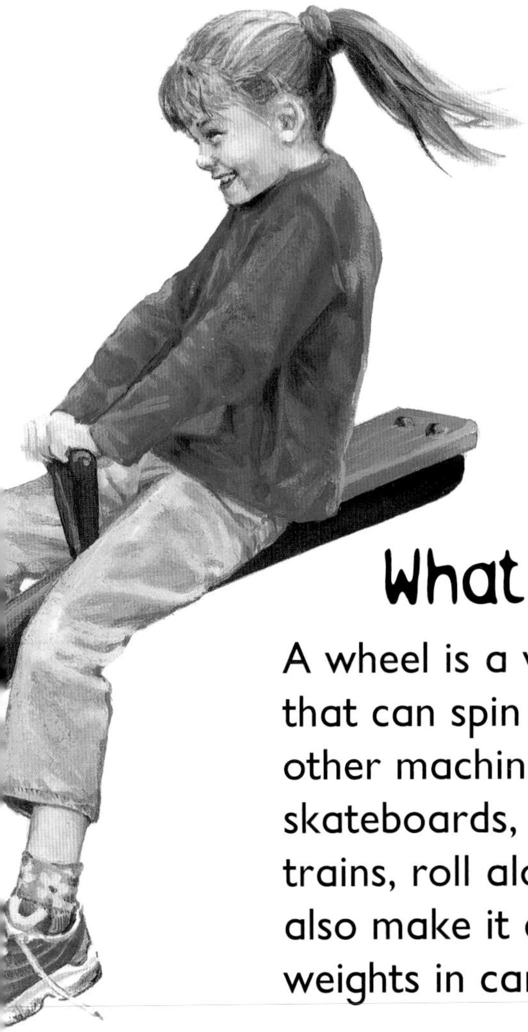

What is a wheel?

A wheel is a very simple machine that can spin around. Wheels let other machines, such as skateboards, bicycles, cars and trains, roll along smoothly. They also make it easy to move heavy weights in carts and wheelbarrows.

Feel

Press the palm of your hand onto a table. A force called friction stops you sliding your hand along.

What makes things stop and start?

Pushes and pulls make things stop and start. Scientists use the word 'force' for pushes and pulls. Forces are all around us. The force of gravity pulls things downwards. It makes a rollercoaster car hurtle downhill. It also slows the car on the uphill parts of the track.

Why do fireworks flash and bang?

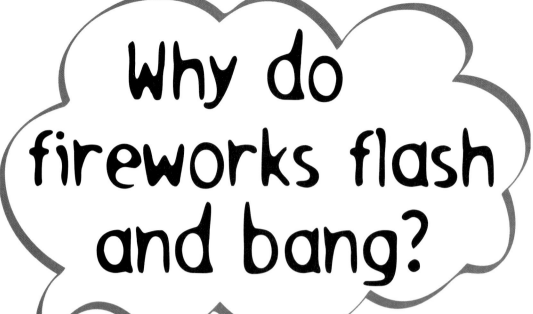

Fireworks flash and bang because they are full of chemicals that burn. The chemicals have lots of energy stored in them. When they burn, the energy changes to light, heat and sound. We use chemicals that burn in other places too, such as cookers, heaters and car engines.

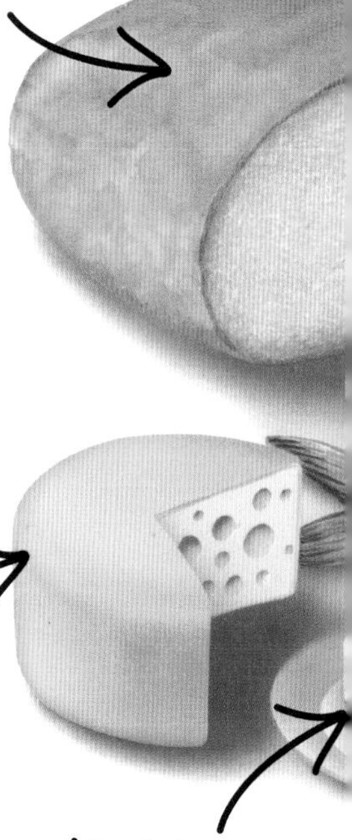

Do I need energy?

Yes, you do. Your body needs energy to keep working. It even uses energy when you are fast asleep! You get energy from food. Some food, such as bread, is full of energy. You have to eat other kinds of food as well. They have chemicals in them that keep your body healthy.

Hot! Hot! Hot!

The hottest-ever temperature recorded was in a science laboratory. It was four hundred thousand million degrees Celsius (400,000,000°C). Now that's hot!

What is a thermometer?

A thermometer tells us how hot something is. This is called temperature. The numbers written on a thermometer are normally degrees Celsius (°C). If you put a thermometer in cold water, it shows 0°C. If you put it in boiling water it shows 100°C. A thermometer can also measure your body temperature.

Remember

Look at the picture of food above. Can you remember a food that gives energy?

What is in an electric motor?

Magnets and wires. Electricity from a battery passes through the wires. This turns the wires into a magnet. Two more magnets on each side of the motor push and pull against the wires. This makes a thin metal rod (spindle) spin around.

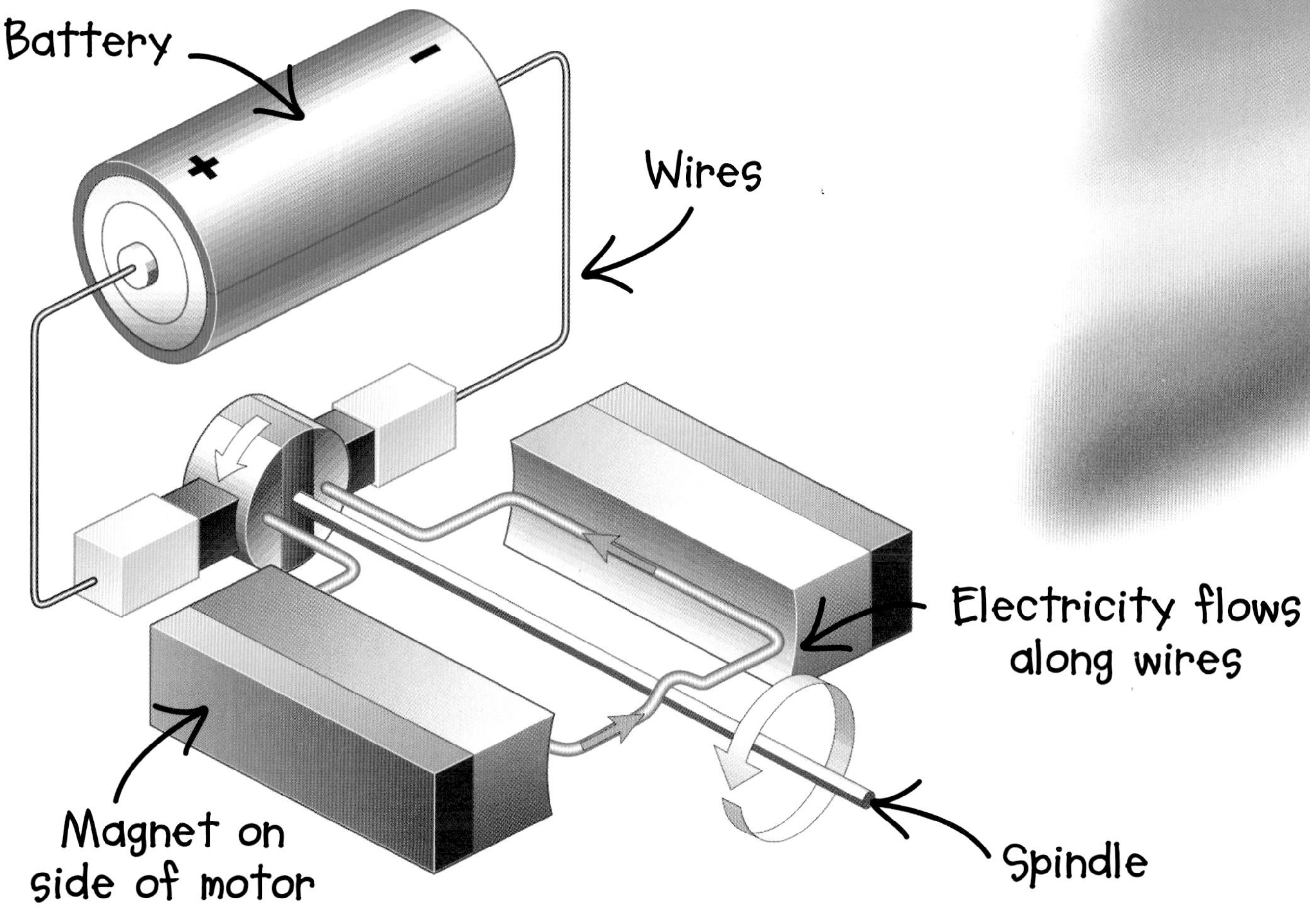

Where do rainbow colours come from?

The colours of a rainbow are in light that comes from the Sun. This light is called white light. It is made up of lots of colours mixed together. We can see the colours if we send a beam of sunlight through a glass triangle called a prism, or when there's a rainbow in the sky.

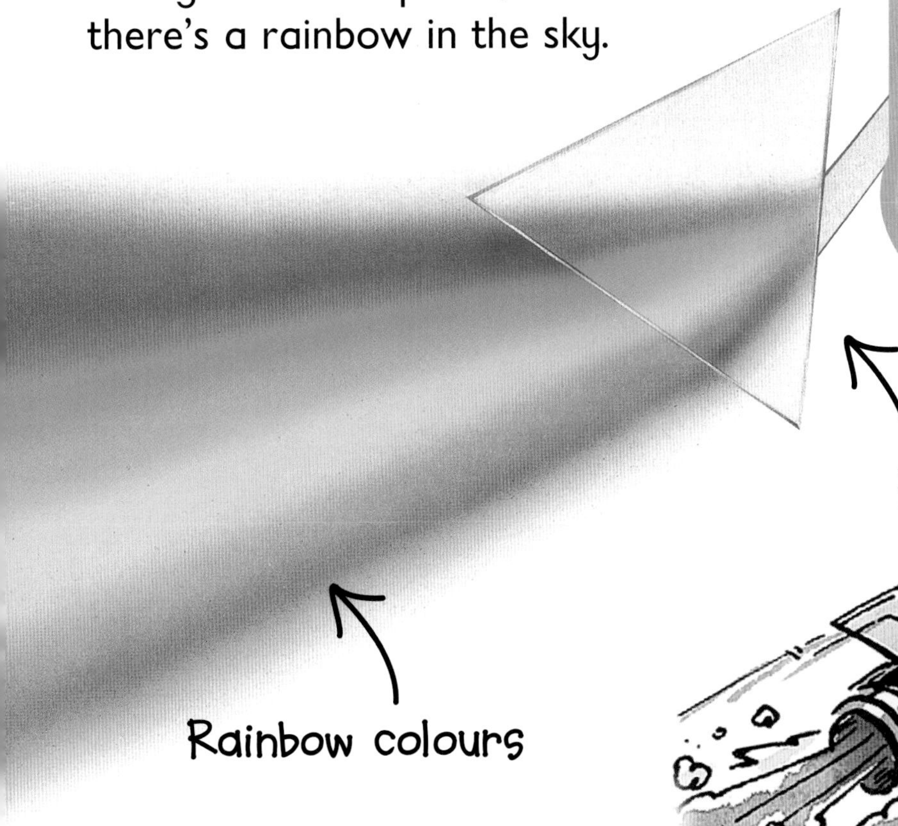

Fast as light!

Light is the fastest thing in the Universe. It travels 300,000 kilometres every second. That means it could travel around the Earth seven times in less than a second!

Make

On a sunny day, stand with your back to the Sun. Spray water into the air and you should see a rainbow!

What is the loudest sound?

The roar of a jet engine is the loudest sound we normally hear. It is thousands of times louder than someone shouting. Sounds this loud can damage our ears if we are too close to them. The quietest sounds we can hear are things like rustling leaves.

Where is science in a city?

Everywhere! In a big city, almost every machine, building and vehicle is based on science. Cars, buses and trains help us move around the city. Scientists and engineers have also worked out how to build tall skyscrapers where people live and work.

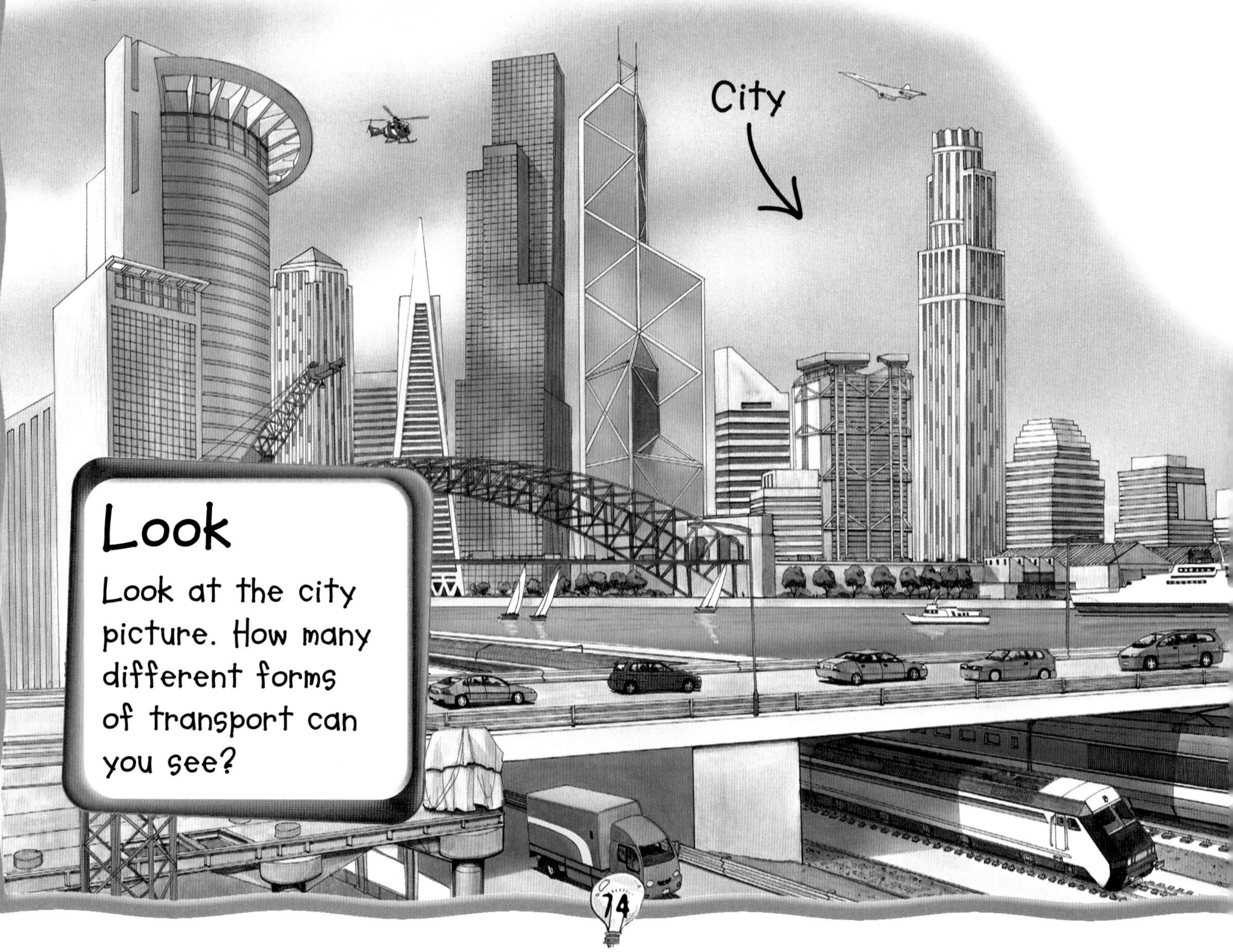

Look

Look at the city picture. How many different forms of transport can you see?

Who works railway signals?

Nobody does! The signals work by themselves. Electronic parts on the track work out if a train is passing. Then a computer changes the signals to red, to stop another train moving onto the same piece of track.

How do skyscrapers stay up?

Skyscrapers stay up because they have a strong frame on the inside. The frame is made from steel and concrete. These are very strong materials. Normally you can't see the frame. It is hidden by the skyscraper's walls. The walls hang on the frame.

Plane spotters!

There's science at an airport, too. A radar machine uses radio waves to find aircraft in the sky. This helps people at the airport to guide the aircraft onto the runway.

How do you make magnets?

By using another magnet! Magnets are made from lumps of iron or steel. You can turn a piece of iron into a magnet by stroking it with another magnet. A magnet can also be made by sending electricity through a coil of wire. This is called an electromagnet. Some electromagnets are so strong, they can pick up cars.

Electromagnet picking up scrap cars

Count

Find a magnet at home (you can use a fridge magnet). How many paper clips can your magnet pick up?

Does a magnet have a field?

Yes – but it's not a field of grass! The area around a magnet is called a magnetic field. A magnetic field is shown by drawing lines around a magnet. The Earth has a magnetic field, too. It is as though there is a giant magnet inside the Earth.

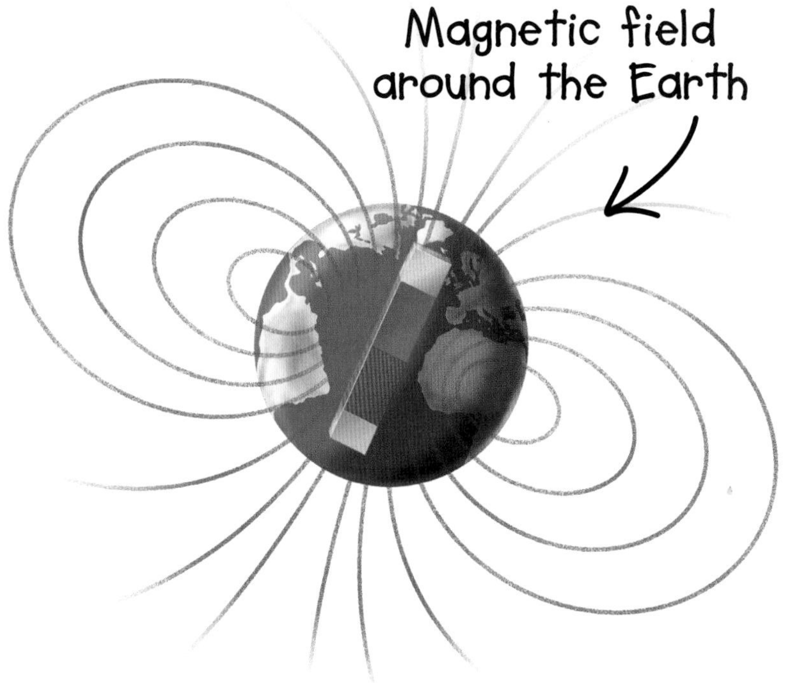

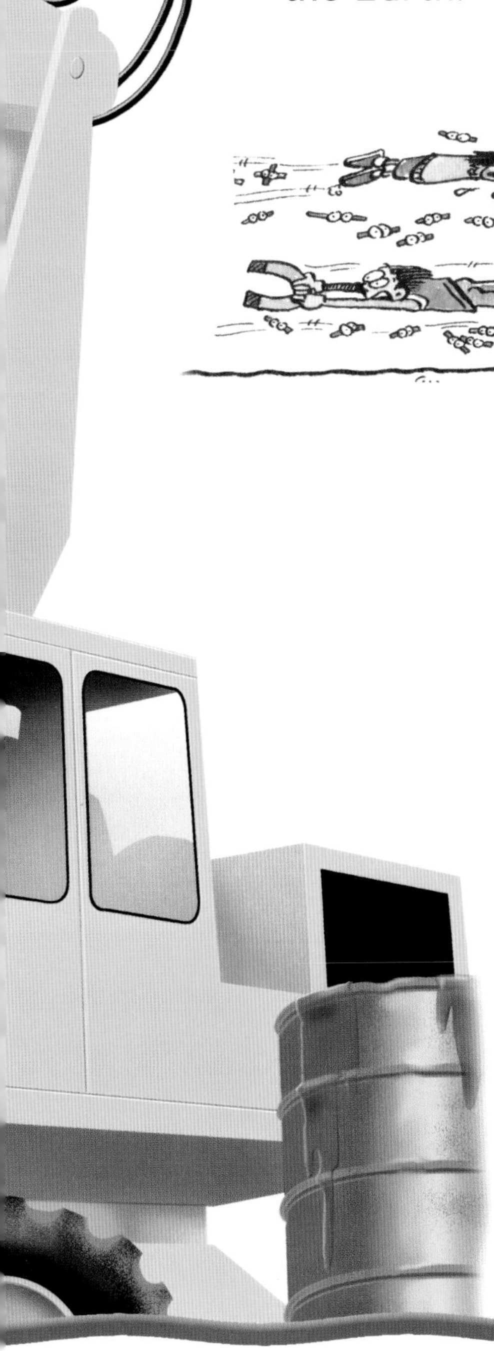

What are poles?

Every magnet has two poles. These are where the pull of a magnet is strongest. They are called the north pole and the south pole. A north pole and a south pole always pull towards each other. Two north poles always push each other away. So do two south poles.

Handy rock!

Some rocks act like magnets. Years ago, people used magnetic rocks to find their way. If they let the rock spin round, it always pointed in the same direction.

Where does electricity come from?

Battery

Electricity comes to your home along cables from power stations. The cables are held off the ground by pylons. Around your home are holes in the wall called sockets. When a machine is plugged into a socket, electricity flows out to work the machine.

Electric!

Our homes are full of machines that work using electricity. If there was no electricity we wouldn't have televisions, lights, washing machines or computers!

Power station

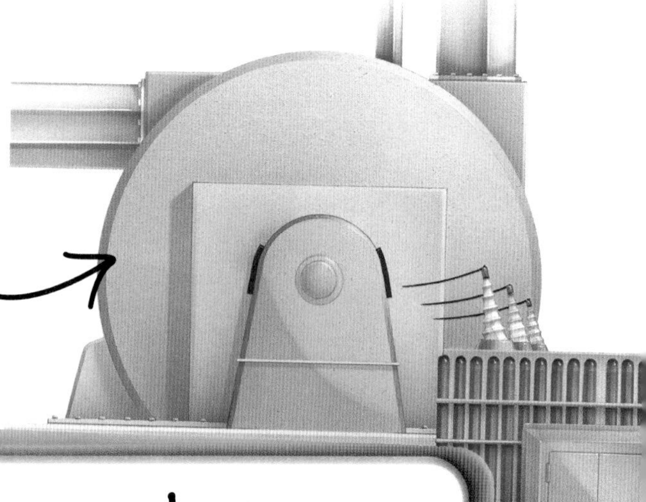

Remember

Mains electricity is very dangerous. It could kill you. Never play with mains sockets in your home.

Light bulb
Switch

What is a circuit?

A circuit is a loop that electricity moves around. This circuit is made up of a battery, a light bulb and a switch. If the switch is turned on, the loop would be broken. Then the electricity would stop moving and the light would go out.

When is electricity in the sky?

When there's a thunderstorm! During a storm, a kind of electricity called static electricity builds up. This can make a big flash, that lights up the sky. This is lightning. The hot lightning heats up the air around it and this makes a loud clap. This is thunder.

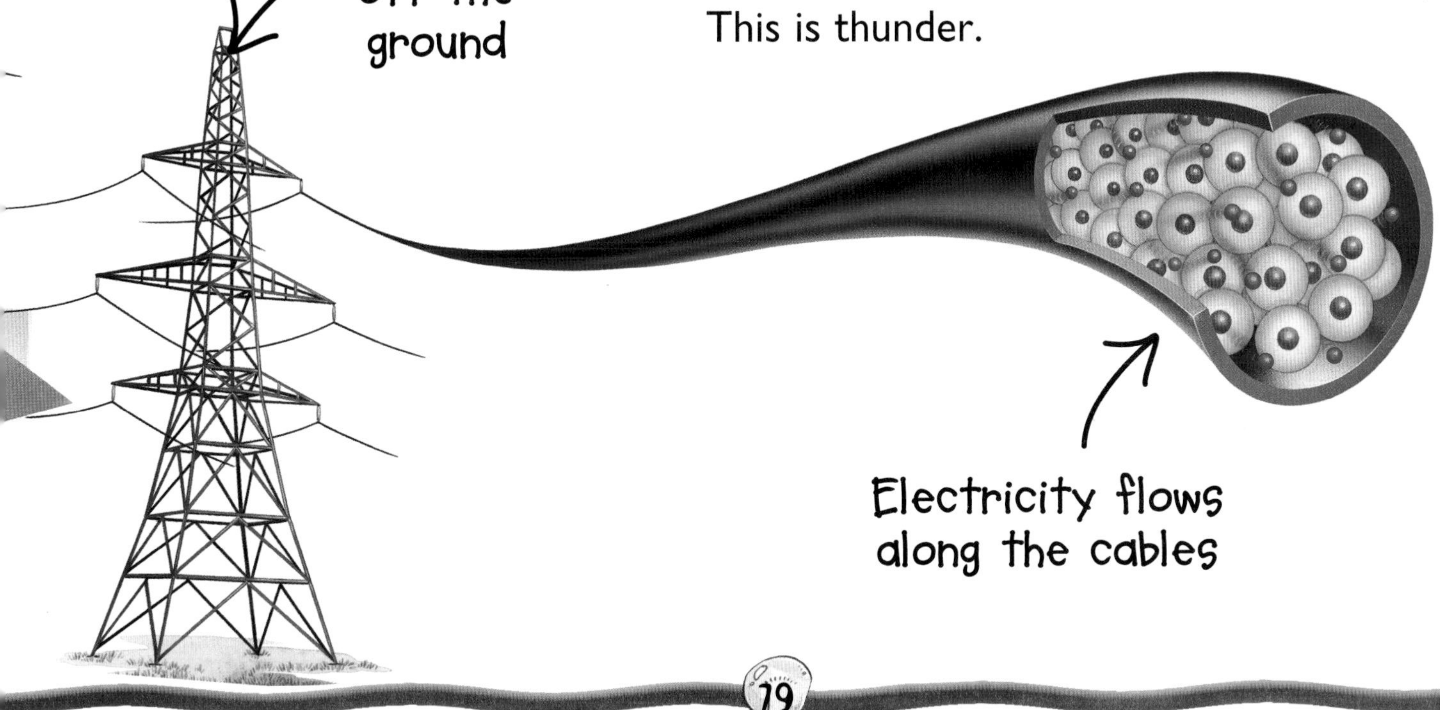

Pylon holds cables off the ground
Electricity flows along the cables

What waves are invisible?

Radio waves are all around us, but we can't see them. We use radio waves to send sounds and pictures to radios and televisions. Some radio waves come from satellites in space. A radio set receives radio waves through a metal rod called an aerial. A dish-shaped aerial picks up radio waves for television programmes.

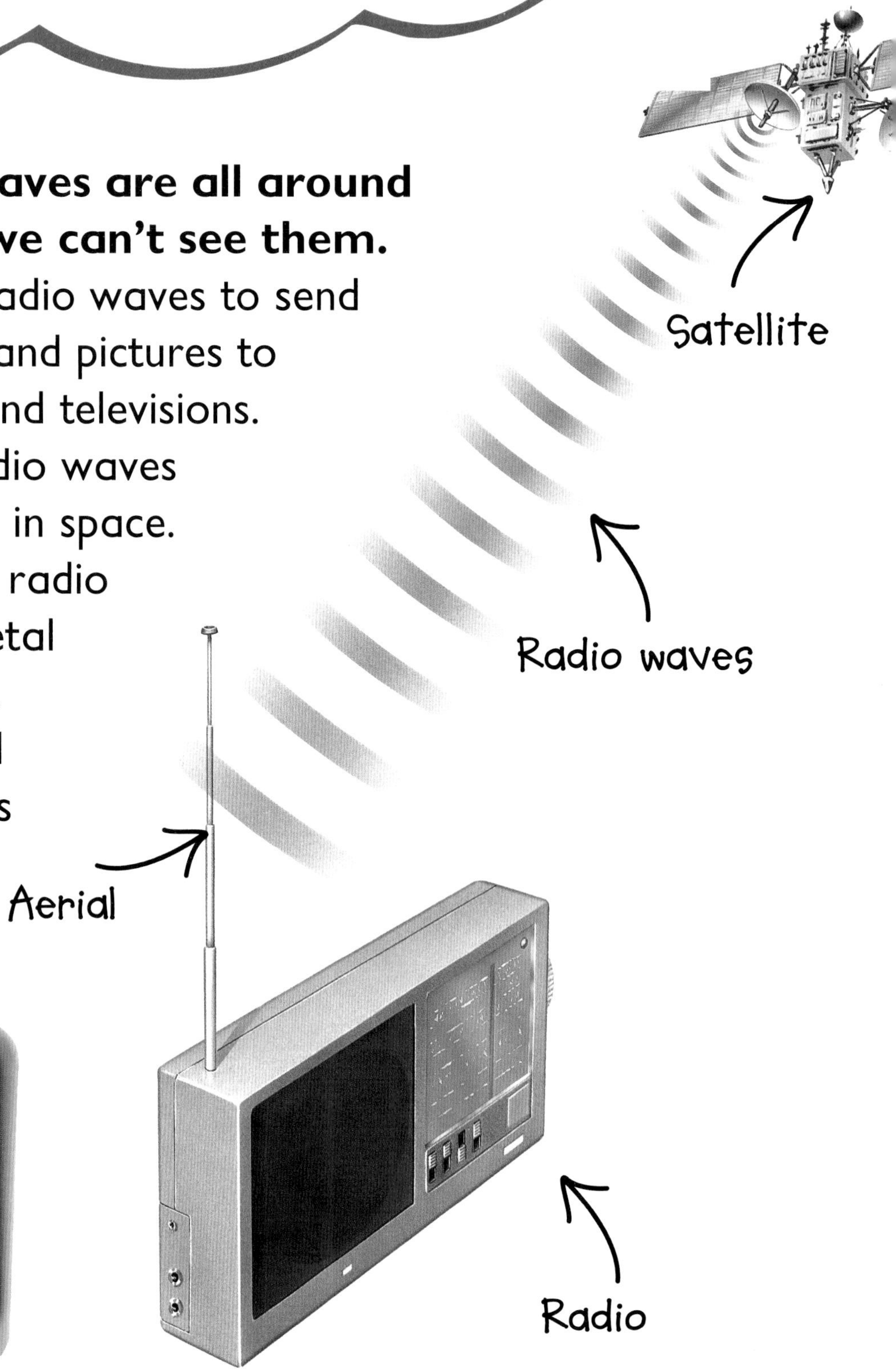

Remember

Which part of your body would stop an X-ray? Skin or bone?

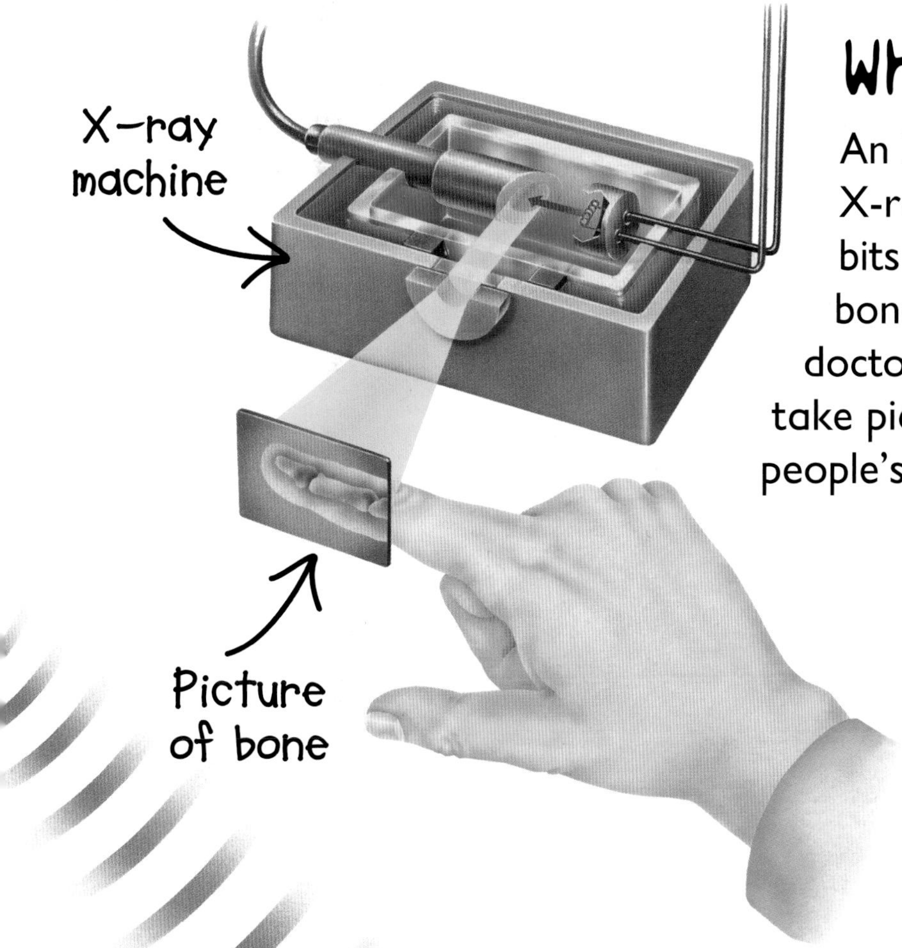

What is an X-ray?

An X-ray is like a radio wave. X-rays can go through the soft bits of your body. However, hard bones stop them. That's why doctors use X-ray machines to take pictures of the inside of people's bodies.

Space radio!

Radio waves can travel through space. But they can't travel through water. So you can listen to a radio in a space station, but not in a submarine!

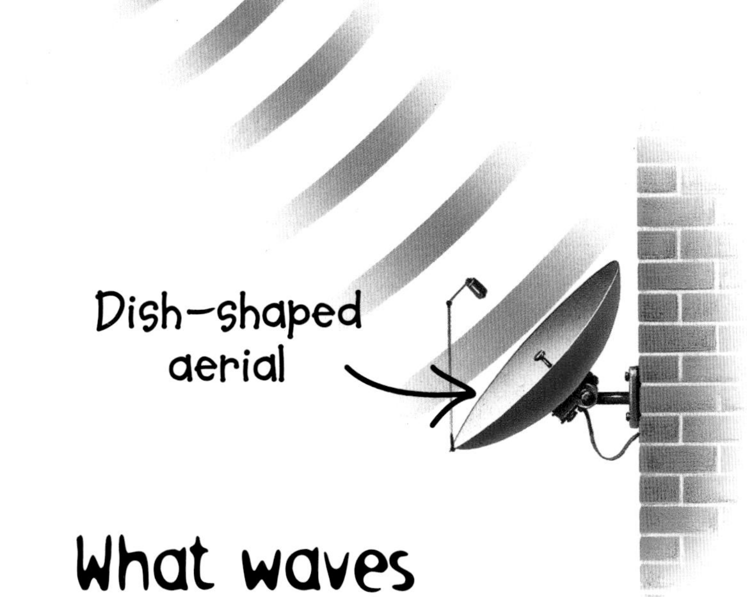

What waves can cook food?

Microwaves can. These are a kind of radio wave. They have lots of energy in them. A microwave uses this energy to cook food. Microwaves are fired into the oven. They make the particles in the food jiggle about. This makes the food hot.

Are computers clever?

Not really! Computers are amazing machines, but they can only do what they are told. They carry out computer programs written down by people. These are full of instructions that the computer follows. You can also tell a computer what to do by using its keyboard and mouse.

Remember

Can you remember the name for a computer's electronic brain? Read these pages again to help you.

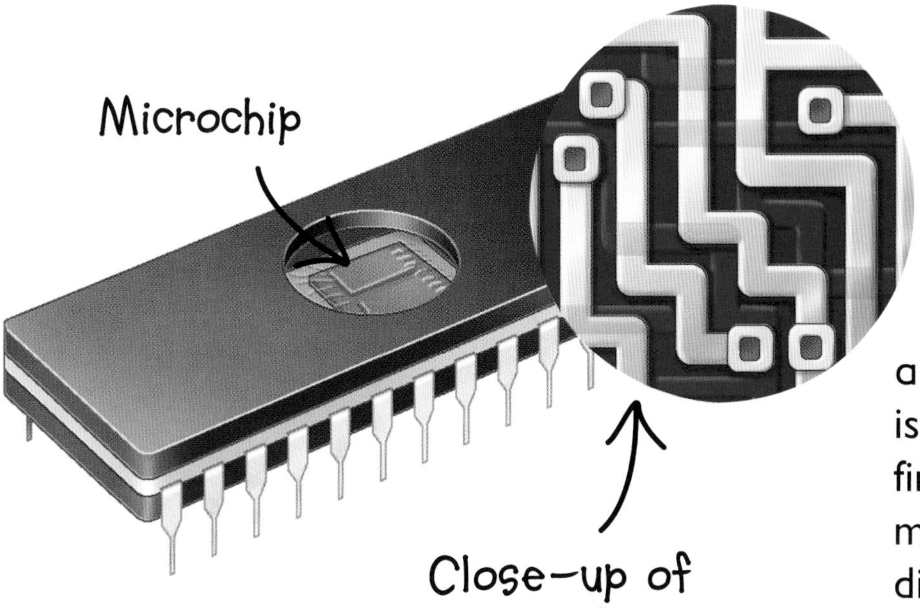

Does a computer have a brain?

A computer doesn't have a brain like yours. It has an electronic brain called a central processing unit. This is a microchip the size of your fingernail. This amazing mini machine can do millions of difficult sums in a split second.

Computer room!

The first computer was made 60 years ago. It was so big that it filled a whole room. A modern calculator can do sums much more quickly!

How does a computer remember?

A computer remembers with its electronic memory. This is made up of lots of tiny microchips. When you turn the computer off, everything in the memory is lost. So you have to save your work on a disc, otherwise you lose it when you switch off.

Is the Internet like a web?

The Internet is made up of millions of computers around the world. They are connected like a giant spider's web! A computer connects to a machine called a modem. This sends signals to a server. The server lets you connect to the Internet. People can send emails and open web pages.

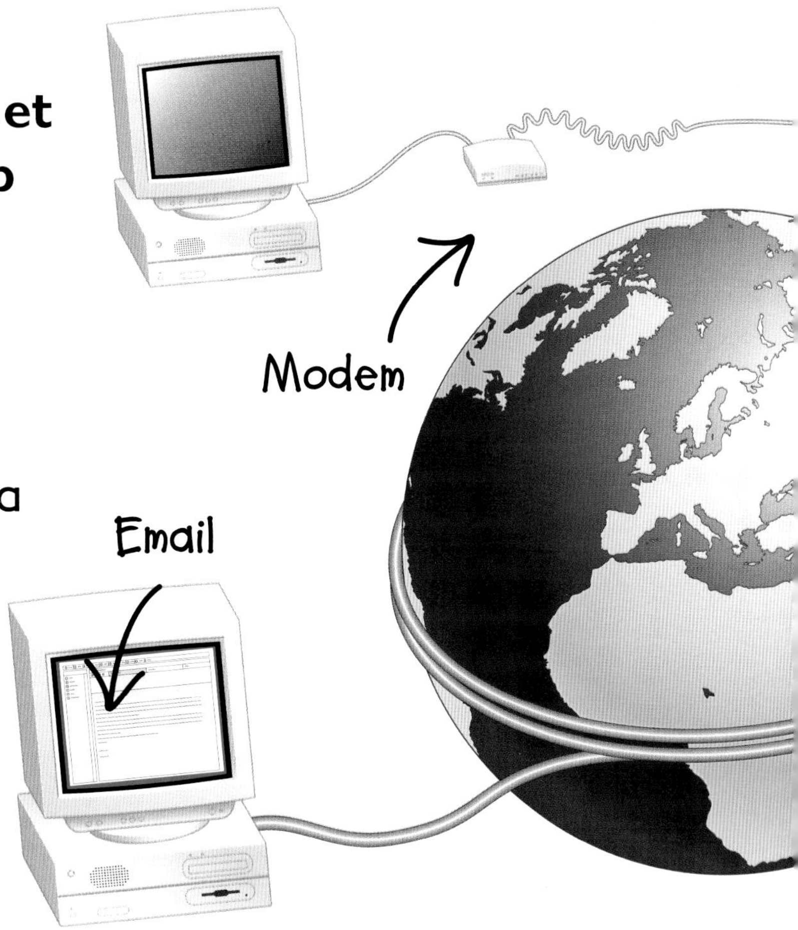

Find out

Look at the main picture on these pages. See if you can find out what the word 'email' is short for.

What does www stand for?

The letters www are short for World Wide Web. The World Wide Web is like a giant library of information, stored on computers all over the world. There are also thousands of shops on the World Wide Web, where you can buy almost anything.

Can I use the Internet without a computer?

Yes. Other machines can link to the Internet, too. You can see simple information from the Internet on a mobile phone. You can send and get emails, too. A mobile phone connects to the Internet by radio.

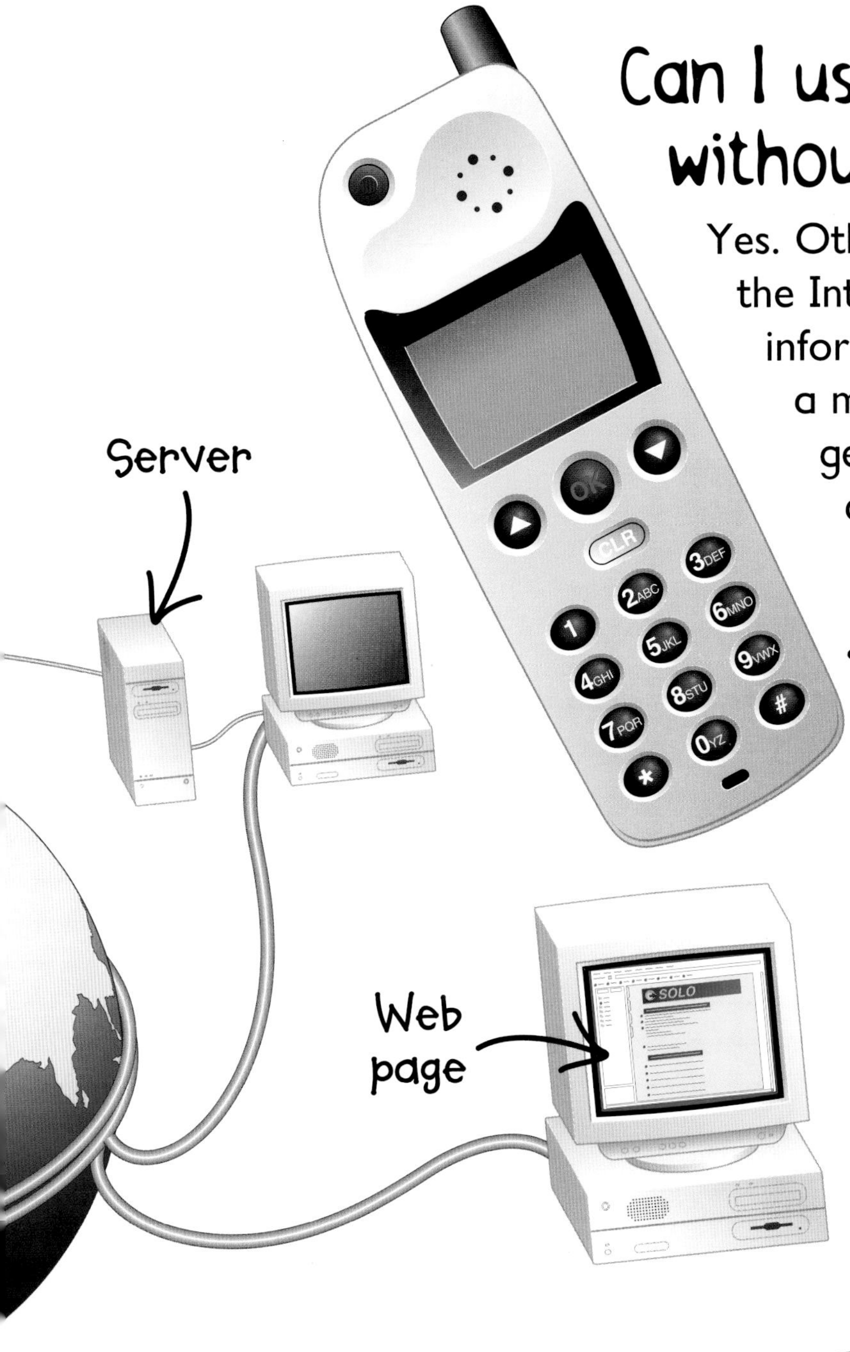

Millions of pages!

The World Wide Web has more than 8000 million pages of information. That's two pages for every person on the planet!

Can a car be made from card?

Yes, it can – but it would break if you sat inside it! It is always important to use the right material to make something. Cars are made from tough, long-lasting materials. Metal, plastic and rubber are all materials used to make cars.

A racing car is made up of hundreds of parts and different materials

Think

Think of three more materials from which things are made. If you get stuck, ask an adult.

Cotton plants make clothes

What materials grow?

Many of the materials we use every day come from plants. Wood comes from the trunks and branches of trees. Cotton is made from the seeds of cotton plants to make clothes such as T-shirts. Some rubber is made from a liquid (sap) from rubber trees.

Rubber tree makes tyres

Tree trunks and branches make wooden bats

Does glass grow?

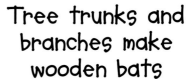

Glass doesn't grow! It is made from sand and two other materials called limestone and soda. These materials are mixed together and melted to make a gooey liquid. When the mixture cools down, it forms the hard glass that we use to makes windows, drinking glasses and other objects.

Bullet proof!

Some glass is extra-strong. Toughened glass is so hard that even a bullet from a gun bounces off it!

What do scientists do at work?

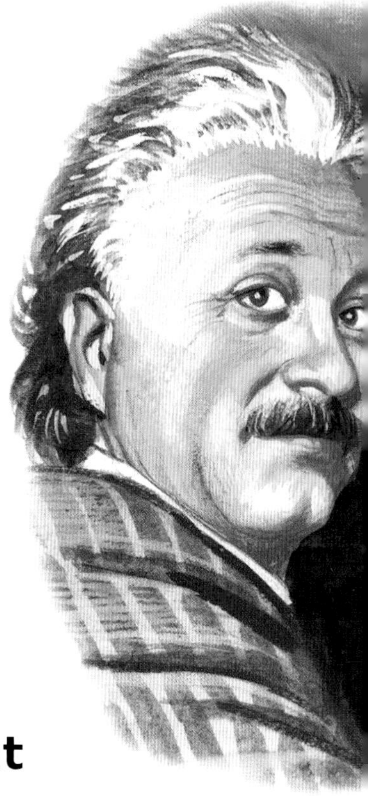

Some scientists try to find out about the world around us. Others find out about space, planets and stars. Some scientists discover useful materials that we can use. Scientists carry out experiments in laboratories to test their ideas.

Scientist in a laboratory

Who is the most famous scientist?

The most famous scientist is called Albert Einstein (1879–1955). He made many discoveries about time, space, the force of gravity and nuclear energy. The ideas that Einstein wrote down were so amazing that they made him famous across the world.

Albert Einstein

Atom pie!

One hundred years ago, scientists thought that the pieces in an atom were all spread out, like the raisins in a pudding. Now we know they are all bunched together.

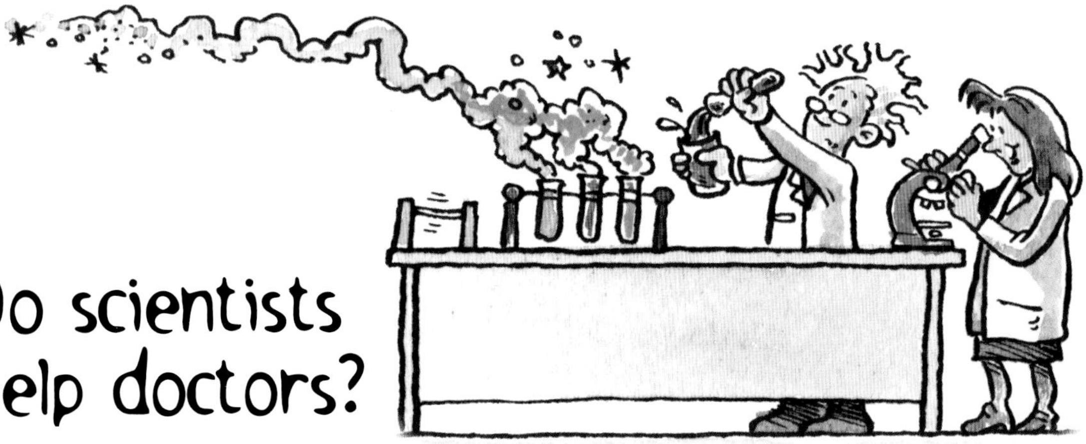

Do scientists help doctors?

Yes, they do. Many scientists make medicines that the doctor gives you when you are ill. They also help to make the complicated machines that doctors use in hospitals. Scientists also try to find out what makes us ill, and how we can stay healthy.

Find

Find out the name of the country where Albert Einstein was born. An encyclopedia will help you.

Are we harming the Earth?

Many of the things we do are harming the world around us. Machines such as cars put dangerous gases into the air. These gases can harm plants and make people ill. They are also making the weather change.

Scientists are always looking for new ways to reduce damage to the Earth.

Dirty cars!

Cars and other vehicles can produce so much pollution that in some cities it has become difficult for people to breathe.

What is recycling?

Recycling is using materials again, instead of throwing them away. This helps to make less waste. Ask your parents to take empty glass bottles to a bottle bank. The glass in the bottles is made into new bottles. Paper, metal and plastic are also recycled.

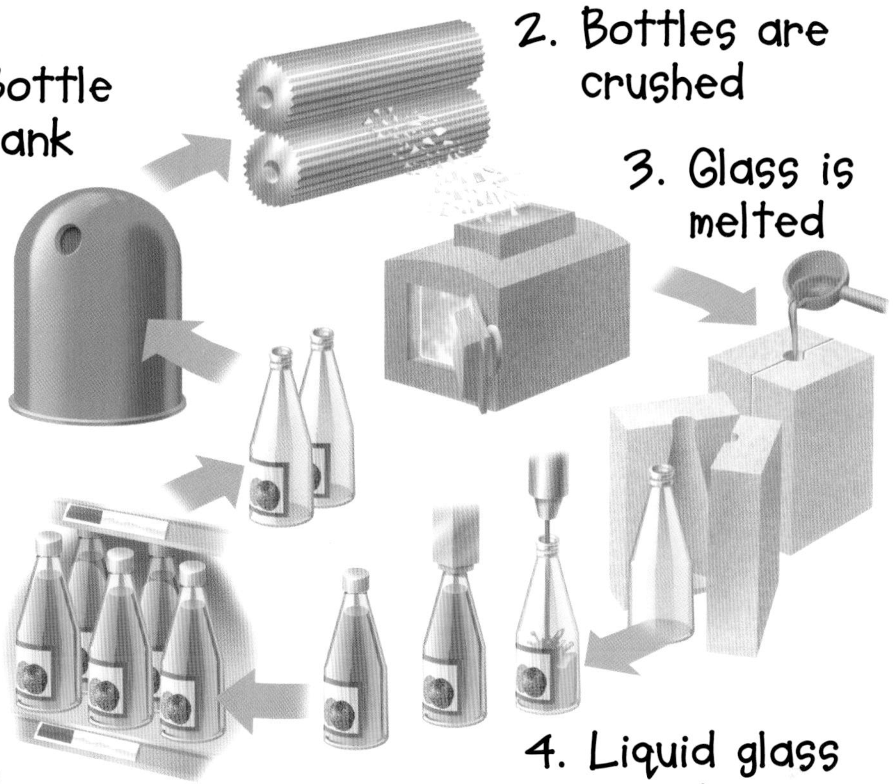
1. Bottle bank
2. Bottles are crushed
3. Glass is melted
4. Liquid glass is put in moulds
5. New bottles are ready

Glass recycling

Save

Ask your family to save electricity. Get them to switch off the lights when nobody is in the room.

Does electricity harm the Earth?

Yes, it does. Lots of coal, oil and gas are burned to make electricity. These make harmful gases that go into the air. You can help by turning things off to save electricity. Scientists are inventing new ways of making electricity from the wind, the Sun and water.

Quiz time

Do you remember what you have read about science? These questions will test your memory. The pictures will help you. If you get stuck, read the pages again.

1. Is science in the playground?

page 68

2. Do I need energy?

page 71

3. What is a thermometer?

page 71

page 72

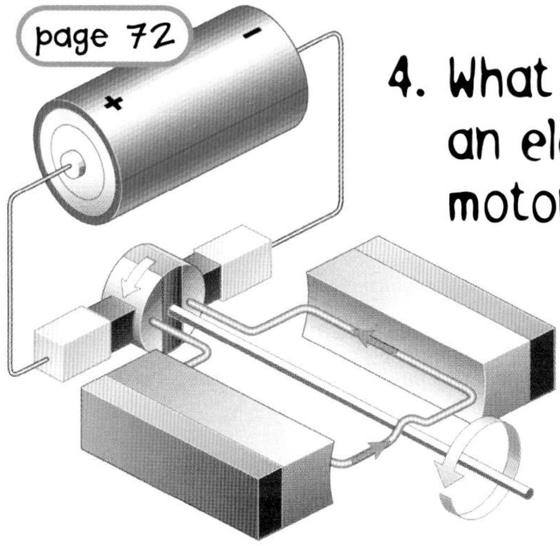

4. What is in an electric motor?

5. How do skyscrapers stay up?

page 75

page 77

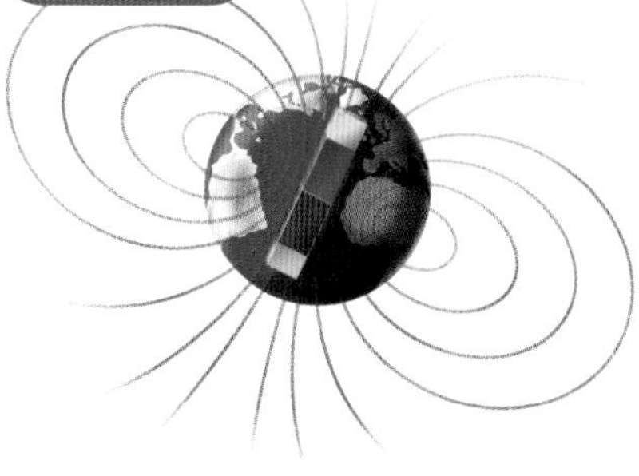

6. Does a magnet have a field?

7. What is a circuit?

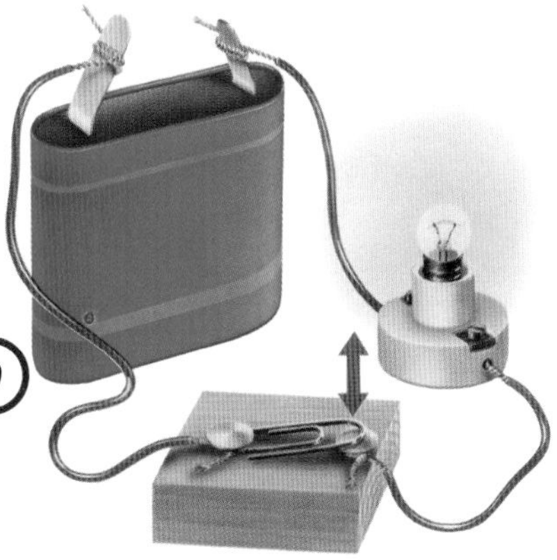

page 79

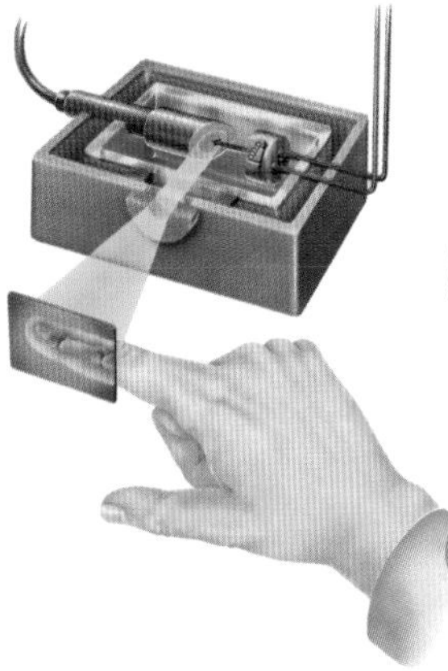

8. What is an X-ray?

page 81

9. What waves can cook food?

page 81

page 82

10. Are computers clever?

page 84

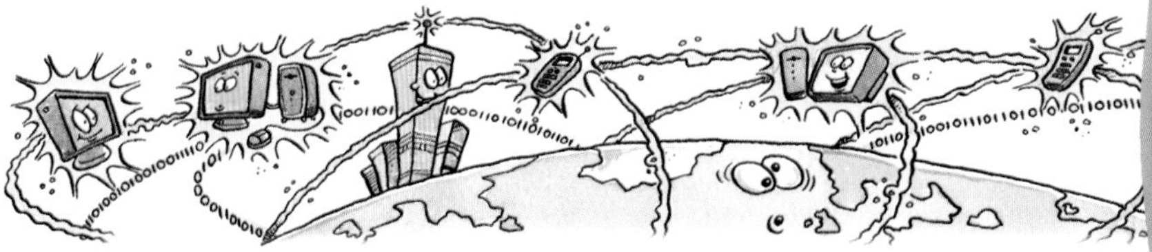

11. What does www stand for?

12. Who is the most famous scientist?

page 89

13. Does electricity harm the Earth?

page 91

Answers

1. Yes it is, in rides such as see-saws
2. Yes, you need energy for your body to work
3. A machine that measures heat
4. Magnets and wires
5. They have a strong frame that supports them
6. Yes, a magnetic field
7. A loop that electricity moves around
8. It is a radio wave
9. Microwaves
10. No, but they can follow instructions
11. World Wide Web
12. Albert Einstein
13. Yes, it can

Brainy questions about...

Your Body

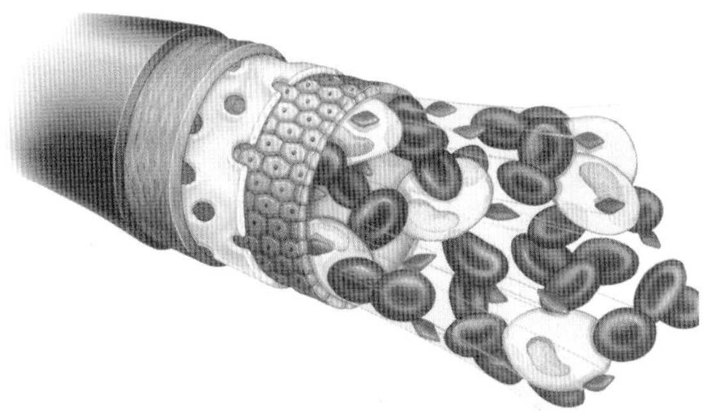

What does my skin do?

Skin protects you from bumps and scratches. It stops your body from drying out, and prevents germs from getting in. When you play on bikes or skateboards, you should wear gloves and knee pads to protect your skin.

Knee pads protect from cuts
Gloves protect from scrapes

Ouch! Ouch! Ouch!

There are millions of tiny touch sensors in your skin. They tell your brain when something touches your skin. Some sensors feel hot and cold. Others feel pain. Ouch!

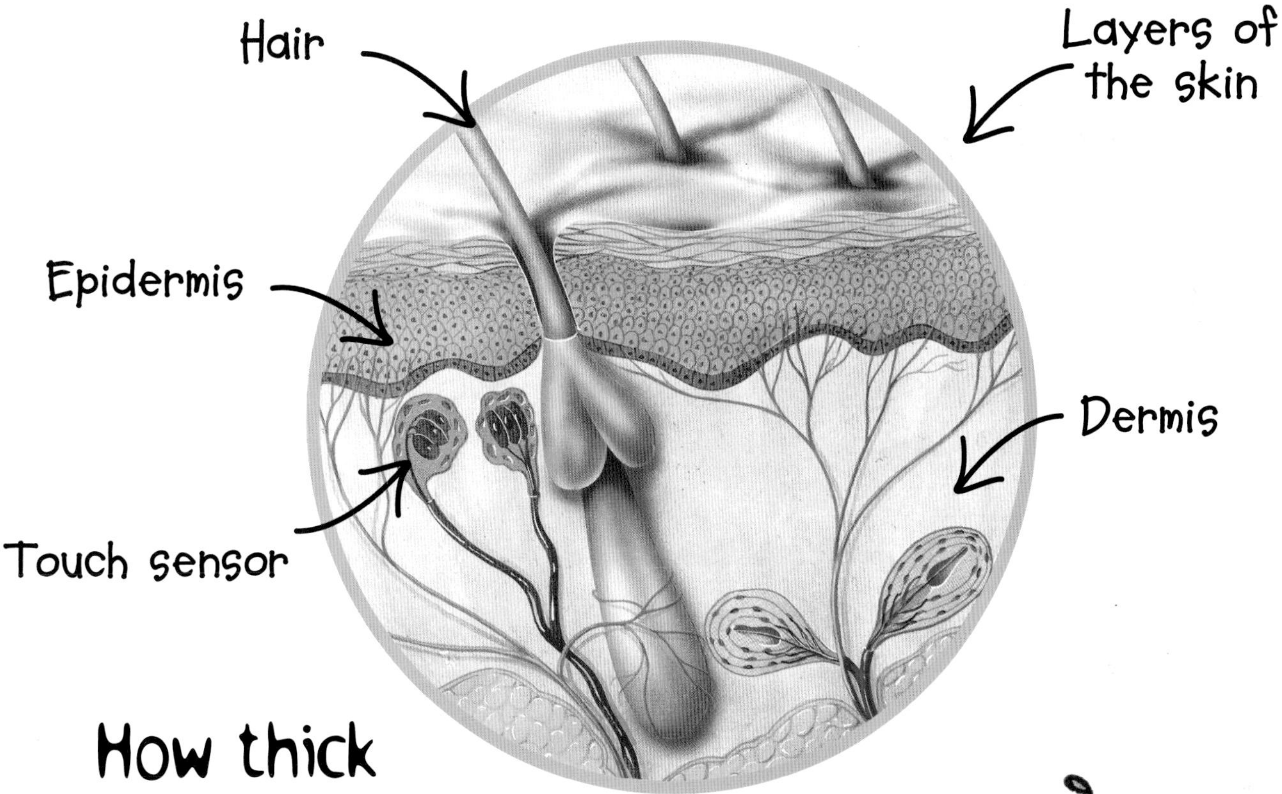

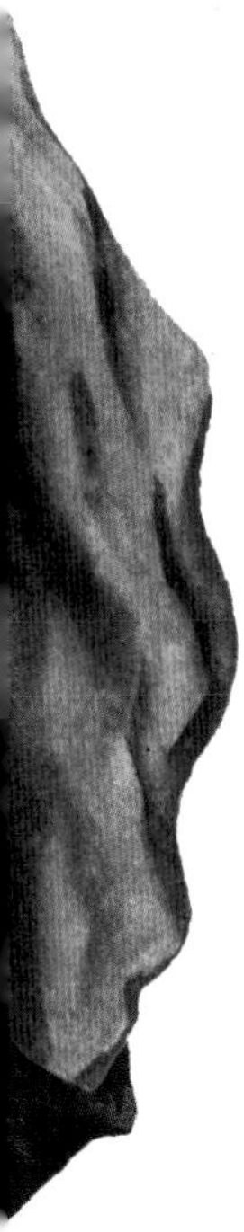

How thick is my skin?

Your skin is very thin. It is only 2 millimetres thick. On top is a layer of tough, dead cells called the epidermis. These cells gradually rub off. New cells grow underneath to replace them. Underneath is another layer of skin called the dermis. This contains areas that give you your sense of touch.

Think

If you are riding a bike or playing on a skateboard, what should you wear on your head, and why?

Why do I sweat when I'm warm?

To cool down again. Your body warms up on a hot day or when you run about. You sweat to get rid of the heat. Your body lets sweat out through your skin. As the sweat dries, it takes away heat. This cools you down.

How much hair do I have?

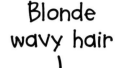

Your whole body is covered in about five million hairs! You have about 100,000 hairs on your head. Hair grows out of tiny pits in your skin, called follicles. Hair grows in different colours and it can be wavy, curly or straight.

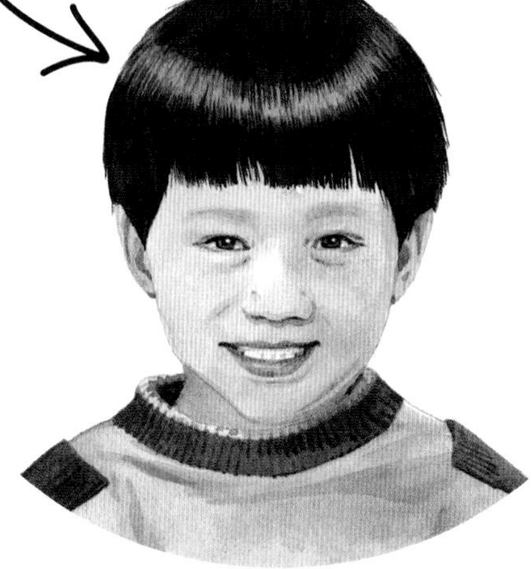

For the chop!

The hair on your head grows about 2 millimetres a week. If a hair is never cut, it reaches about one metre in length before it falls out. It is replaced by a new hair.

What are nails made from?

Fingernails and toenails are made from a hard material called keratin. It is the same material that hair is made from. Nails grow out of the nail root. In a week, a nail grows by about half a millimetre. They grow faster at night than in the day!

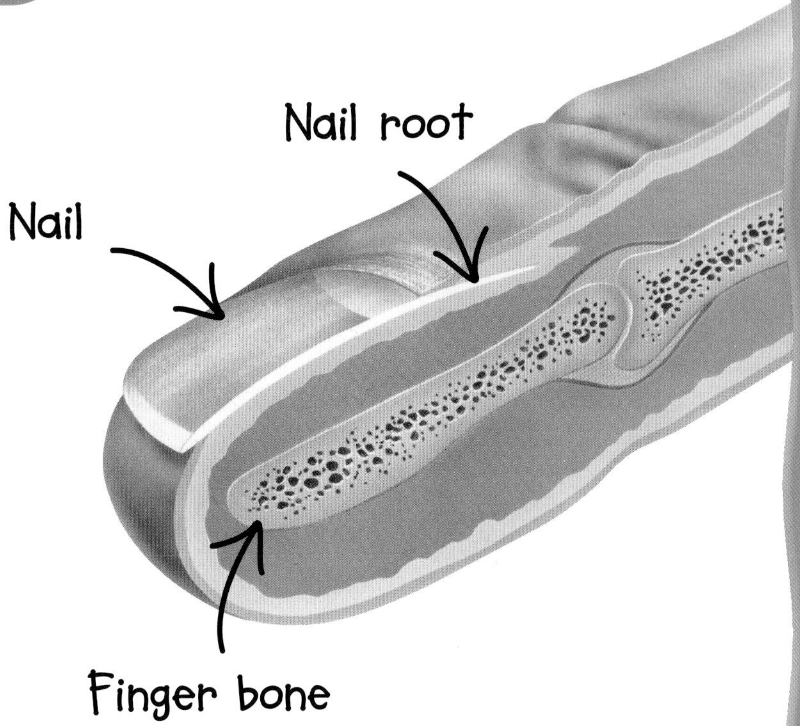

Look

Have a look in the mirror. Is your hair straight, wavy or curly? Use the pictures on page 8 to help you.

Why do we have fingernails?

Fingernails protect your fingertips. The nail stops your fingertip bending back when you touch something. This helps your fingers to feel things. Nails are useful for picking up tiny objects.

How many bones do I have?

Most people have 206 bones. Half of them are in your hands and feet. All your bones together make up your skeleton. The skeleton is like a frame. It holds up the other parts of your body. It also protects the squashy bits inside.

Find

Can you find your collarbone? It starts at your shoulder and runs to the top of your rib cage.

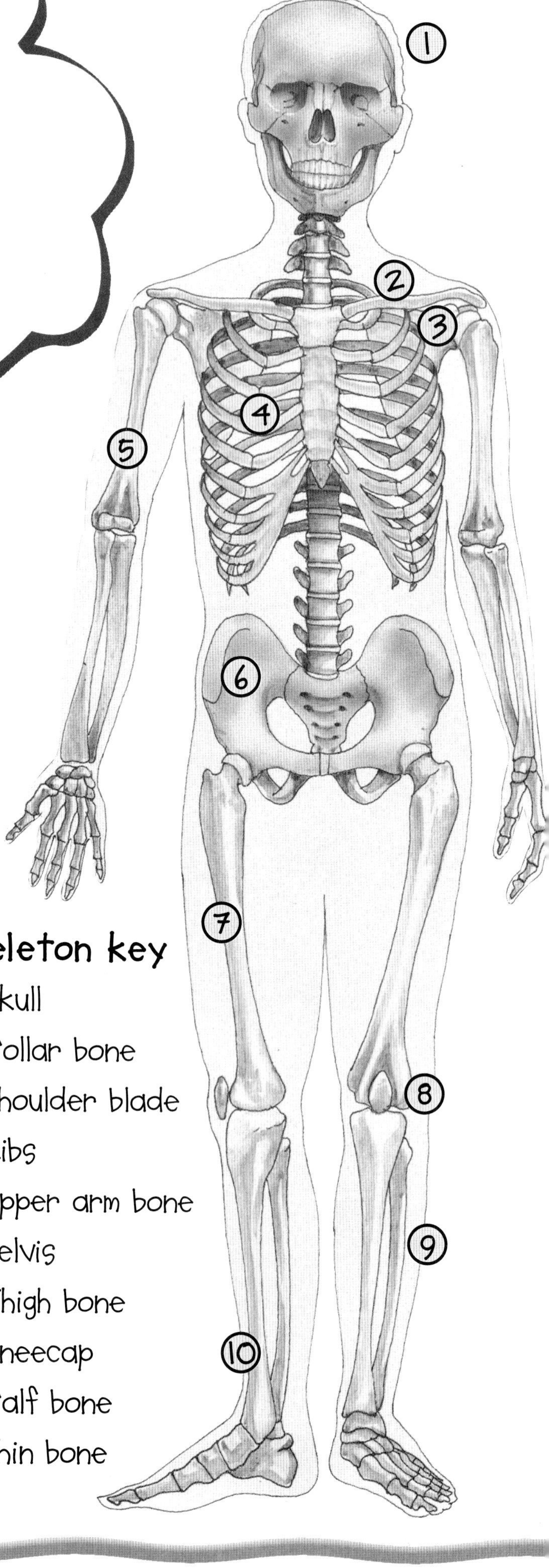

Skeleton key

1. Skull
2. Collar bone
3. Shoulder blade
4. Ribs
5. Upper arm bone
6. Pelvis
7. Thigh bone
8. Kneecap
9. Calf bone
10. Shin bone

What are bones made from?

Bones are made from different materials mixed together. Some of the materials are very hard and some are tough and bendy. Together they make bones very strong. There is a kind of jelly called marrow inside some bones. This makes tiny parts for your blood, called red and white cells.

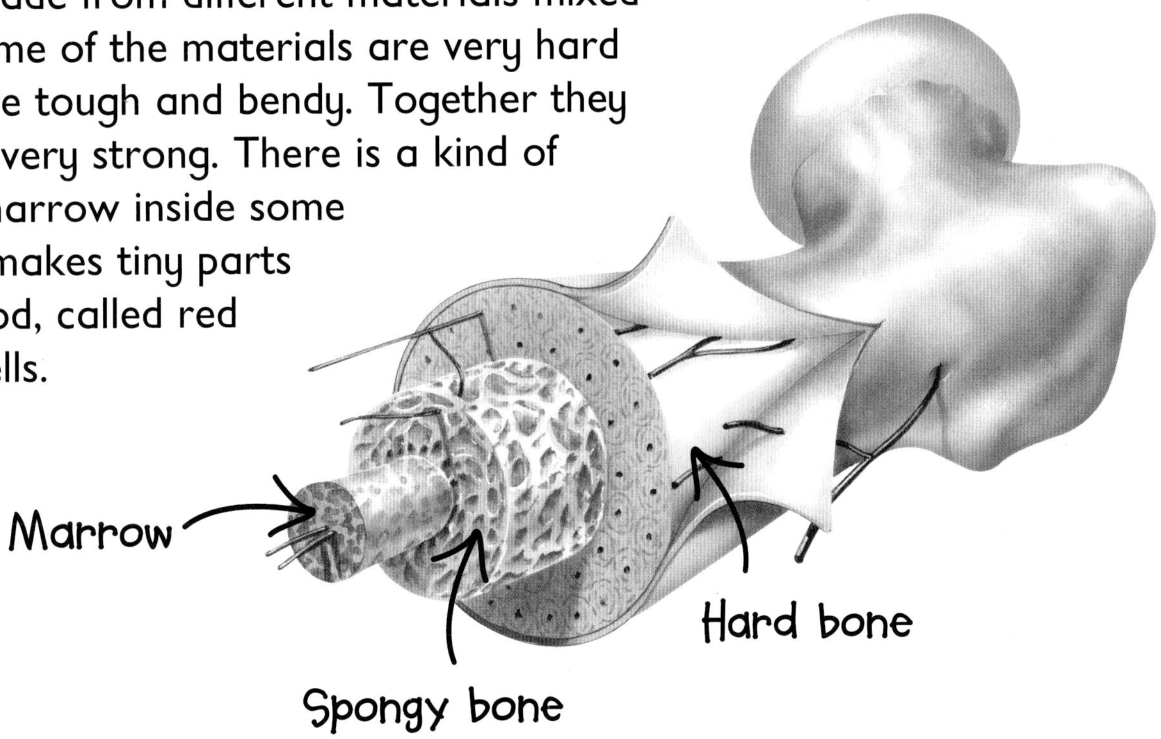

Strong bones!

Your bone is lightweight but super-strong. It is stronger than concrete or steel, which are used for making buildings and bridges! But bones can still break if they are bent too much.

How are bones joined together?

Your bones are connected by joints. They let your back, arms, legs, fingers and toes move. You have about 100 joints. The largest joints are in your hips and knees. The smallest joints are inside your ear.

How do muscles work?

Muscles are made from fibres that look like bits of string. The fibres get shorter to make the muscle pull. Many muscles make your bones move. They help you to run, jump, hold and lift things. Some muscles move your eyes, your heart and other body parts.

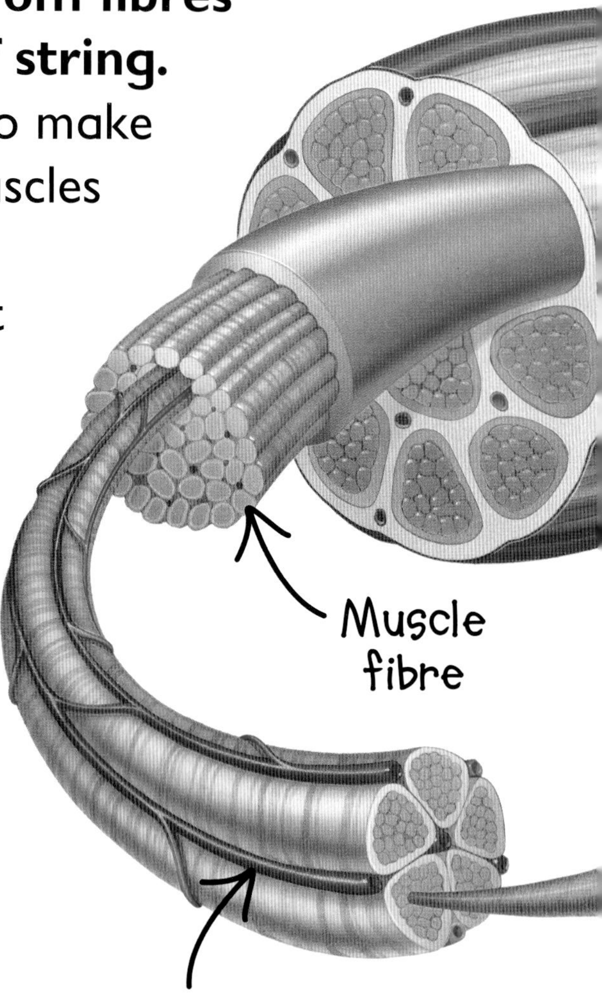

What is my biggest muscle?

The biggest muscles in your body are the ones that you sit on – your bottom! You use them when you walk and run. The strongest muscle in your body is in your jaw. It scrunches your teeth together.

Cheeky muscles!

Your face is full of muscles. You use them to smile, to wrinkle your nose, or to cry. You use more muscles to frown than to smile!

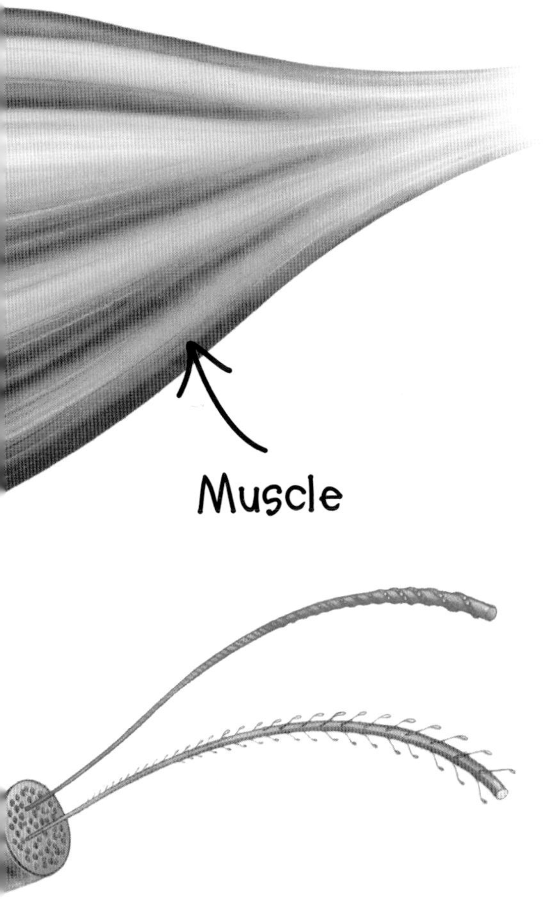

What makes my muscles move?

Your brain does. It sends messages along nerves to your muscles. Lots of muscles are needed, even for small movements, like writing with a pen. Your brain controls other muscles without you thinking about it. For example, the muscles in your heart keep working even when you are asleep.

Feel

Bend and unbend your arm. Can you feel your arm muscles getting shorter and longer?

Why do I need to breathe?

You breathe to take air into your body. There is a gas in the air called oxygen that your body needs to work. The air goes up your nose or into your mouth. Then it goes down a tube called the windpipe and into your lungs.

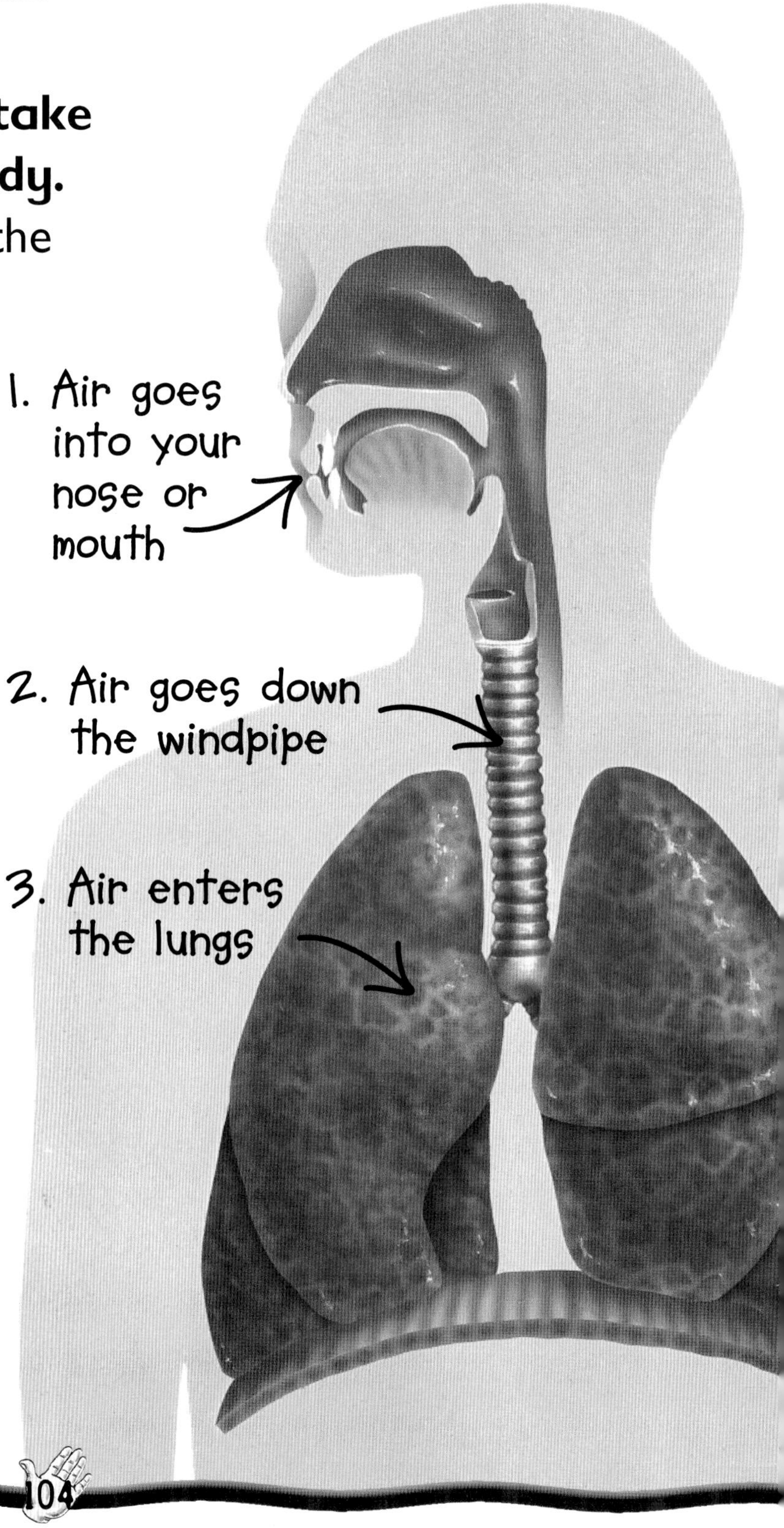

1. Air goes into your nose or mouth
2. Air goes down the windpipe
3. Air enters the lungs

Count

How many times do you breathe in and out in one minute?

Is my voice kept in a box?

Not quite! The real name for your voicebox is the larynx. It's at the top of the windpipe, and makes a bulge at the front of your neck. Air passing through the voicebox makes it shake, or vibrate. This is the sound of your voice. Your voice can make lots of sounds, and helps you to sing!

Singing

Fill 'em up!

When you are resting, you take in enough air to fill a can of fizzy drink in every breath. When you are running, you breathe in ten times as much air.

What makes air go into my lungs?

There is a big muscle under your lungs that moves down. More muscles make your ribs move out. This makes your lungs bigger. Air rushes into your lungs to fill the space. When your muscles relax, the air is pushed out again.

What food is good for me?

Lots of food is good for you! Different foods give your body the goodness it needs. Fruit and vegetables are very good for you. Bread and pasta give you energy. Small amounts of fat, such as cheese, keep your nerves healthy. Chicken and fish keep your muscles strong.

Fats keep nerves healthy
Vegetables help digestion
Fruit is full of goodness

Eating elephants!

You eat about one kilogram of food every day. During your life, you will eat about 30 tonnes of food. That's the same weight as six elephants!

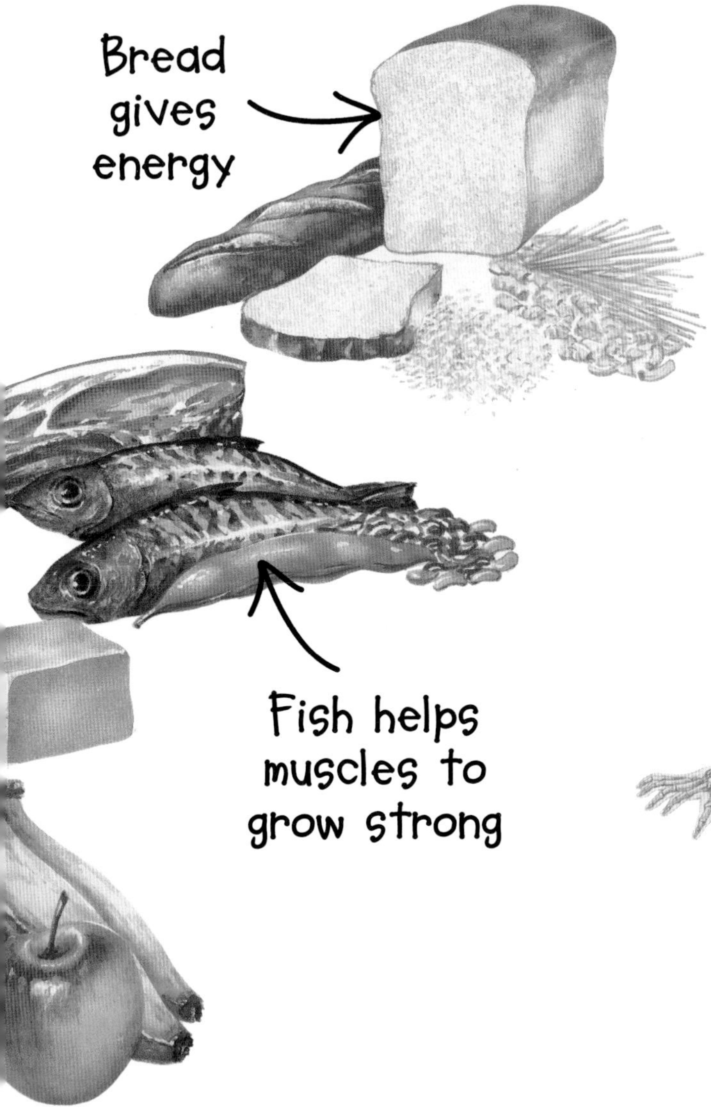
Bread gives energy
Fish helps muscles to grow strong

Why do I need to eat food?

Food keeps your body working. It is like fuel for your body. It keeps your body going through the day and night, and works your muscles. Food also contains things your body needs to grow, repair itself and fight illness.

Your whole body needs food

What happens when I swallow?

The first thing you do with food is chew it. Then you swallow lumps of the chewed food. When you swallow, the food goes down a tube called the gullet. Muscles in the gullet push the food down into your stomach.

Draw

Look at some of the pictures on these pages. Can you draw a healthy meal that you would like to eat?

What are teeth made of?

Teeth are covered in a material called enamel. This is harder than most kinds of rock! Teeth are fixed into your jaw bones by roots. Sharp front teeth (incisors) bite food into small pieces. Tall, pointy teeth (canines) tear and pull food. Flat back teeth (molars) chew food to a mush.

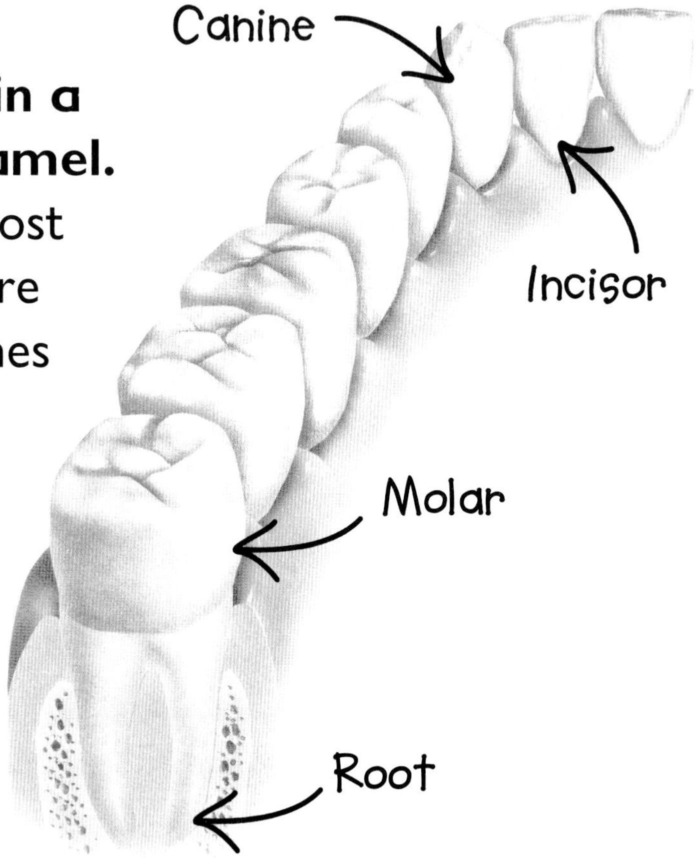

How many sets of teeth do I have?

You have two sets. A baby is born without teeth. The first set of teeth appears when a child is six months old. This set has 20 teeth. These teeth fall out at about seven years old. They are replaced by 32 adult teeth.

Discover

Do you still have your first set of teeth, or have your baby teeth begun to fall out?

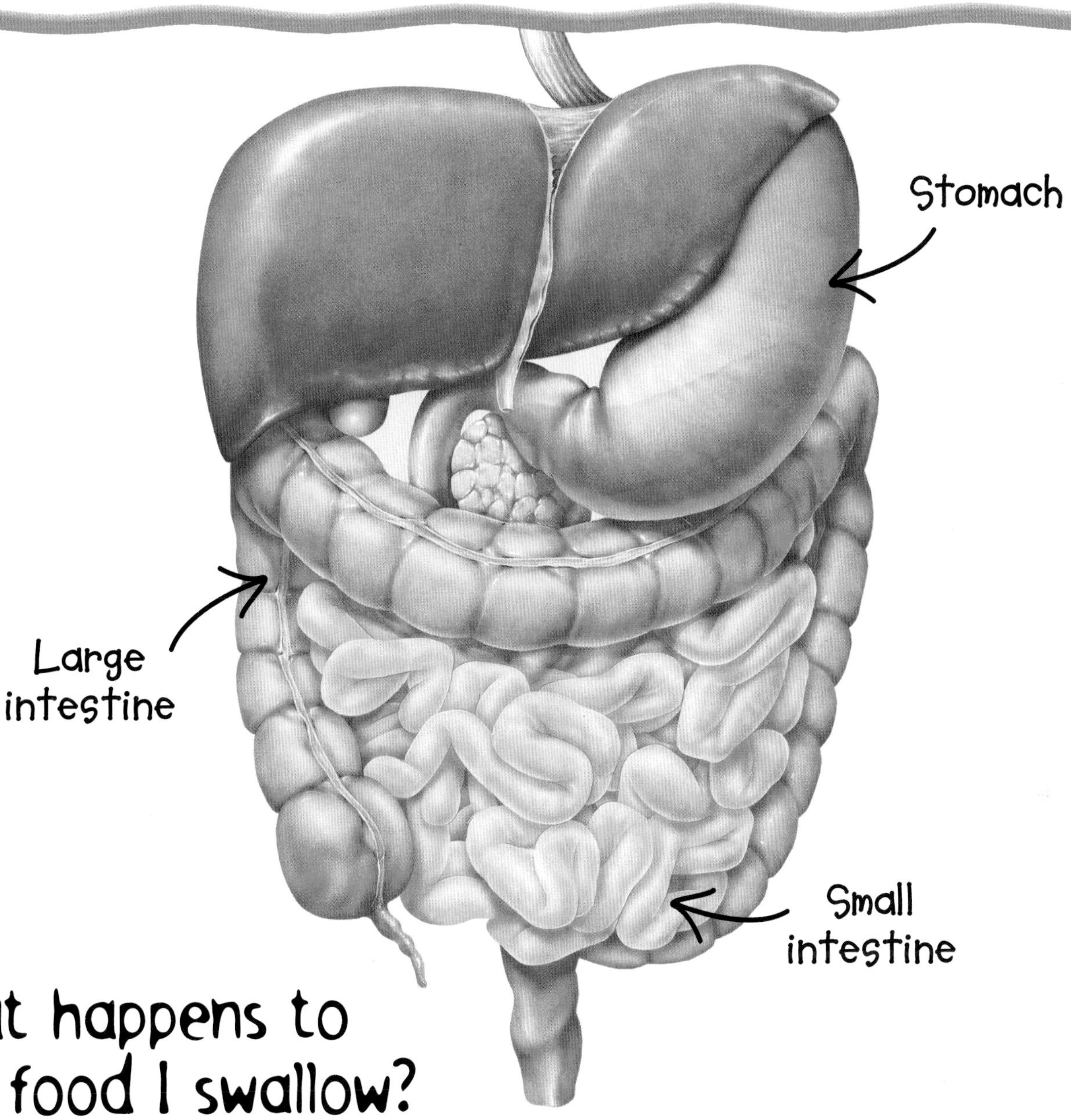

What happens to the food I swallow?

The food you swallow goes into your stomach. Here, special juices and strong muscles break the food up into a thick mush. The mushy food then goes into a long tube called the intestines. Here, all the goodness from the food is taken out, to be used by our body.

All gone!

When you go to the toilet, you get rid of waste. This is leftover food. It is stored in your large intestine until you go to the toilet.

Why does my heart beat?

To pump blood and oxygen around your body. Your heart is about the size of your fist and is made of muscle. When it beats, your heart squeezes blood into tubes. These carry blood and oxygen around your body. The blood then comes back to the heart from the lungs, with more oxygen.

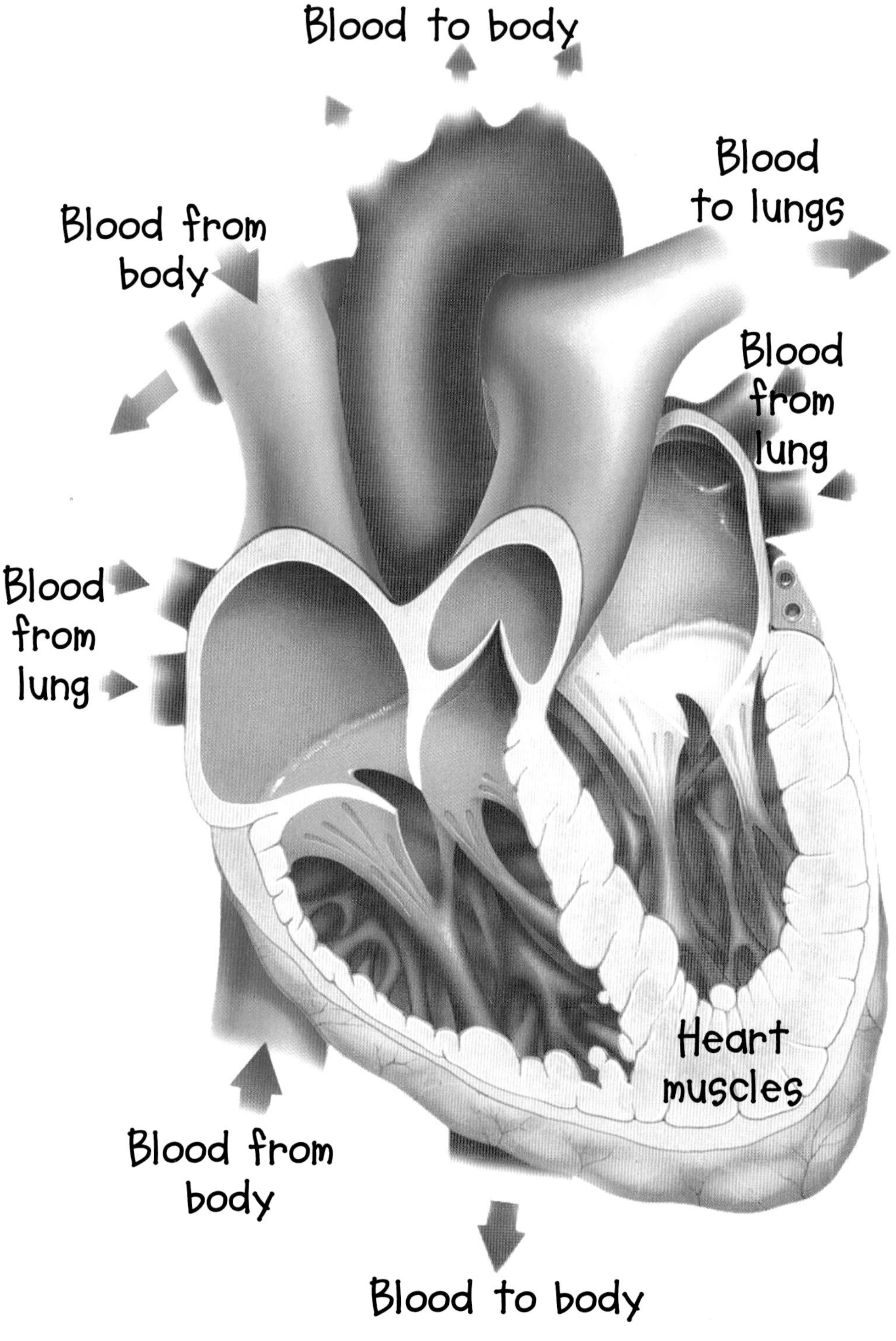

Beat of life!

Your heart beats once a second for the whole of your life. That is 86,000 beats a day, and 31 million beats a year. In total, this is 2000 million beats in your life.

What does blood do?

Your whole body need oxygen to work. Blood carries oxygen to every part of your body in its red cells. Blood also contains white cells that fight germs. Tubes called arteries and veins carry blood around your body.

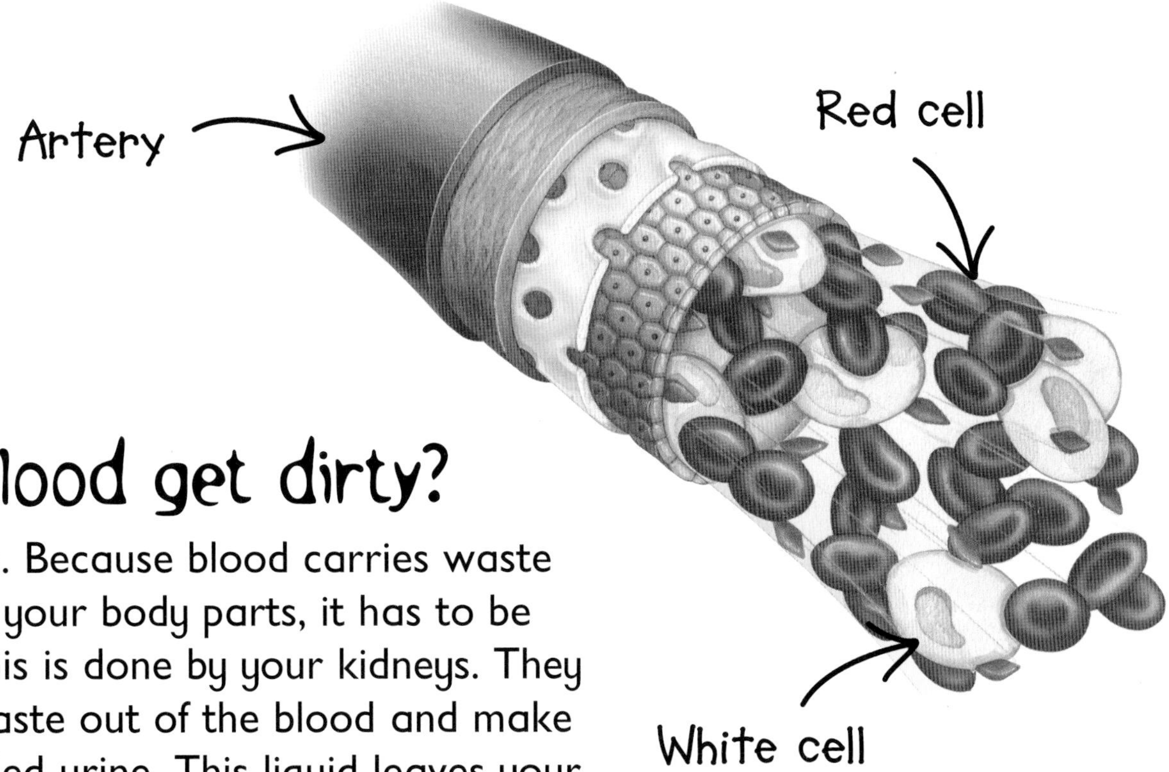

Does blood get dirty?

Yes, it does. Because blood carries waste away from your body parts, it has to be cleaned. This is done by your kidneys. They take the waste out of the blood and make a liquid called urine. This liquid leaves your body when you go to the toilet.

Feel

Touch your neck under your chin. Can you feel the blood flowing through an artery to your brain?

Are my eyes like a camera?

Your eyes work like a tiny camera. They collect light that bounces off the things you are looking at. This makes tiny pictures at the back of the eyes. Here, millions of sensors pick up the light. They send a picture to your brain along a nerve.

In a spin!

Inside your ear are loops full of liquid. They can tell when you move your head. This helps you to balance. If you spin around, the fluid keeps moving. This makes you feel dizzy!

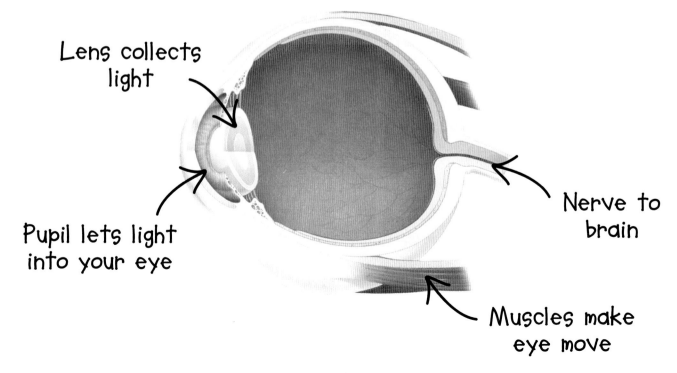

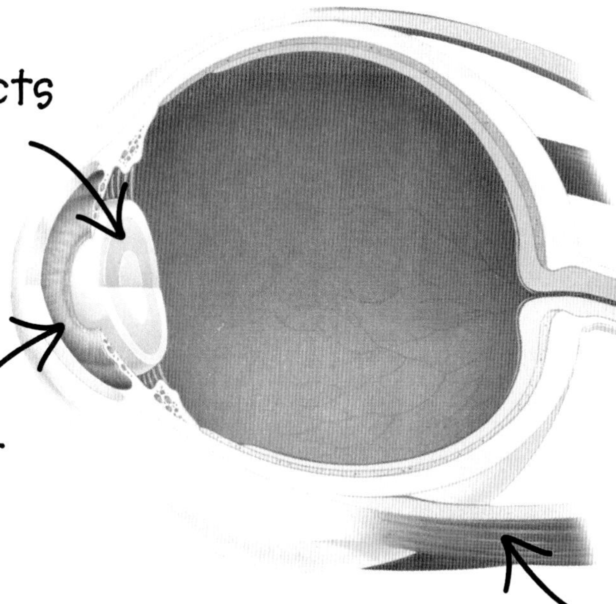

What is inside my ears?

The flap on your head is only part of your ear. The hole in your ear goes to a tiny piece of tight skin, called an eardrum. Sounds enter your ear and make the eardrum move in and out. Tiny bones pass these movements to the cochlea, which is shaped like a snail. This is filled with liquid.

Look

Look in the mirror at your eye. Can you see the dark pupil where light goes in?

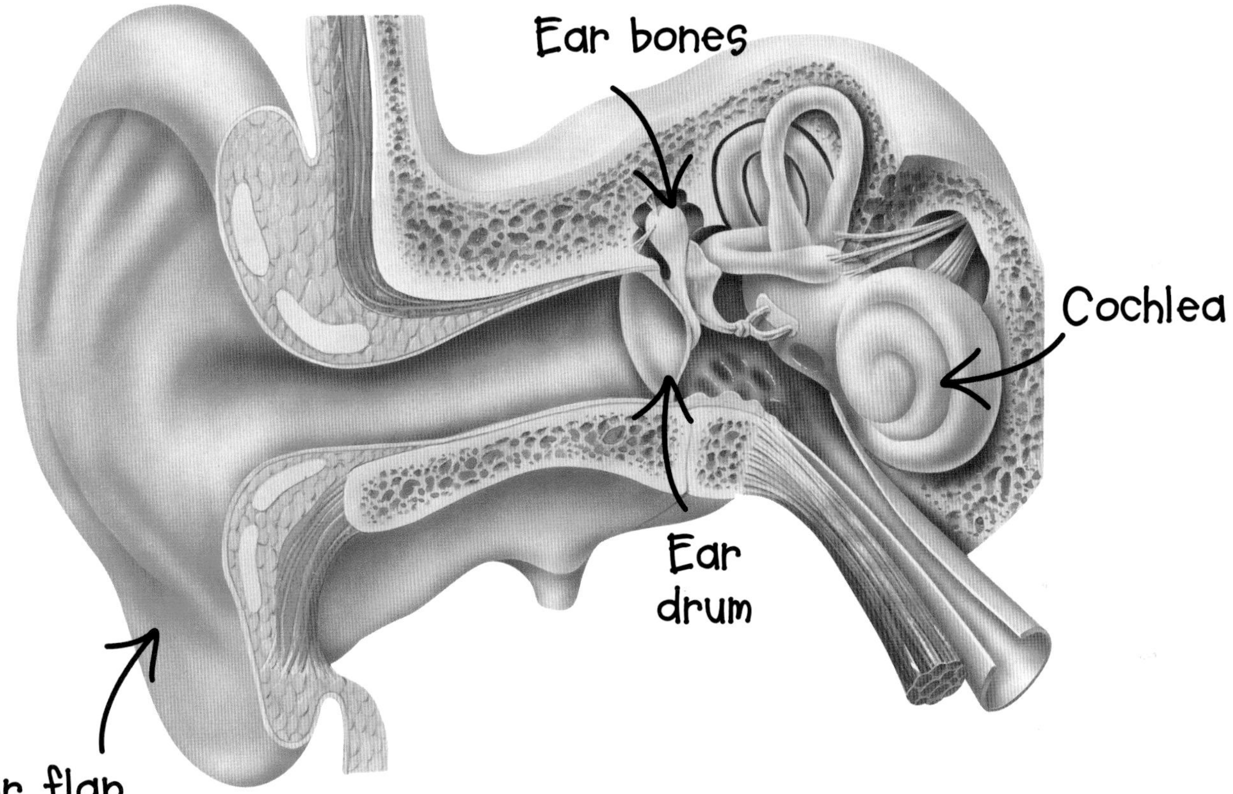

How do I hear sounds?

The cochlea in your ear contains thousands of tiny hairs. It is also is full of liquid. Sounds make the liquid move. This makes the hairs wave about. Tiny sensors pick up the waving, and send messages to your brain so you hear the sound.

Why can't I see smells?

Because they're invisible! Smells are tiny particles that float in the air. Inside the top of your nose are sticky smell sensors. When you sniff something, the sensors collect the smell particles. They send messages to your brain, which tell you what you can smell.

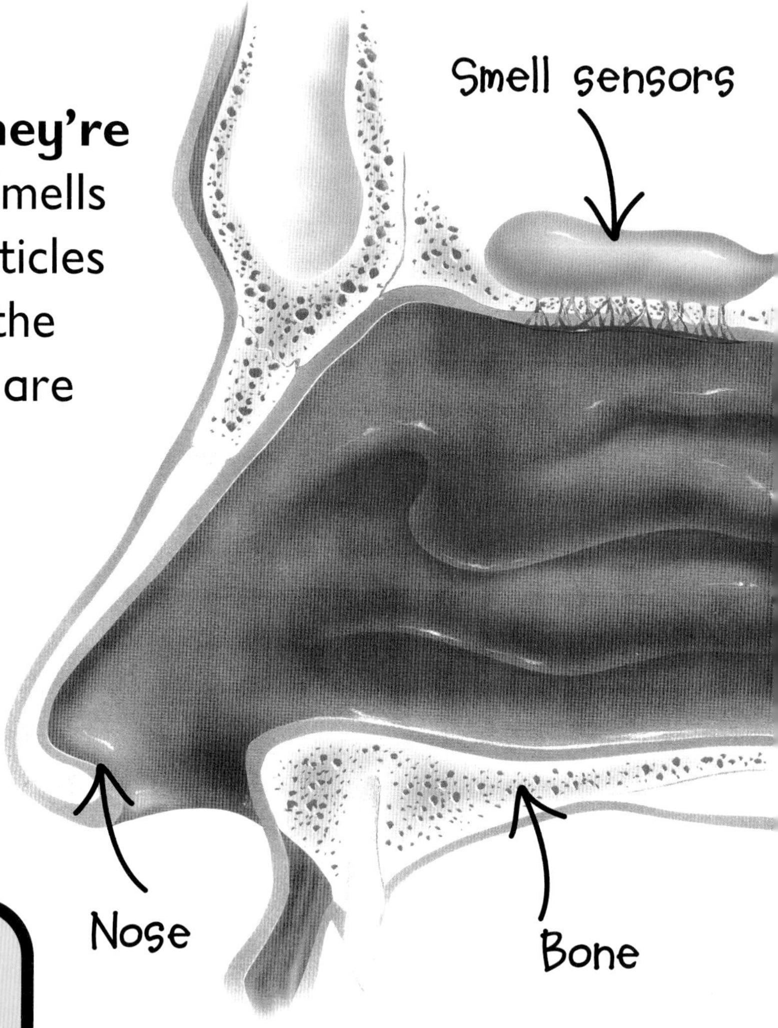

A blocked dose!

Smell and taste work together when you eat. Your sense of smell helps you to taste flavours in food. When you have a cold, your smell sensors get blocked, so you cannot taste, either.

How do I taste things?

With your tongue. Your tongue is covered with tiny taste sensors. These are called taste buds. Buds on different parts of your tongue can sense different tastes, or flavours. Your tongue also moves food around your mouth and helps you to speak.

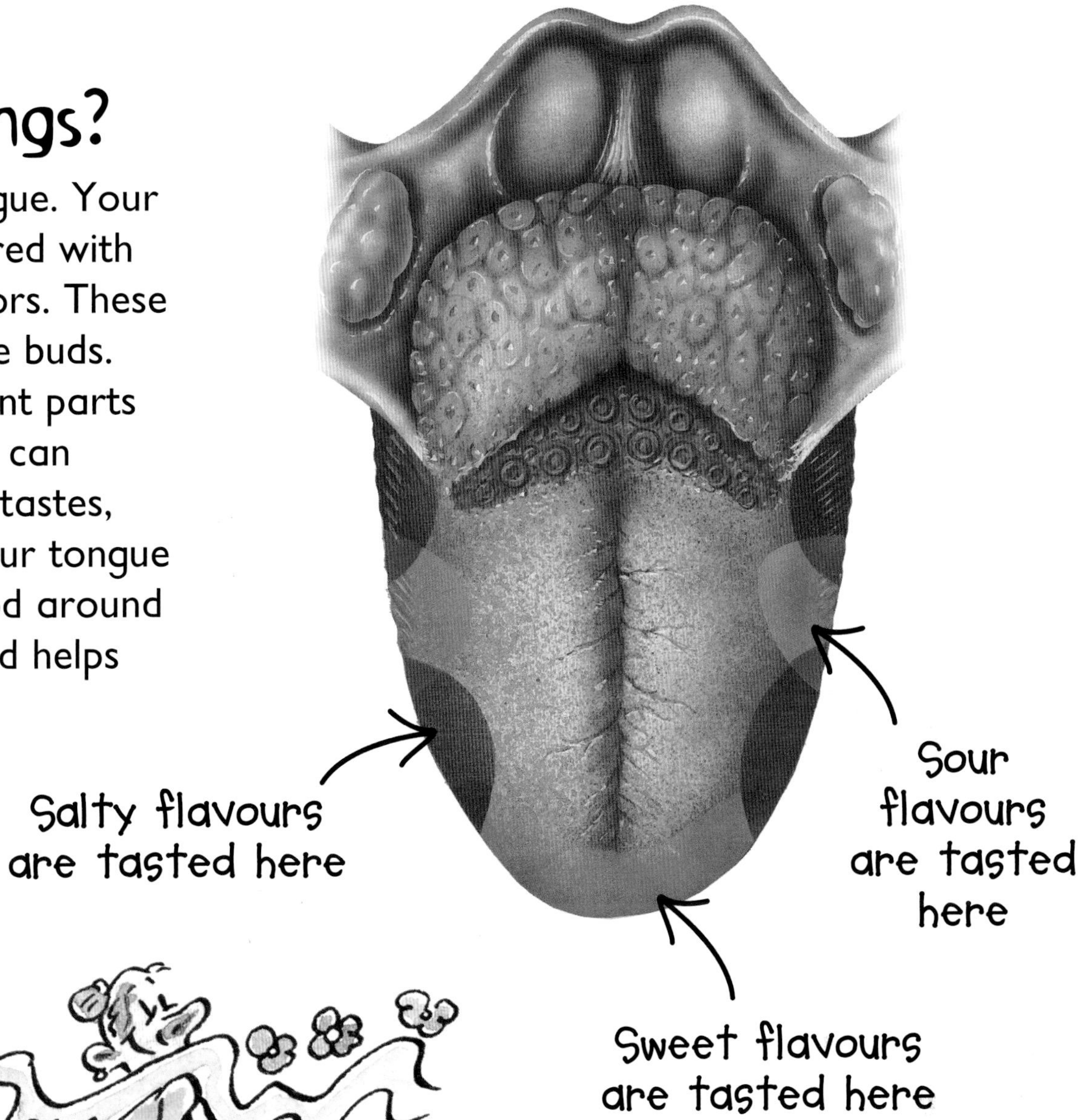

How many smells can I sense?

Your nose can sense about 3000 different smells. You don't just have a sense of smell so you can smell nice things, such as flowers and perfumes! Your sense of smell warns you if food is rotten before you eat it.

Think

Look at the picture of the tongue. Can you think of three different things that taste sour, sweet and salty?

Is my brain really big?

Your brain is about the same size as your two fists put together. It is the place where you think, remember, feel happy or sad – and dream. Your brain also takes information from your senses and controls your body. The main part is called the cerebrum.

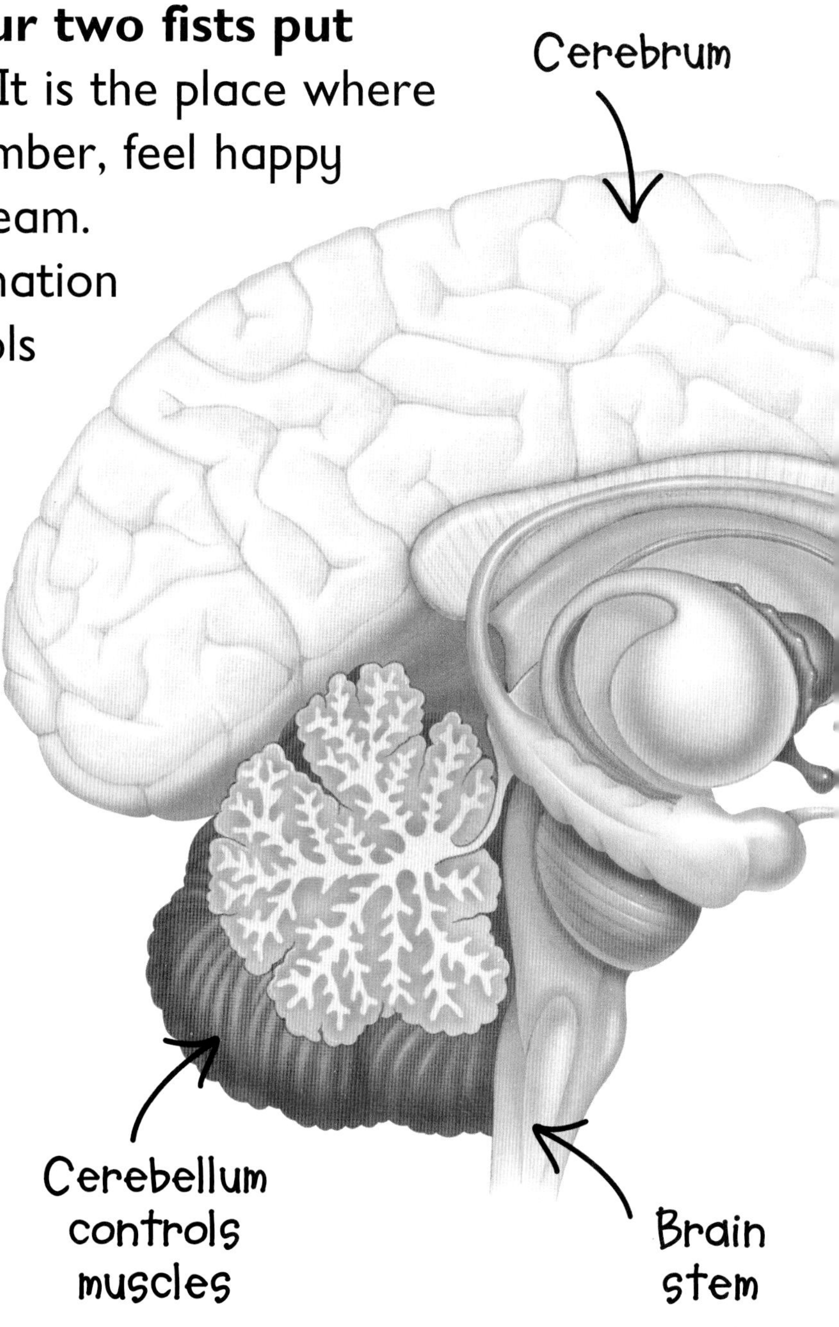

Right and left!

The main part of your brain is divided into two halves. The left half helps you to play music and to draw. The right half is good at thinking.

Can my brain really wave?

Well, sort of! Your brain works using electricity. It has about 10,000 million tiny nerve cells. Tiny bursts of electricity are always jumping around between the cells. Doctors can see your brain working by looking at the electricity with a special machine called an EEG. It shows the electricity as waves on a screen.

Remember

Your brain controls the five senses – smelling, tasting, touching, hearing – can you remember your fifth sense?

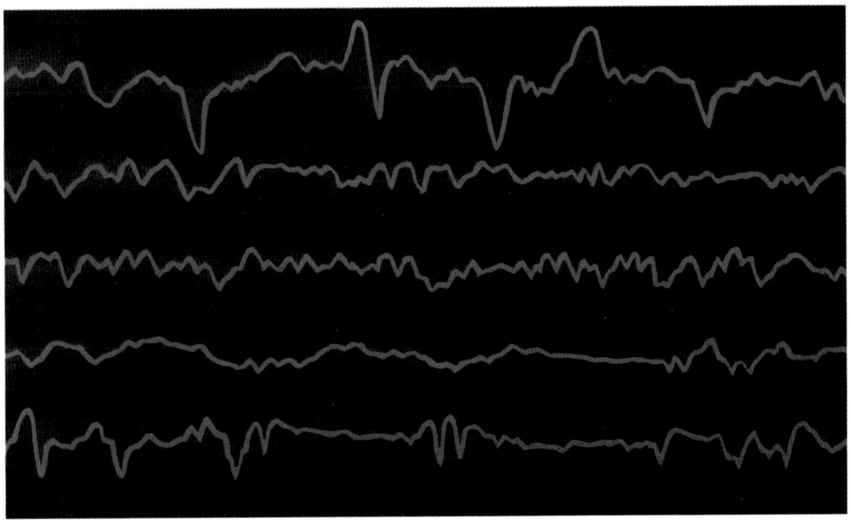

Brain waves from an EEG machine

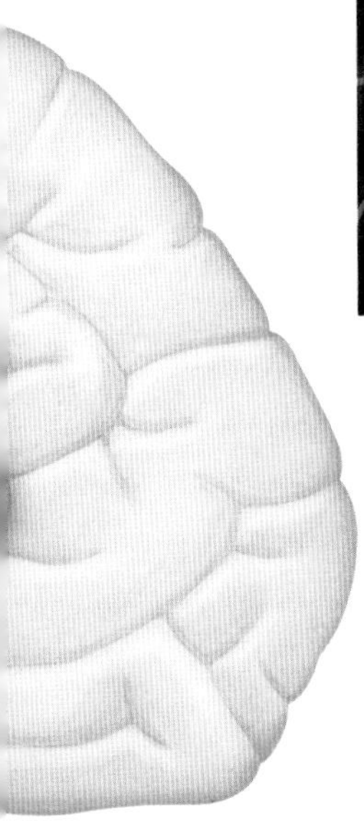

How does my brain help me to play?

Different parts of your brain do different jobs. One part senses touch. Another part deals with thinking. Speaking is controlled by a different part. The cerebellum controls all your muscles. When you play and run, the cerebellum sends messages to your muscles to make them move.

Quiz time

Do you remember what you have read about your body? These questions will test your memory. The pictures will help you. If you get stuck, read the pages again.

1. What does my skin do?

page 96

2. Why do I sweat when I'm warm?

page 97

3. How much hair do I have?

page 98

4. How are bones joined together?

page 101

page 102

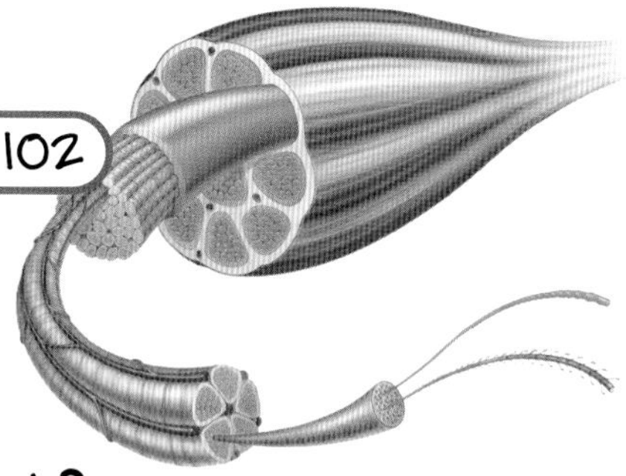

5. How do muscles work?

page 105

6. What makes air go into my lungs?

7. Why do I need to eat food?

page 107

8. How many sets of teeth do I have?

page 108

9. What does blood do?

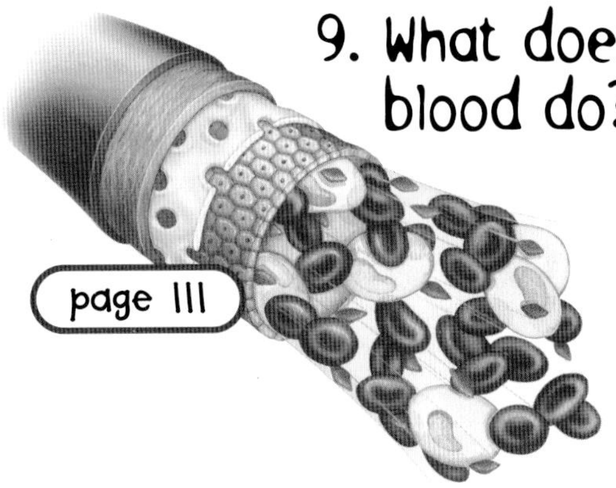

page 111

10. How do I hear sounds?

page 113

11. How do I taste things?

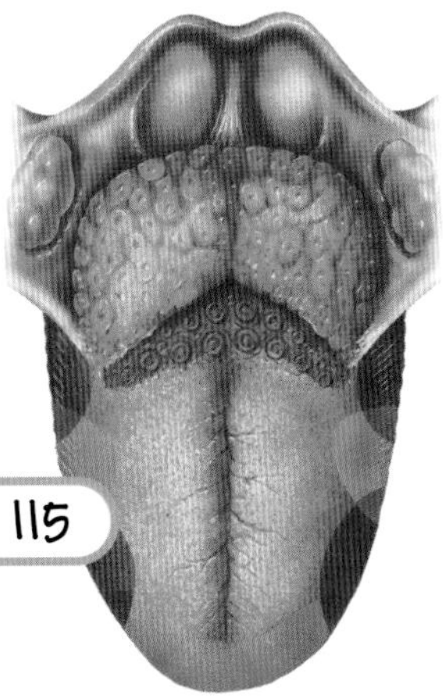

page 115

12. Is my brain really big?

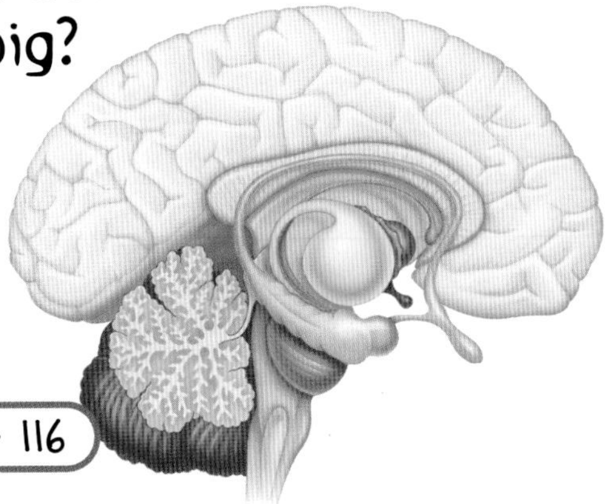

page 116

13. How does my brain help me to play?

page 117

Answers

1. It protects you
2. To help you cool down again
3. You have five million hairs on your body
4. They are connected by joints
5. The fibres inside get shorter and pull
6. Muscles
7. To keep your body working
8. Two sets
9. Carries oxygen around your body
10. With the parts that are inside your ear
11. With your tongue
12. It's as big as your fists put together
13. It tells your muscles to move

Prehistoric questions about...

Dinosaurs

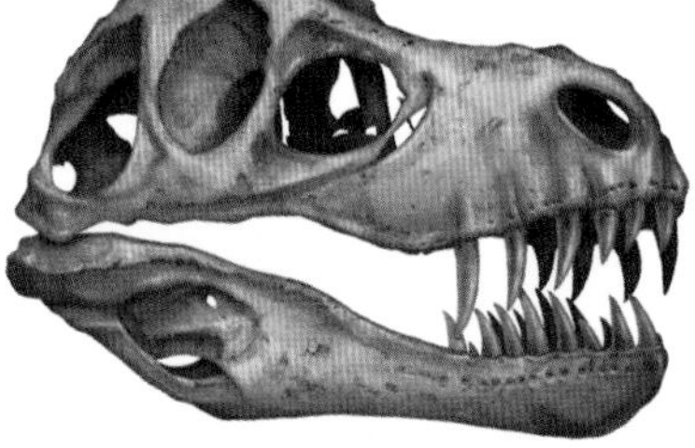

What is a dinosaur?

Dinosaurs were animals that lived millions of years ago. There were lots of different types of dinosaur – little ones, big ones, fierce ones and shy ones. All dinosaurs lived on land – and they died out a long time ago. There are no dinosaurs living today.

Make

Use salt dough or plasticine to make some dinosaur models. Use a picture or a toy dinosaur as a guide.

When did dinosaurs live?

It is thought that the first dinosaurs lived around 230 million years ago. They roamed the Earth for the next 165 million years, before becoming extinct (dying out) about 65 million years ago. Humans haven't been around for two million years yet!

Where did the dinosaurs live?

Dinosaurs lived all over the world. At that time, the weather was much hotter than it is today. There were plants such as ferns, mosses and large evergreen trees, but there were no flowers.

What a terror!

The word 'dinosaur' means 'terrible lizard', even though dinosaurs weren't lizards! Many of the plant-eating dinosaurs were about as terrible as today's sheep!

Did any dinosaurs eat plants?

Many dinosaurs ate plants. *Plateosaurus* grew up to 8 metres long. It had a long neck and could reach high up into trees by standing on its back legs. It grabbed branches with the hooks on its thumbs and nibbled at the tastiest leaves.

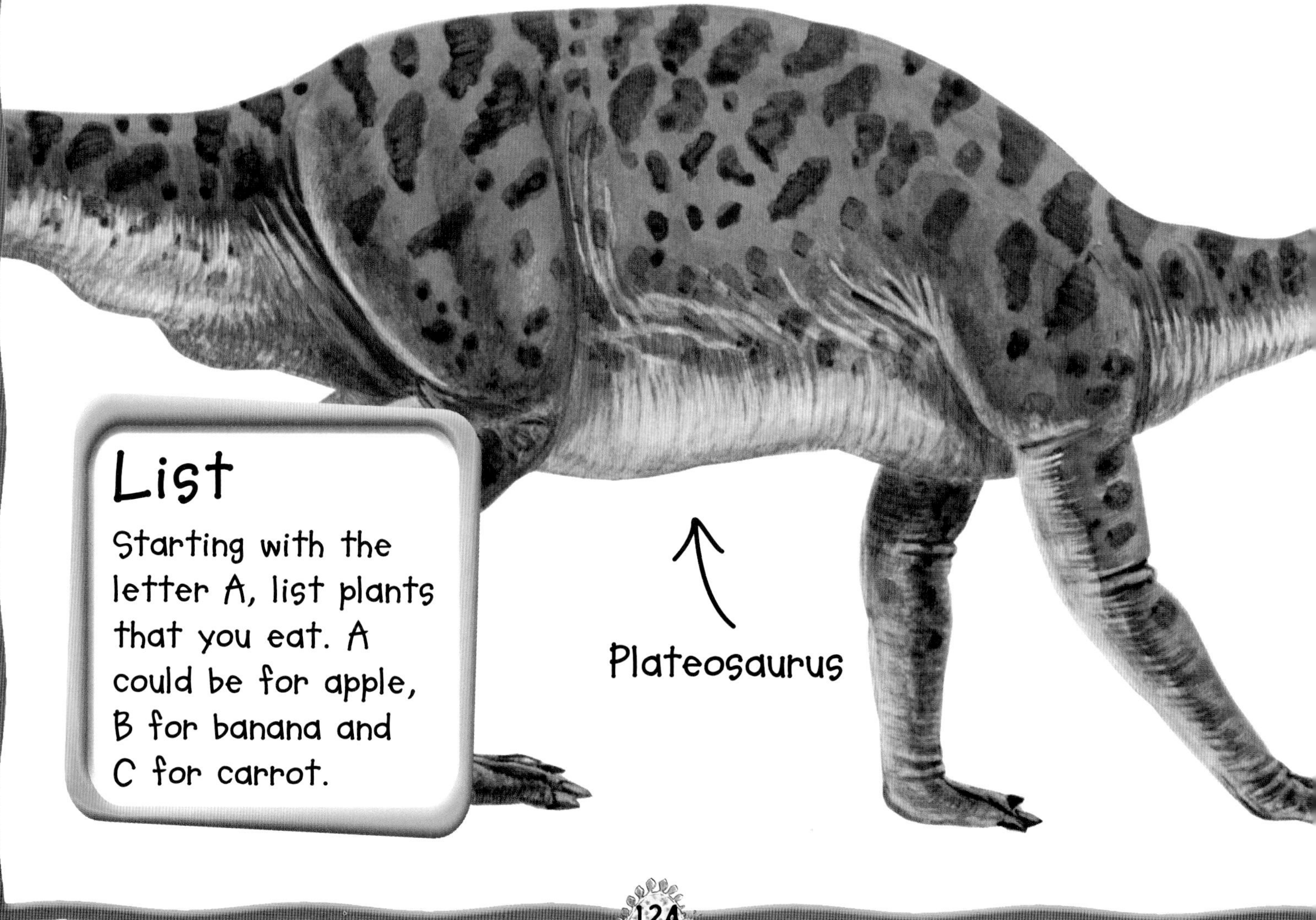

List

Starting with the letter A, list plants that you eat. A could be for apple, B for banana and C for carrot.

Why were dinosaurs so big?

Riojasaurus (ree-oh-ja-saw-rus) was a giant dinosaur that measured 10 metres from its nose to the tip of its tail. Being tall meant that it could reach high into trees for food. Big dinosaurs could fight off enemies, such as *Rutiodon,* a big crocodile that lived at the time.

No fruit!

Early plant-eating dinosaurs did not eat fruit or grass – none had appeared yet! Instead, they ate plants called horsetails, ferns, cycads and conifer trees.

Why did dinosaurs eat stones?

Lots of plant-eating dinosaurs swallowed their food without chewing. Instead, they gobbled stones and pebbles, which stayed in their stomachs. When they swallowed food, the stones helped to mash the food up, turning it into a pulp.

How big is a dinosaur tooth?

Dinosaur teeth were different sizes. Meat eaters, such as *Tyrannosaurus rex*, needed large, sharp and pointed teeth for tearing flesh. Each tooth measured up to 15 centimetres! When scientists look at dinosaur teeth they can work out what type of food the dinosaur ate.

Toothy!

Baryonyx had small, pointed, cone-shaped teeth. These are like the teeth of a crocodile or dolphin today. They were good for grabbing slippery food such as fish.

Did plant eaters need sharp teeth?

Plant-eating dinosaurs, such as *Apatosaurus*, had long, thin teeth that were blunt, not sharp. They used these teeth to pull leaves off branches. Herds of these dinosaurs could strip all the plants clean in one area, before moving on.

Tyrannosaurus rex fossil

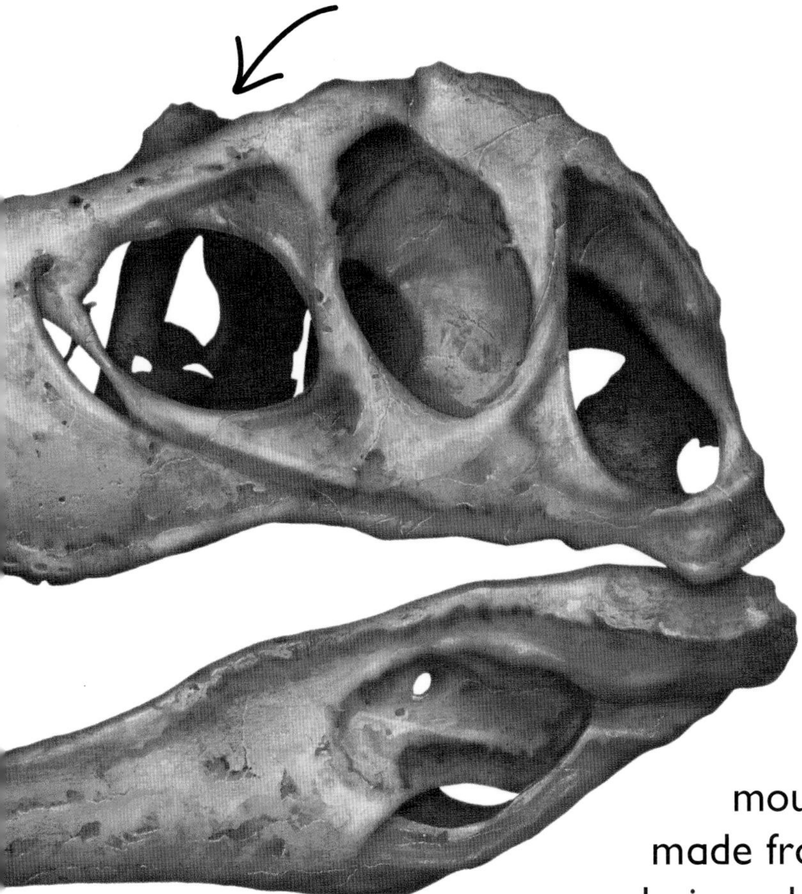

> **Think**
>
> You have different types of teeth. Think about which ones you use to cut food, and which ones you use to chew.

Did all dinosaurs have teeth?

Not all dinosaurs needed teeth. *Ornithomimus* had a beak-shaped mouth without teeth. Its mouth was made from the same tough substance as our hair and nails. This bird-like dinosaur probably pecked at seeds, worms and bugs. Its large eyes helped it to find food.

Ornithomimus

What were the biggest dinos?

The biggest dinosaurs, called sauropods, were ENORMOUS! Each one could weigh as much as ten elephants. *Brachiosaurus* was one of the largest dinosaurs that ever lived and was 25 metres long. It was twice as tall as a giraffe and could reach the tops of the tallest trees.

Draw

Lots of animals eat plants and live in groups, or herds. Draw some modern animals that spend all day eating plants.

What was the biggest dinosaur that ever lived?

The biggest dinosaur ever discovered is *Argentinosaurus*. Not much is known about this giant, but it is thought that it may have measured 40 metres from head to tail! *Argentinosaurus* had a huge body but a small head and brain.

Scary tail!

Diplodocus is also known as 'Old Whip-tail'! It could swish its tail so hard that it made a CRACK! like a whip. This would scare off enemies or even rip off their skin.

What did sauropods eat?

All sauropods ate plants. They probably had to spend most of the day eating, just to get enough energy for their enormous, heavy bodies. They may have spent 20 hours every day just grazing and nibbling at plants.

Why did dinosaurs have claws?

Most dinosaurs had claws on their fingers and toes. Meat-eating dinosaurs, such as *Deinonychus* (die-non-ee-kus) used their claws for catching and killing other animals. These dinosaurs were fast, clever and strong. Their claws could cut like knives and their teeth were razor-sharp.

Discover

Look at books to find pictures of elephants' feet. Do their toenails look like the claws of Apatosaurus?

Were all claws sharp?

Even plant-eating dinosaurs, such as sauropods, had claws. They didn't need claws to catch other animals, so they were flat and blunt rather than sharp. *Apatosaurus* had claws to protect its feet from stones, just like nails protect your fingertips and toes.

Thumb nose!

When scientists discovered remains of *Iguanodon*, they found a bone shaped like a horn. They put this on *Iguanadon's* nose. Now they think it is a thumb claw!

Which dinosaur had a spike on each hand?

Iguanodon was a plant-eating dinosaur. It didn't need spikes to kill other animals, but it could use them as weapons to defend itself.

If meat-eating dinosaurs attacked *Iguanodon*, it could fight back with its strong arms, using its spikes like daggers.

What was the scariest dinosaur?

***Tyrannosaurus rex* – known as *T-rex* for short – is one of the scariest dinosaurs.** This dinosaur was a large meat eater. It had powerful legs that helped it run fast and a huge mouth filled lots of sharp, pointed teeth.

Colour

No one knows what colour dinosaurs were. Draw your favourite dinosaur, then colour it in using spots, stripes and colours!

Giganotosaurus

What was the biggest meat-eating dinosaur?

Giganotosaurus was even bigger than *T-rex* – it is the largest meat-eating dinosaur ever found. Its huge legs could carry more than 8 tonnes of weight, even when it was chasing its prey. It had small arms and both had three claws for grabbing and stabbing.

How did meat eaters get their food?

Some meat eaters hunted and captured their prey using their powerful claws and sharp teeth. Others were scavengers. This means that they ate any dead animals that they found. It is thought that *T-rex* both hunted, and scavenged, for food.

Bite marks!

Some meat-eating dinosaurs not only bit their prey, but also each other! Remains of a T-rex had bite marks on its head. Perhaps the dinosaurs fought each other to become leader of the pack.

Which dinosaur had big eyes?

Dinosaurs used their senses to see, touch, hear, smell and taste. *Troodon* was a bird-like dinosaur that had HUGE eyes. Scientists think it may have hunted at night, and that its large eyes helped it to find food in the dark.

Troodon

Play

Play a game of hide and seek. Use your senses, such as seeing and hearing, to hunt your prey!

What were the noisiest dinosaurs?

We can't be sure what sounds dinosaurs made, but *Parasaurolophus* was probably one of the noisiest! It had a large crest on its head that was made of hollow bone. *Parasaurolophus* could have blown air through the crest to make a bellowing noise, like a giant trumpet.

Were dinosaurs clever or stupid?

Animals with big brains are usually cleverer than those with small brains. *Apatosaurus* had a tiny brain. *Troodon* had a large brain, compared to the size of its body. It may have been one of the cleverest dinosaurs that ever lived.

Dino rap!

Small meat-eating dinosaurs are called 'raptors'. These dinos lived and hunted in packs. They were slim, clever and fast. Some even had feathers to keep them warm!

How fast could dinosaurs move?

Some dinosaurs could run very fast – up to 80 kilometres an hour. That is faster than a horse at full gallop! *Ornithomimus* could run this fast because it had a slim body, hollow bones and long, thin legs. It ran fast so it could chase other animals, and escape being eaten itself!

Print

Dip feathers in paint and press them on paper to make your own prints. Try making handprints, too.

Could big dinosaurs move quickly?

Large dinosaurs were often slower. Heavy bodies were harder to move! *Muttaburrasaurus* was a big dinosaur that may have run on its hind legs, holding its head up to look for enemies. Its long tail may have helped it to keep its balance.

Speedy!

Coelophysis (co-el-off-ee-sis) could trot, jump and leap. It ran upright on its two back legs. It could also bound along on all four legs like a dog, at speeds of 30 kilometres an hour.

Were some dinosaurs small?

All dinosaurs were quite small when they first hatched from their eggs! Some fully-grown dinosaurs were not much bigger than a pet cat. *Compsognathus* was a small, light dinosaur that ate little creatures, such as lizards and bugs.

Did dinosaurs wear armour?

Dinosaurs needed to protect themselves from their enemies. Some of them did this by growing great pieces of bone over their bodies. These bony plates protected the dinosaurs' soft bodies underneath, like huge shields, or suits of armour.

Which dinosaur had a lumpy tail?

Euoplocephalus (you-o-plo-seff -a-lus) had a tail that was strengthened with lumps of bone. When this dinosaur swung its tail, it could hit an attacker with such force that it could break a leg!

Blink!

The armoured dinosaur Euoplocephalus (you-oh-ploh-sef-al-us) was so well-protected that it even had bony plates on its eyelids, which could snap open and closed, just like shutters!

Which dinosaur had three horns?

Triceratops was a plant eater and it probably used its three horns to frighten away attackers. It would also have used them for fighting enemies. *Triceratops* looked scary, but it probably spent most of its time quietly eating plants.

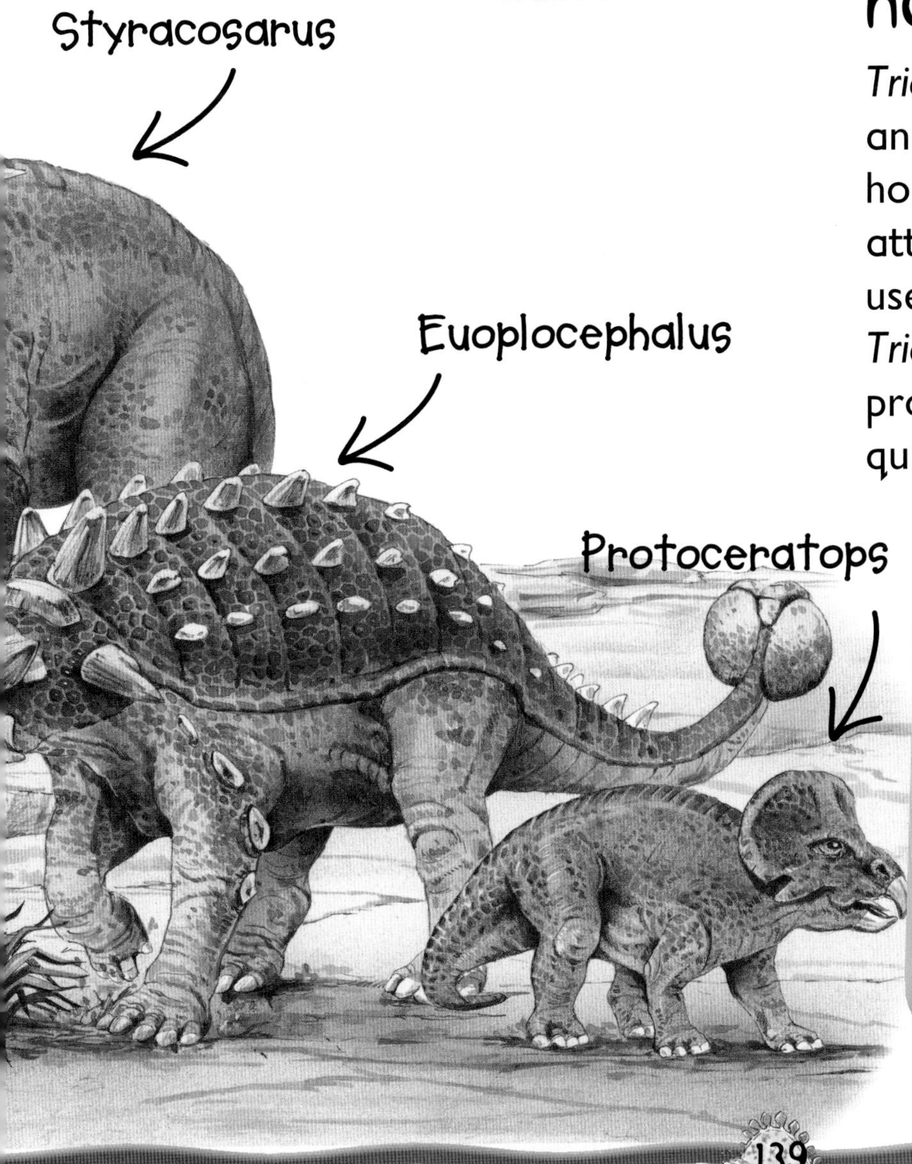

Make

Make a dinosaur model from clay or dough and then add a suit of armour. Include horns and a tail-club, using cardboard or pebbles.

How did dinosaurs have babies?

Dinosaurs laid eggs, just like birds, lizards and crocodiles do today. *Protoceratops* was a small dinosaur, the size of a pig. It lived in the desert. The female made a bowl-shaped nest in the warm sand and then laid her eggs inside it.

Find out

Find out how much you weighed and how long you were when you were born. Ask how quickly you grew!

Did dinosaurs look after their babies?

Some dinosaurs did look after their babies, until they were old enough to look after themselves. *Maiasaura* collected food for its newly hatched young and fed it to them, rather like birds feed their chicks today. The parents probably guarded their babies, too.

How do we know about dinosaur babies?

Scientists have found dinosaur eggs, and the remains of nests that have lasted for millions of years. They have even discovered large areas where many *Maiasaura* mothers came to lay their eggs, year after year.

Big baby!

Baby dinosaurs grew up to five times faster than human babies! A baby dinosaur, such as Diplodocus, was already one metre long and 30 kilograms in weight when it came out of its egg!

Did dinosaurs live alone?

Some dinosaurs lived alone, but many lived in groups, or herds. *Velociraptor* was a fast runner and meat eater that lived in packs. Just like today's lions and wolves, *Velociraptor* could kill bigger animals than itself. These dinosaurs hunted together.

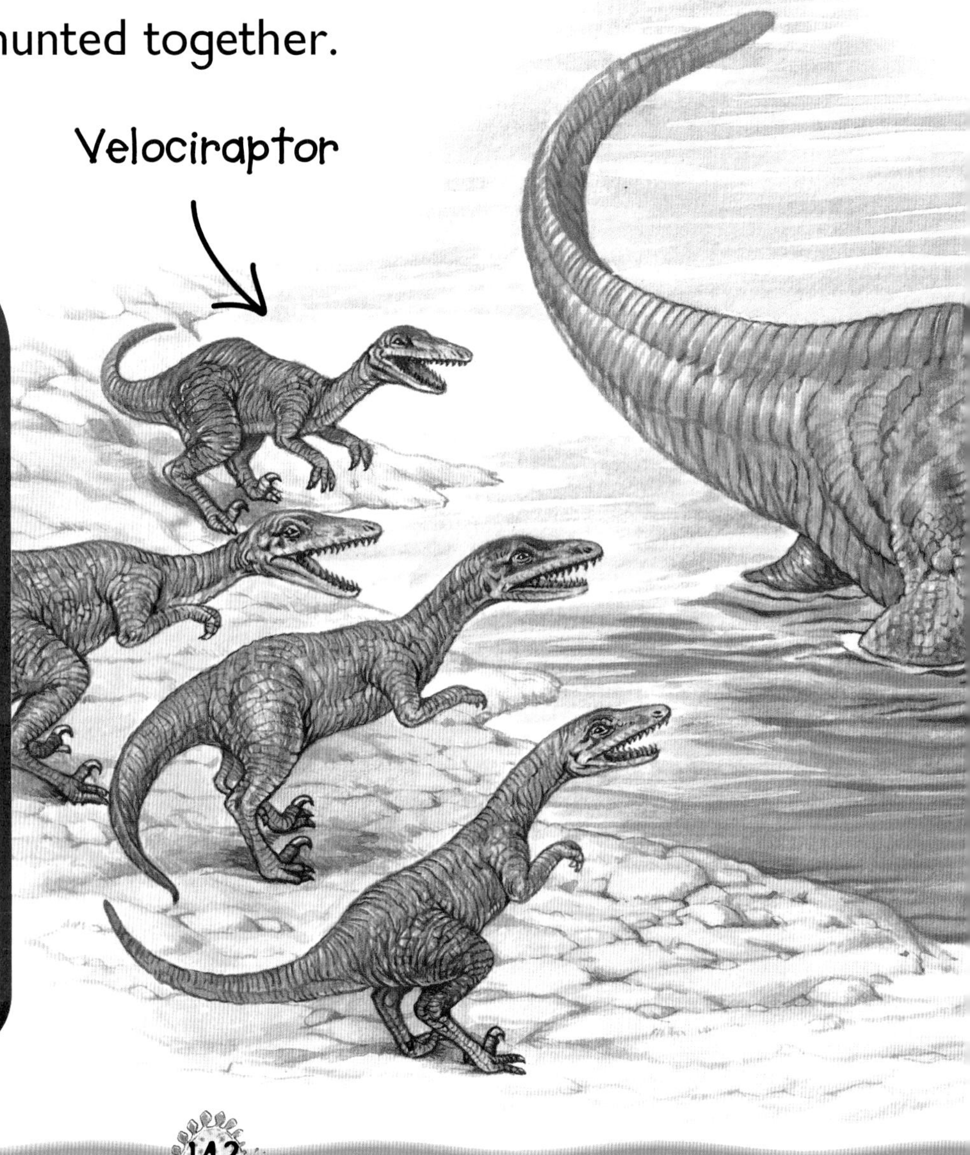

Fossil poo!

Dinosaur droppings also form fossils! These have pieces of food inside such as bones or plants. Some fossil droppings are as big as TV sets!

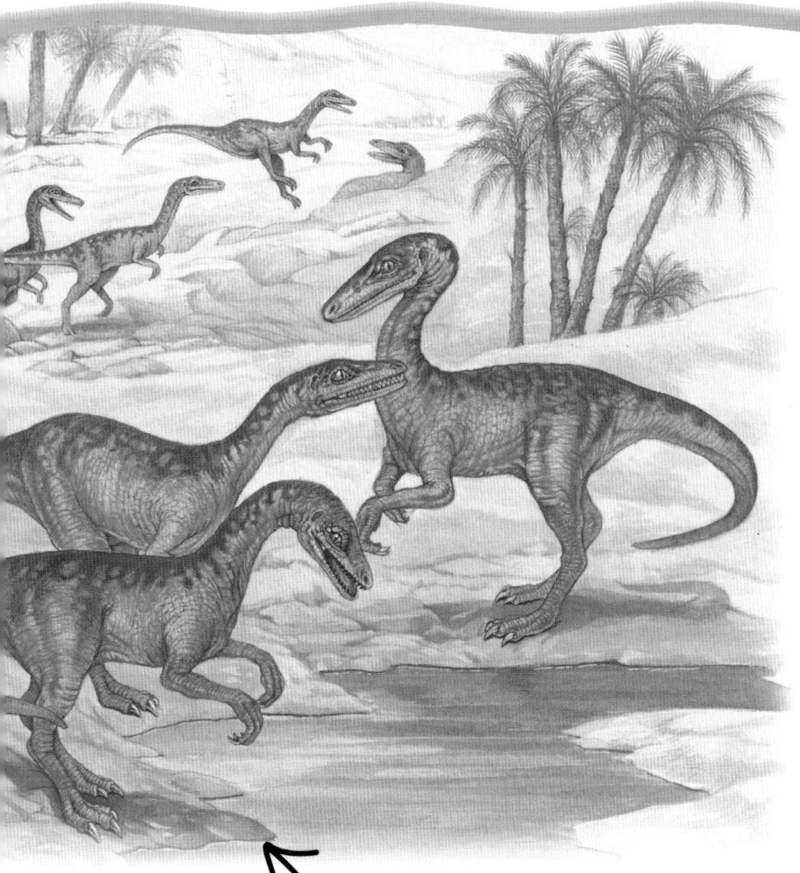

Coelophysis

Could dinosaurs leap and jump?

Scientists work out how dinosaurs moved by looking at their bones. The bones of *Coelophysis* are small, hollow and light so it was probably able to dart about easily. The shapes of its teeth and jaw bones suggest that *Coelophysis* ate insects or fish.

Anatosaurus

Look

Look at some pictures of birds such as ostriches. Do they remind you of any dinosaurs in this book?

Why are some dinosaurs like birds?

Some dinosaurs had feathers, large eyes and beaks. They even laid eggs and ate insects. It is believed that some changed (evolved) over time and became the very first birds on Earth.

Why did the dinosaurs die?

About 65 million years ago the dinosaurs suddenly died (became extinct). No one knows for sure why this happened, but something HUGE must have taken place to affect all life on the planet.

Read

Go to the library to find out about animals today that are in danger of becoming extinct. Find out why.

The dinosaurs may have been killed by a giant rock from space

Erupting volcanoes

What killed millions of animals?

Maybe volcanoes erupted, spitting out enormous clouds of ash and poisonous gas. Maybe a large lump of rock from space (a meteorite) smashed into the Earth. These things can change the weather, so perhaps the dinosaurs died because it got too cold for them.

Egg hunters!

Some dinosaurs might have become extinct because their eggs were eaten by other animals. Shrew-like creatures around at the time may have eaten the eggs at night as dinosaurs slept.

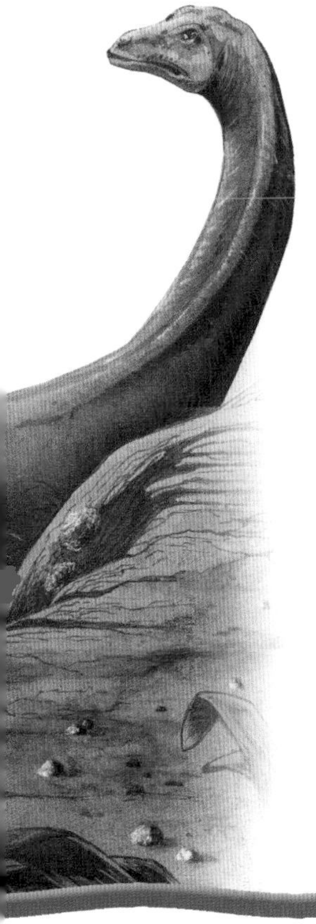

Could the dinosaurs have died from a disease?

This is unlikely because it wouldn't explain why so many millions of other animals died too. It is thought that more than two-thirds of all living things died at the same time as the dinosaurs, including sea creatures and plants.

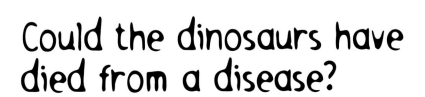

Can we find new dinosaurs?

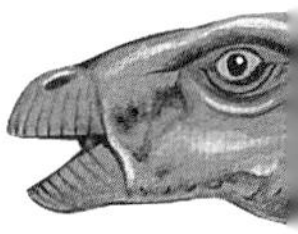

The remains of animals and plants that lived long ago are called fossils. These remains are bones, teeth, eggs and footprints – that have turned to rock over millions of years. Fossils of new dinosaurs such as *Jobaria* and *Janenschia* have been found in Africa.

Think

If you found fossils from a new dinosaur, think of what name you would give your own dinosaur.

Dino girl!

Leaellynasaura (lee-ell-in-oh-saw-ra) was named after the daughter of the scientists who found its fossils!

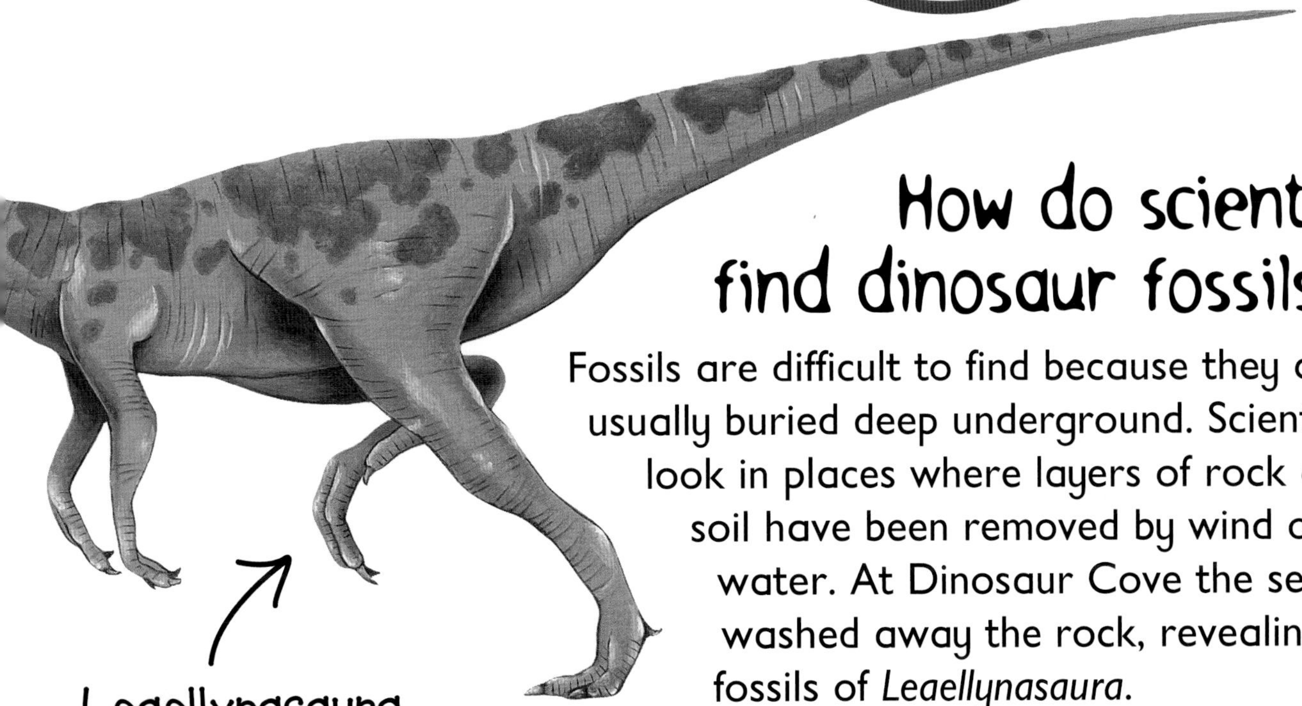

How do scientists find dinosaur fossils?

Fossils are difficult to find because they are usually buried deep underground. Scientists look in places where layers of rock and soil have been removed by wind or water. At Dinosaur Cove the sea has washed away the rock, revealing the fossils of *Leaellynasaura*.

Could dinosaurs ever come back to life?

It is unlikely that dinosaurs will ever walk the Earth again. However, scientists are still finding fossils and using them to uncover new facts about the lives of these magnificent creatures. Dinosaurs live on, but only in our imaginations!

Quiz time

Do you remember what you have read about dinosaurs?
These questions will test your memory. The pictures will help you. If you get stuck, read the pages again.

page 125

1. Why did dinosaurs eat stones?

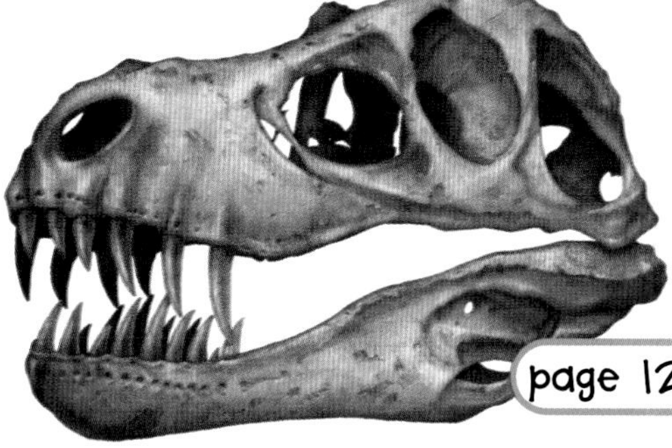

page 126

2. How big is a dinosaur tooth?

3. What were the biggest dinos?

page 128

4. What was the scariest dinosaur?

page 132

5. What was the biggest meat-eating dinosaur?

page 133

6. Which dinosaur had big eyes?

page 134

7. Were some dinosaurs small?

page 137

page 144

11. Why did the dinosaurs die?

12. How do scientists find dinosaur fossils?

page 147

8. Which dinosaur had a lumpy tail?

page 139

13. Could dinosaurs ever come back to life?

page 147

9. Did dinosaurs look after their babies?

page 141

10. Could dinosaurs leap and jump?

page 143

Answers

1. To mash food up in their stomachs
2. Different sizes
3. Sauropods
4. Tyrannosaurus rex
5. Giganotosaurus
6. Troodon
7. Yes, some were not much bigger than pet cats
8. Euoplocephalus
9. Yes, some did
10. Yes, Coelophysis could
11. Volcanoes may have erupted, or a meteorite may have smashed into the Earth
12. In rocks
13. No

Chirpy questions about...

Birds

What is special about birds?

Birds can fly, walk, run and even swim!

Because they have wings, birds are able to fly to all parts of the world, from steamy rainforests to the icy Arctic. There are about 9000 different types of bird, from beautiful barn owls to giant ostriches.

Do birds have teeth?

Birds don't have teeth. Instead, they have really strong mouths that are called beaks, or bills. Sharp, pointed beaks are good for grabbing bugs and short, strong beaks are great for cracking nuts open!

Discover

Beaks and feathers are made of a special tough material. See if you can you discover what it's called.

The early bird!

The oldest-known bird lived about 150 million years ago. Archaeopteryx (ark-ee-op-ter-ix) had feathers and wings, but it had teeth instead of a beak.

Why do birds lay eggs?

Birds lay eggs so that their babies can grow. Baby birds are called chicks and they begin life in an egg. The eggs are kept safe in a nest until they hatch.

How do birds fly?

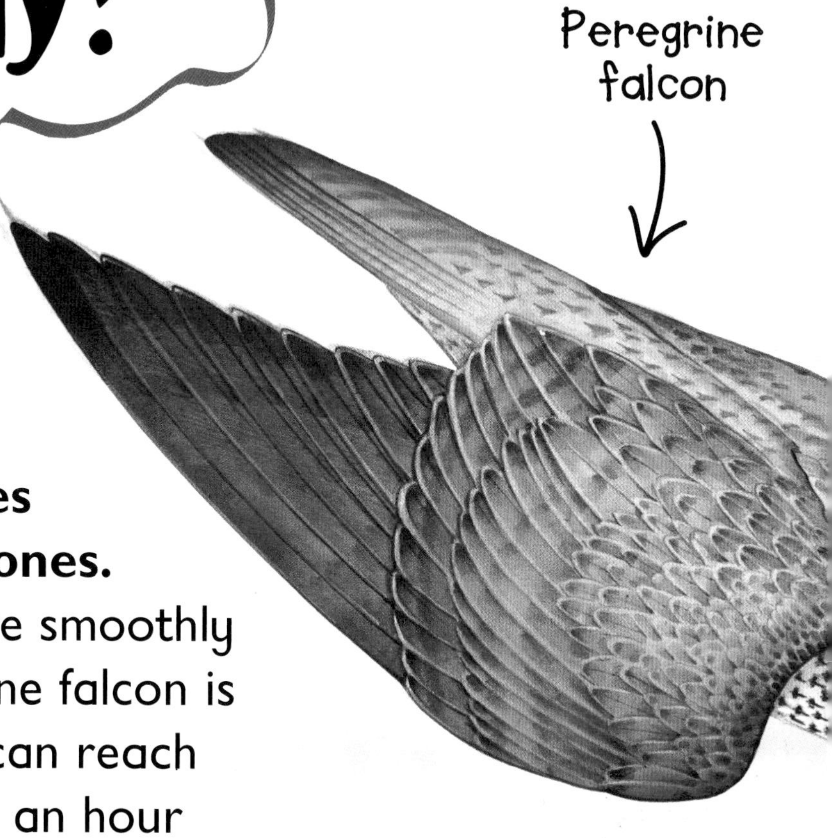

Birds can fly because they have wings, powerful muscles and very light bones. Feathers also help birds move smoothly through the air. This peregrine falcon is the fastest of all animals. It can reach top speeds of 180 kilometres an hour as it swoops and dives.

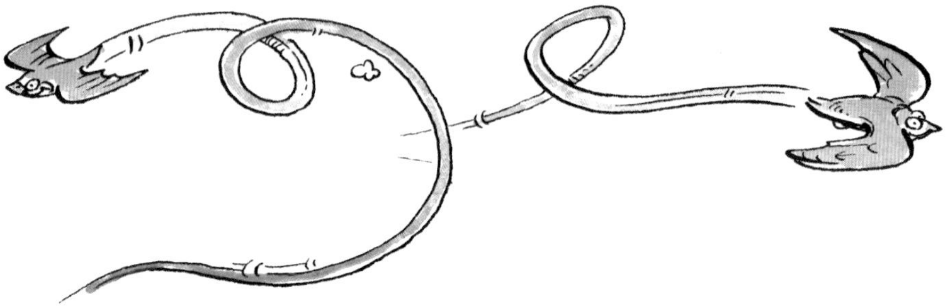

How far can a bird fly?

Birds can fly very long distances. Swifts are super fliers and even eat and mate while they swoop through the clouds. When young swifts leave the nest they may fly for the next two years and travel more than 500,000 kilometres!

Count

If a bird beats its wings ten times in one second, how many times would it beat its wings in two seconds?

Do all birds fly?

All birds have wings, but not all of them fly. This speedy roadrunner lives in the desert. It can fly, but it prefers to walk or run as it looks for lizards, snakes and bugs in the sand.

Roadrunner

Hum that tune!

Hummingbirds beat their wings 50 times a second. As the wings slice through the air they make the humming noise that gives the birds their name.

Why are some birds colourful?

Birds can be big show-offs and they use bright colours to make themselves look attractive. Male birds are usually more colourful than females. When this peacock sees a female (a peahen) he displays his fine tail and shakes it, so she can admire his great beauty.

Peacock

Love birds!

Great crested grebes are water birds that dance for each other. During the dance they offer each other gifts – beakfuls of water weed. Lovely!

Which birds strut around and coo?

Male birds puff up their feathers, strut around and make cooing noises to impress the females. These cocks-of-the-rocks also dance and spread their wings to show off to the female birds. They live in the South American rainforest.

Cocks-of-the-rocks

Why do birds sing?

Birds sing to get the attention of other birds. Like their colourful feathers, they may use songs to attract mates. Some birds squawk loudly if they are being attacked. Most baby birds learn to sing by copying their parents.

Dress-up

A bird's feathers are called its plumage. Put on some bright clothes and see if anyone notices your plumage!

Why do birds lay eggs in nests?

Birds lay their eggs in a nest to keep them safe. Once the eggs have hatched, the little chicks stay in the nest until they have grown enough to be able to fly. These bald eagles build giant nests up to 2.5 metres across.

Why are cuckoos lazy?

Cuckoos don't bother making their own nests. Instead, they lay their eggs in other birds' nests. This way cuckoos do not have all the hard work of looking after their own chicks – other birds do it for them!

How do birds build nests?

Birds build their nests in different ways, but most of them use twigs and sticks. African weaver birds make their delicate nests using strips of leaves and grass. They knot and weave the strips together to make a cosy, safe home.

Make it

Use sticks and twigs to make a nest. Make a soft lining with grass or straw. Pop some chocolate eggs in the middle.

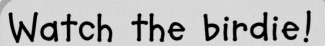

1. The weaver bird twists strips of leaves

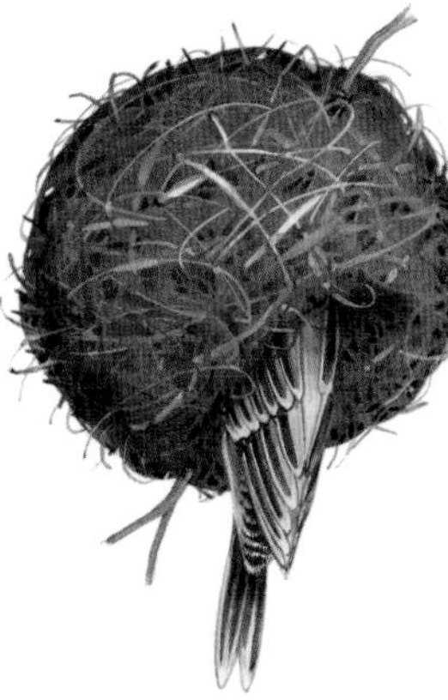

2. The roof is made

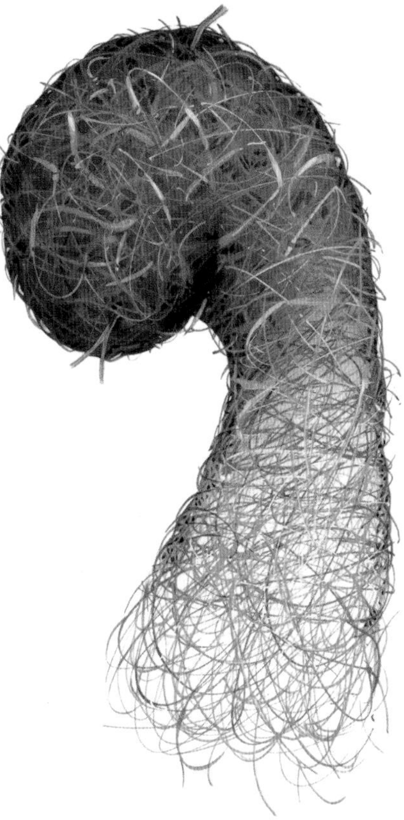

3. The finished nest

Watch the birdie!

Most birds take minutes to lay an egg. The mother cuckoo can lay an egg in 9 seconds! This allows her to quickly pop it in the nest of another bird.

What is a bird of prey?

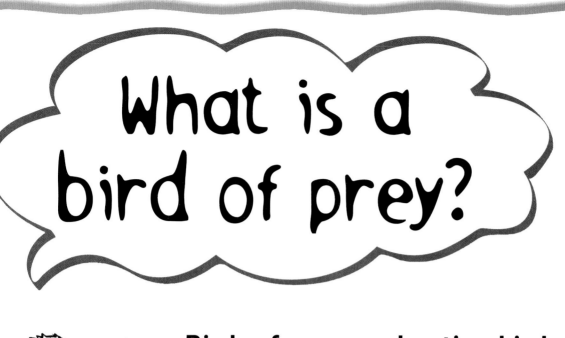

Birds of prey are hunting birds. As they soar and glide across the sky they search for animals to eat. Golden eagles have extremely good eyesight and can spot food far away. They swoop to the ground and grab rabbits and mice with their sharp claws.

Top bird!

Eagles like to build their nests in high places. One pair of sea eagles made their nest on top of a light-tower by the coast in Norway!

How does a sea eagle catch fish?

Sea eagles need good eyes and strong claws to catch a swimming fish. Each foot has a pointed hook for holding onto a slippery fish. Sea eagles take their fish to a cliff or rocky ledge where they can eat in comfort.

Sea eagle

Do hunting birds live in towns?

It's unusual to see big hunting birds such as eagles in towns. But you might see smaller ones, such as ravens. These black birds are very clever animals. They hunt mice and rats but they will eat almost any food that they can find.

Try it

Eagles use their feet to grab their food. See if you can pick up anything using just your feet.

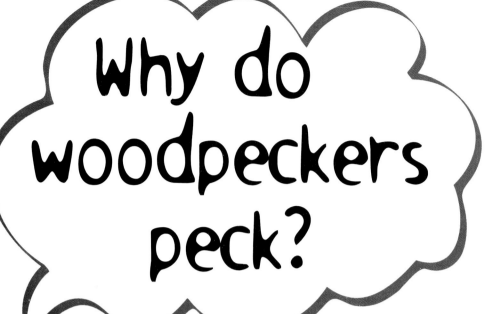

Why do woodpeckers peck?

Woodpeckers peck at trees to disturb the little insects that live in the bark. They then gobble them up. These birds can also use their strong, pointed beaks to hammer at the tree until they have made a hole big enough for a nest.

Hummm, I'm hungry!

Bee hummingbirds beat their wings 200 times a second. If we used up the same amount of energy we would need to eat three times our own weight in potatoes each day!

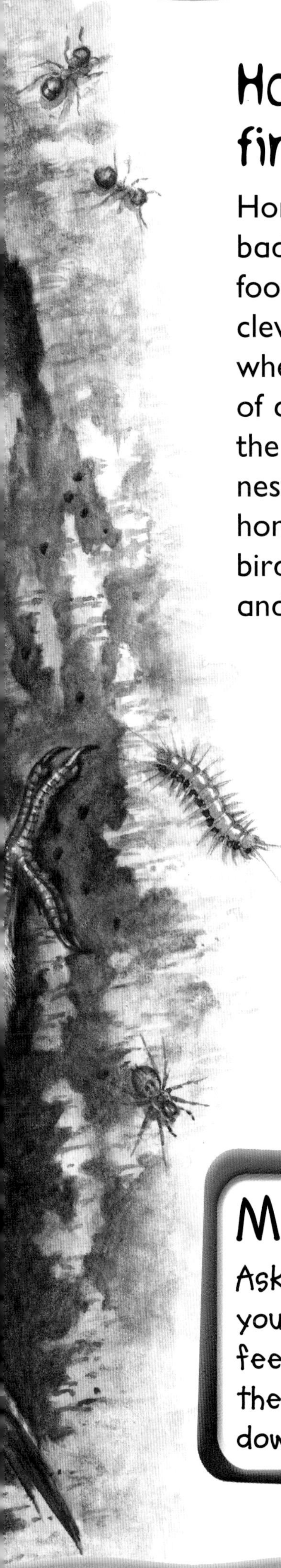

How do honeyguides find their food?

Honeyguide birds follow honey badgers to find their favourite food – delicious bee grubs! The clever birds follow the badgers when they go in search of a bee's nest. When the badger opens the nest it feeds on the honey, while the birds eat the grubs and beeswax.

Make it

Ask an adult to help you make a bird feeder. You can then hang it upside down from a tree.

Do antbirds eat ants?

Antbirds follow army ants as they march through the forest, but they don't usually eat them. The birds perch on trees as the army ants pass by, then they pounce on the other small animals and insects that come to feed on the ants.

How does a bird eat a snail?

Birds that eat snails need to get the soft body out of the hard shell. Some birds smash snails against rocks. This snail kite uses its sharp beak to cut the slimy snail away from its shell and hook it out.

Snail kite

Knobbly knees!

Flamingos look as if they have got back-to-front legs. Actually, what appear to be their knees are really their ankles!

Which bird has a scissor-shaped beak?

The beak of a skimmer is shaped like scissors. This is because the lower beak is much longer and flatter than the top beak. As it flies over water, the skimmer dips its lower beak below the surface. When it touches a fish it snaps its beak shut.

Flamingo

Why do flamingos have long necks?

Flamingos have long necks so that they can reach underwater to find their food. They use their beaks to catch tiny pink creatures called shrimps that float past. Flamingos turn pink after eating lots of these shrimps!

Remember

Can you remember what a skimmer's beak is shaped like? If you can't, read this page again to find out.

Quiz time

Do you remember what you have read about birds?
These questions will test your memory. The pictures will help you. If you get stuck, read the pages again.

page 153

1. Why do birds lay eggs?

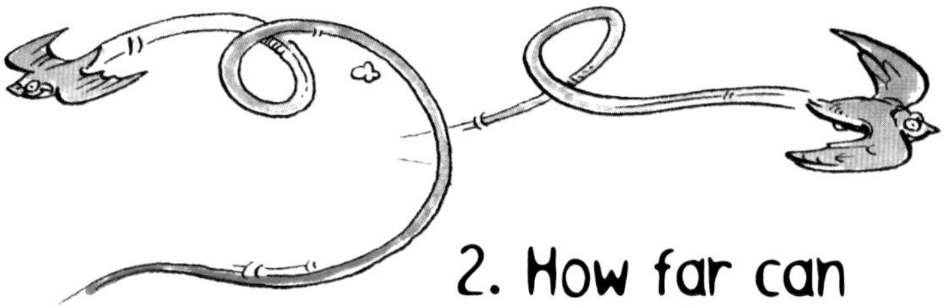

page 154

2. How far can a bird fly?

3. Do all birds fly?

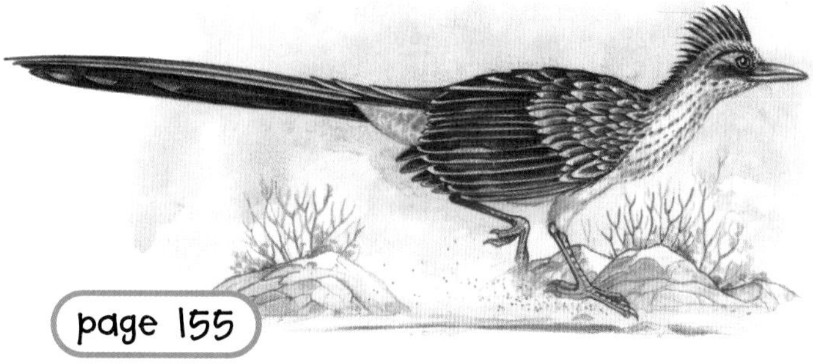

page 155

4. Why do birds sing?

page 157

5. How do birds build nests?

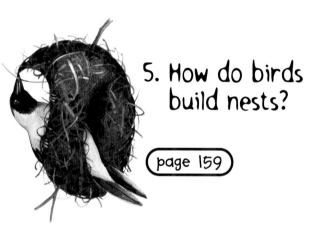

page 159

6. Why are cuckoos lazy?

page 159

7. What is a bird of prey?

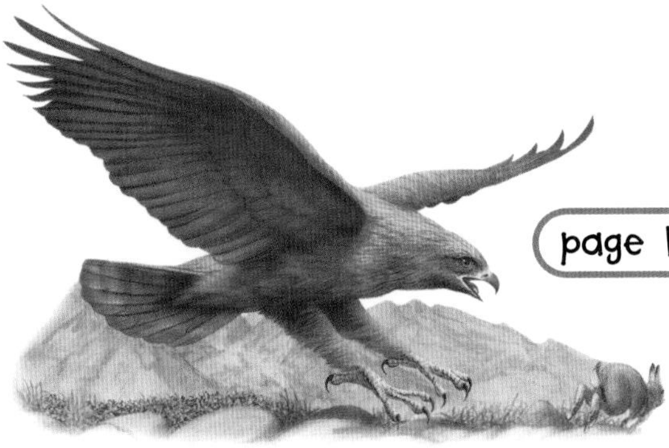

page 160

8. Do hunting birds live in towns?

page 161

9. Why do woodpeckers peck?

page 162

10. Do antbirds eat ants?

page 163

11. How does a bird eat a snail?

page 164

12. Which bird has a scissor-shaped beak?

page 165

13. Why do flamingos have long necks?

page 165

Answers

1. So their babies can grow
2. Very long distances
3. Not all birds can fly
4. To get the attention of other birds
5. With twigs and sticks
6. Because they don't make their own nests
7. A hunting bird
8. Smaller ones do
9. To disturb insects that live in the bark
10. Yes, they eat army ants
11. The snail kite hooks it out with it's beak
12. The skimmer
13. So they can reach underwater to find their food

Fur-raising questions about...

Mammals

Why are some animals furry?

Fur or hair keeps some animals warm. Animals that have fur or hair are called mammals. Fur also protects from the weather. This hairy orang-utan lives in the rainforest. She picks fruit and leaves to eat. She feeds her baby on milk.

What is a joey?

A joey is a baby kangaroo. When a joey is born it is smaller than your big toe! Even though it is tiny and blind, the joey crawls all the way to its mother's pouch and climbs in. It feeds on milk from its mother.

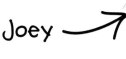

Egg-citing news!

Most mammals give birth. This means that they have babies, cubs or kittens. Some strange mammals, such as the duck-billed platypus, lay eggs.

Find out

Were you a beautiful baby, or did you hatch from an egg? Look at old photos of yourself to find out.

Why do some mammals sniff the air?

Many mammals use their noses to get information about the world around them. Their noses are very sensitive to smells. Wild animals, such as deer and rabbits, sniff the air around them to check for signs of danger.

What is the biggest mammal?

The blue whale is – and it's enormous! In fact, it is the biggest animal that has ever lived. Even a baby blue whale is huge – it measures 7 metres in length. All whales are mammals and give birth to their babies, which are called calves.

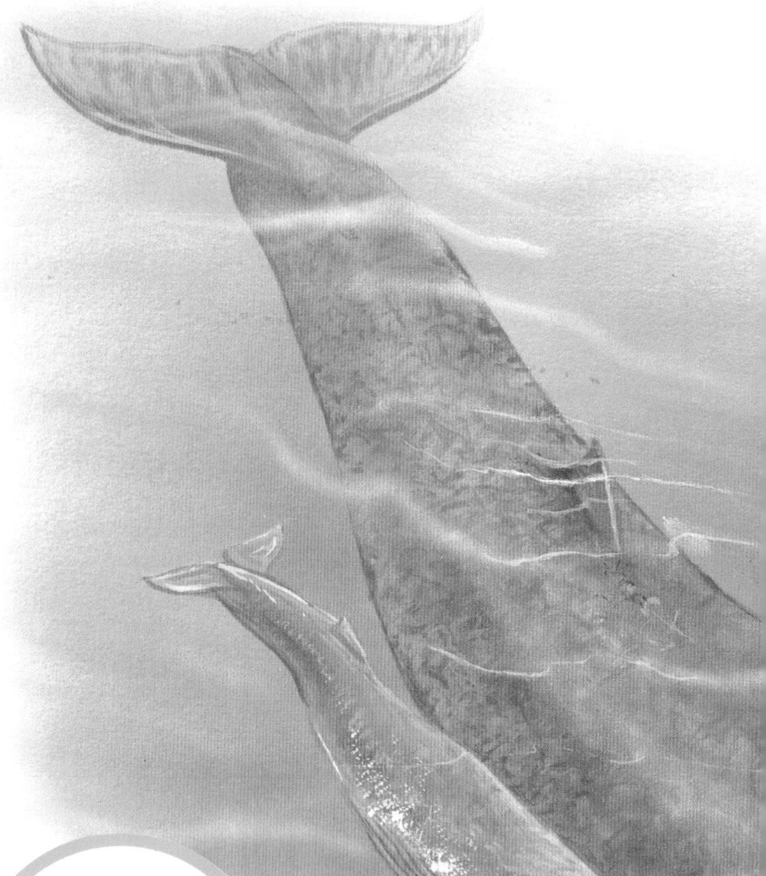

What a hooter!

African elephants have the longest noses! Their noses are called trunks and they can be 2.5 metres long. Trunks are used for smelling, picking up food and drinking.

African elephant

How big is an elephant?

One African elephant can weigh more than 100 people put together. Elephants are the biggest animals that live on land and they can reach 4 metres in height. They spend most of their day eating to keep themselves that huge!

Measure

Using a measuring tape, see if you can mark out how long a blue whale calf is.

Blue whale

What is the smallest mammal?

The tiny hog-nosed bat is not much bigger than your thumb! Bats are the only mammals that can fly. They usually sleep during the day and come out at night to look for food.

How do cheetahs run so fast?

Cheetahs have big muscles in their legs and they can run faster than any other animal. These speedy cats run out of breath quickly. This means that the animals they're chasing, such as gazelles, often manage to escape. Cheetahs can reach speeds of 100 kilometres an hour!

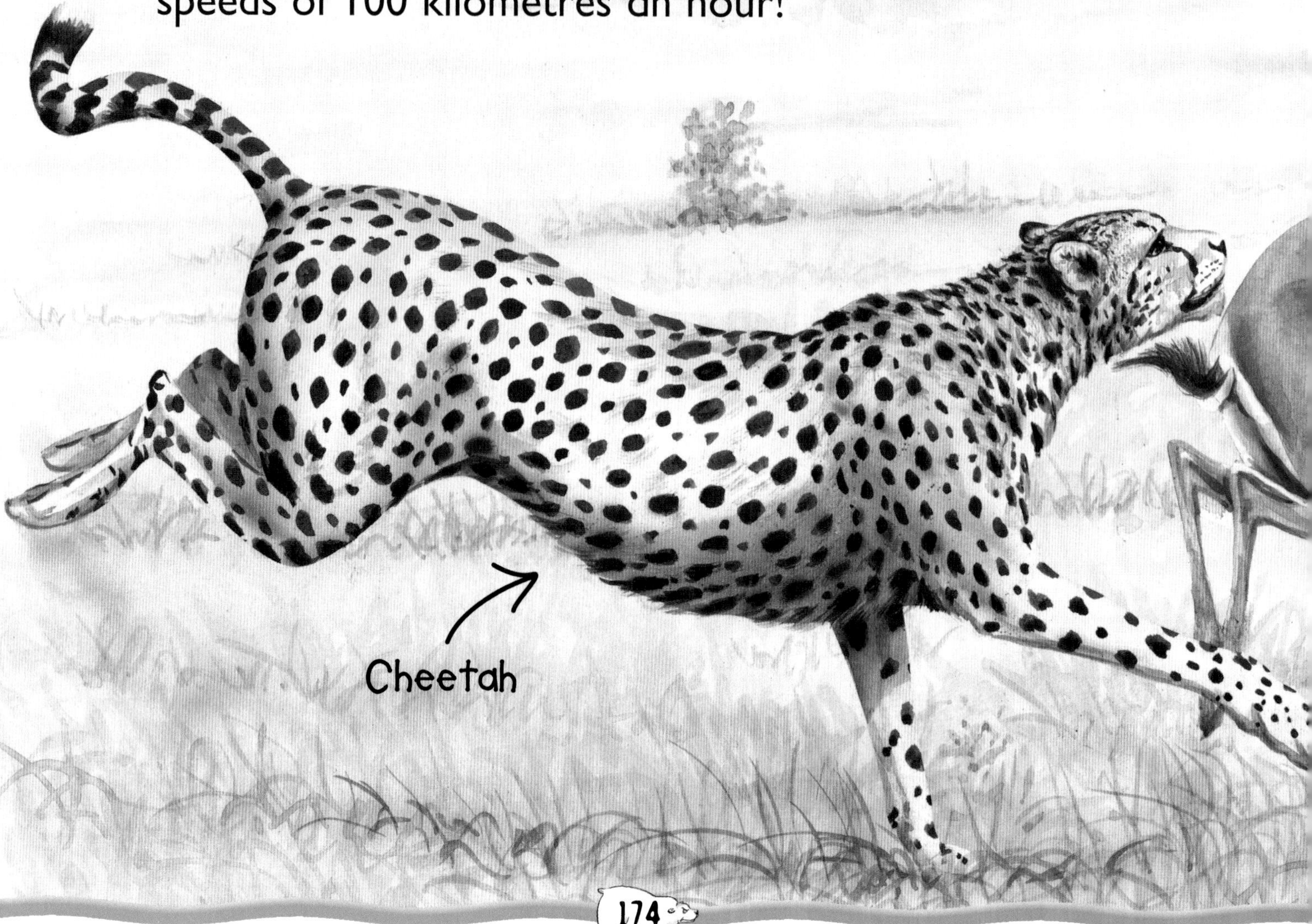

Hare

Why do hares kick?

Hares sometimes kick out at their enemies. Other animals such as foxes try to catch hares to eat them. If the hare sees, smells or hears an enemy, it can run fast to get away, or kick out with its back legs.

Run

How fast can you run? Ask an adult to time you next time you are in the park or garden.

Whoosh!

The pronghorn deer is one of the fastest mammals in North America. It runs fast to escape from wolves, which hunt it for food.

Gazelle

Which mammal is very bouncy?

Kangaroos bounce instead of running. The red kangaroo is a champion jumper and it leaps across the dry deserts of its Australian home. It travels quickly to search for water and food, which are hard to find in a desert.

Are mammals good swimmers?

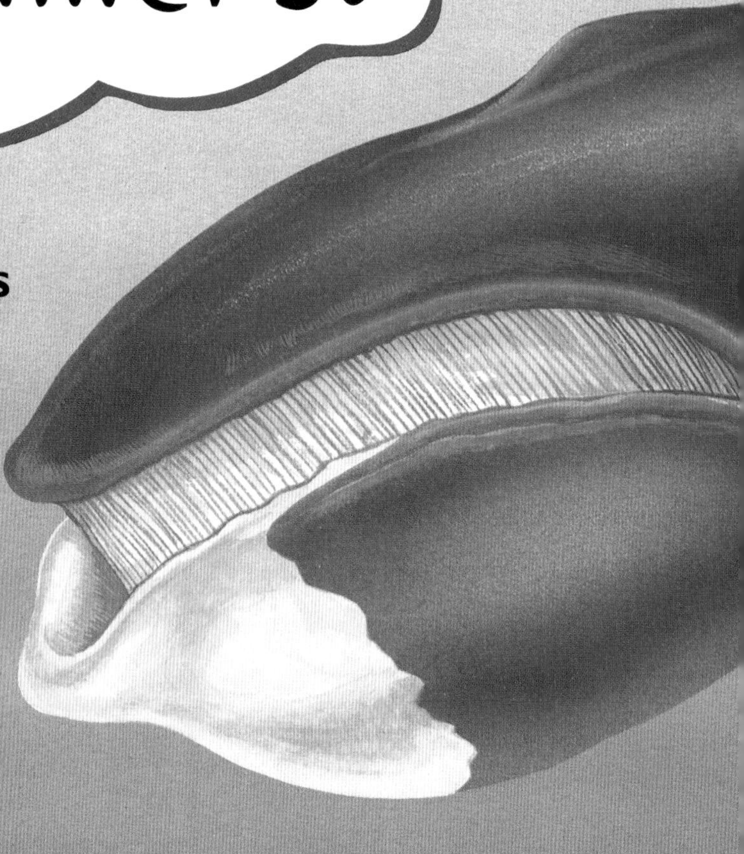

Some mammals are super swimmers! Whales, dolphins and seals have bodies that are perfectly shaped for moving through water smoothly and quickly. They have fins and tails instead of arms and legs. Whales and dolphins spend their whole lives in water.

Can seals breathe underwater?

No mammals can breathe underwater – not even seals, whales and dolphins. Instead, they have to take in all the air they need when they are at the surface of the water, then hold their breath. Some seals can stay underwater for an hour at a time!

Diving deep!

The Weddell seal is a daring diver. It plunges down to the deep, dark, cold water of the oceans as it hunts for fish to eat.

What does a killer whale kill?

Killer whales kill squid, fish, seals and even birds. They are strong swimmers and have sharp, pointed teeth. Killer whales can be friendly. They live in family groups and calves stay with their mothers all their lives!

Swim

You are a mammal and you can learn to swim too! Visit your local pool for some watery fun!

Are polar bears cuddly?

Polar bears may look cuddly with their thick, white fur, but they are fierce hunters. These bears live in the ice-covered lands near the North Pole. Their fur keeps them warm – they even have fur on the soles of their feet so that their toes don't get frost bite!

Polar bear

Lots of lemmings!

A female lemming can have her first babies when she is only 14 days old. From then on, she can have as many as 12 babies every single month!

Why are some animals white?

White animals usually live in places that are covered with snow in winter. A white Arctic hare blends into the snow and hides from enemies. In summer, the snow melts and the hare grows brown fur.

Paint

Paint a snowy scene showing some animals that live in cold places, such as polar bears, seals and penguins.

How do seals stay warm?

Seals spend a lot of their time underwater in cold parts of the world. They can keep warm because they have thick layers of fat, called blubber, under their skin. Seals also have waterproof fur that stops water getting through to their skin.

Why do wolves live in packs?

Wolves live in packs because they hunt together and look after one another. A mother wolf takes good care of her cubs. As the cubs grow, they are brought food from their father and other members of the wolf pack.

Cool cats!

Lions may be fierce, but they are also very lazy. They sleep or doze for more than 20 hours a day, keeping cool in the shade!

How many meerkats live together?

Meerkats live in groups of up to 30 animals. A group is called a colony and each colony is made up of several families. While some meerkats search for food, others stand guard and look for enemies, such as hawks.

What is a group of whales called?

A group of whales is called a pod. Pilot whales live in pods of 20 or more animals that swim and hunt together. Some dolphins live in pods that may have more than 1000 members.

Count

How many people can you count in your family? Include all your grandparents, aunts, uncles and cousins.

How big is a baby panda?

Pandas give birth to tiny babies, or cubs. Each cub could fit inside your hand and weighs the same as an apple. Newborn pandas are blind and helpless. They do not open their eyes until they are two or three months old.

What are baby elephants called?

Baby elephants are called calves. Soon after they are born, elephant calves are able to stand up. Within a few days, they can run around. Elephants live in groups called herds. The adult elephants protect the young from lions and hyenas.

Elephant calf

Big baby!

The baby blue whale is bigger than any other mammal baby. It weighs more than 30 people put together and drinks up to 500 litres of milk every day.

Measure

How much milk do you drink every day? Use a measuring jug to see how much milk fills up a glass.

Which mammal has the most babies at a time?

The Virginia opossum can have up to 21 babies at a time – more than any other mammal. Each baby opossum is no bigger than a fingertip! If it is attacked, a Virginia opossum lies down and pretends to be dead.

How do tigers catch their food?

Tigers are hunters. Their bodies are perfect for finding, chasing and killing other animals. Stripy fur helps the tiger blend in with tall grass so they are difficult to spot. When a tiger sees a meal, it runs and pounces. It uses its claws and teeth to kill.

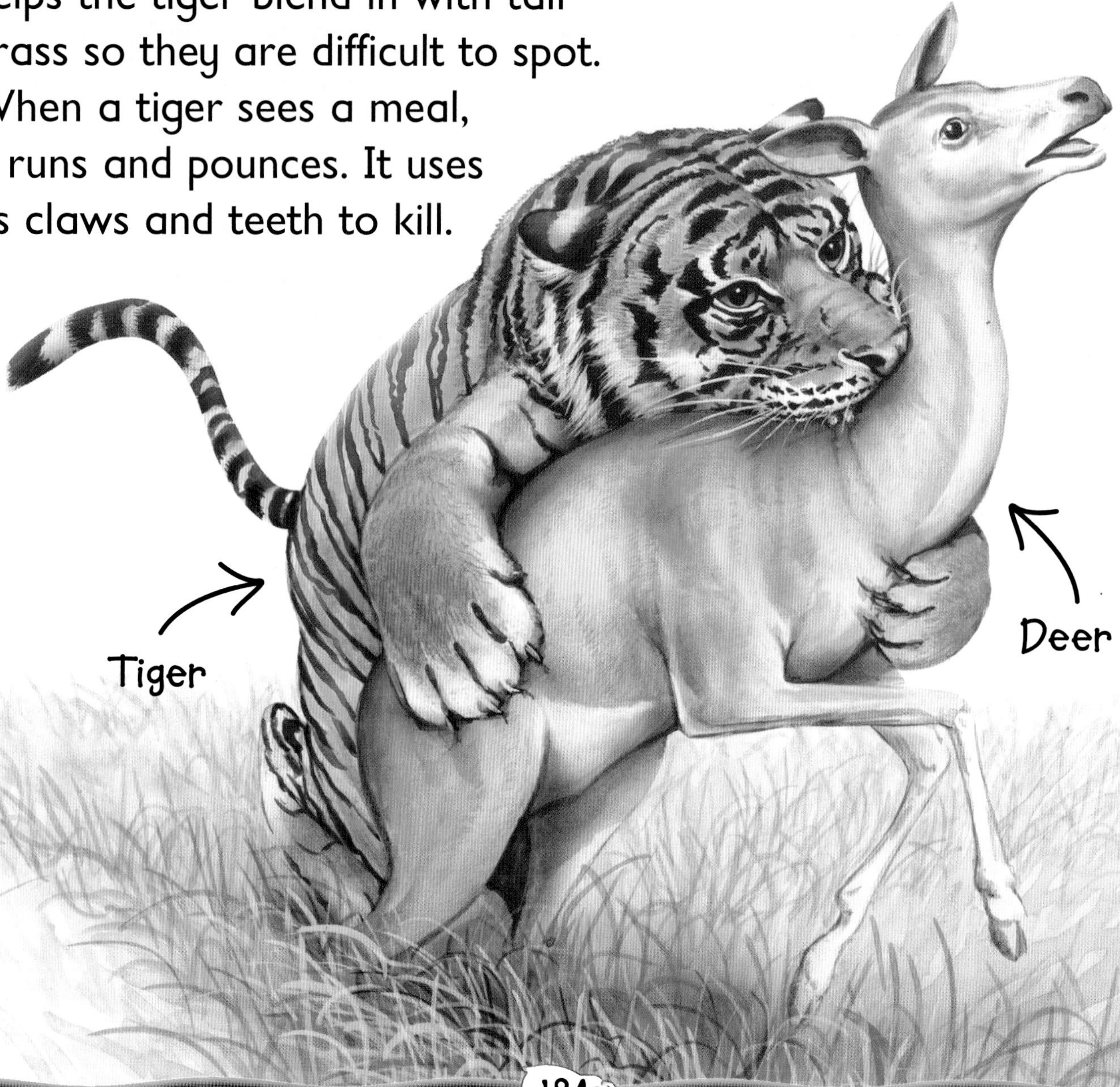

What do bears eat?

Bears eat all kinds of food. Some bears hunt other animals but most eat insects, fruit and leaves. Sloth bears love to eat termites. They have long claws for digging out termite nests. The bears suck the termites up one at a time!

Sloth bear

Great apes!

Chimpanzees live in groups that hunt together. They search for other monkeys, birds and antelopes to eat. They also form groups that attack other groups of chimpanzees.

Why do dogs hunt in packs?

Wild dogs hunt in packs because they are more likely to get something to eat. By working together they can surround an animal. They may catch a bigger animal than one dog alone could catch.

Work

Working together is best. True or false? Help an adult with the shopping or the housework to find out!

Are rhinos dangerous?

A rhinoceros is one of the most dangerous mammals. Mother rhinos may attack people, or other animals, to protect their babies. They can run fast and they have sharp horns for attacking. Male rhinos also use their horns to fight one another.

Bee-eaters!

Smelly skunks sometimes feed on bees. They roll the bees on the ground to remove the stings before eating them.

Why do some mammals have scales?

Some mammals have scales to protect themselves, rather like a suit of armour. Pangolins are strange ant-eating mammals that live in Africa and Asia. Their bodies are covered in overlapping scales that protect them from other animals – and the stinging bites of ants.

Pangolin

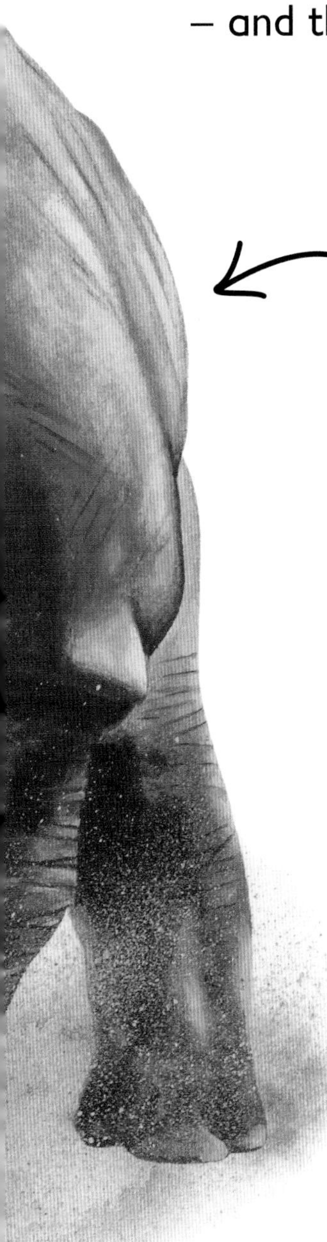

Rhinoceros

What is the stinkiest mammal?

Skunks are very stinky mammals! These stripy creatures shake their tails at an enemy to warn it to stay away. If that doesn't work, the skunk raises its tail and sprays a smelly liquid in its enemy's face!

Make it

Ask an adult to help you make a cardboard suit of armour. How easy is it to move wearing the armour?

Quiz time

Do you remember what you have read about mammals? These questions will test your memory. The pictures will help you. If you get stuck, read the pages again.

1. What is a joey?

page 171

2. What is the biggest mammal?

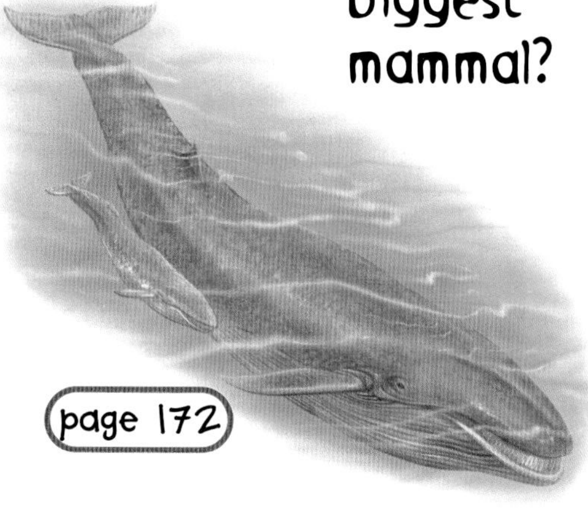

page 172

3. Which mammal is very bouncy?

page 175

4. Can seals breathe underwater?

page 176

5. Are polar bears cuddly?

page 178

6. Why are some animals white?

page 179

7. Why do wolves live in packs?

page 180

page 185

11. What do bears eat?

8. How many meerkats live together?

page 181

12. Why do dogs hunt in packs?

page 185

13. Are rhinos dangerous?

page 186

9. How big is a baby panda?

page 182

page 183

10. What are baby elephants called?

Answers

1. A baby kangaroo
2. The blue whale
3. The kangaroo
4. No
5. No, they are fierce hunters
6. To blend in with their surroundings
7. Because they hunt together and look after each other
8. Up to 30
9. As big as your hand
10. Calves
11. Insects, fruit and leaves
12. They are more likely to get something to eat
13. Yes, rhinos are one of the most dangerous animals

Ancient questions about...

Ancient Egypt

Why were the pyramids built?

Pyramids were tombs (burial places) for Egyptian rulers, called pharaohs. The three great pyramids of Khufu, Khafre and Menkaure were built in Giza, Egypt, 4500 years ago.

The Great Pyramid of Khufu is the biggest. It took 20 years and 4000 workers to build it!

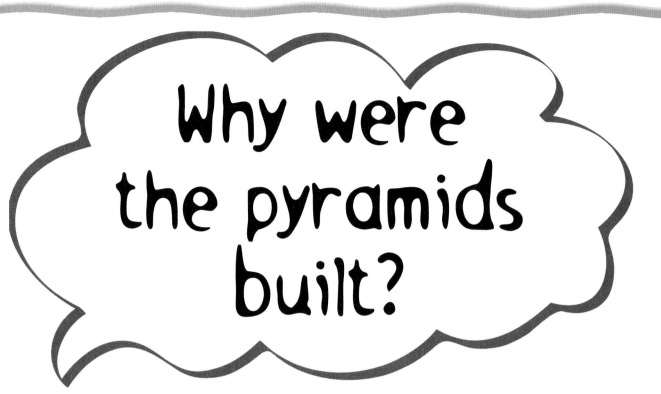

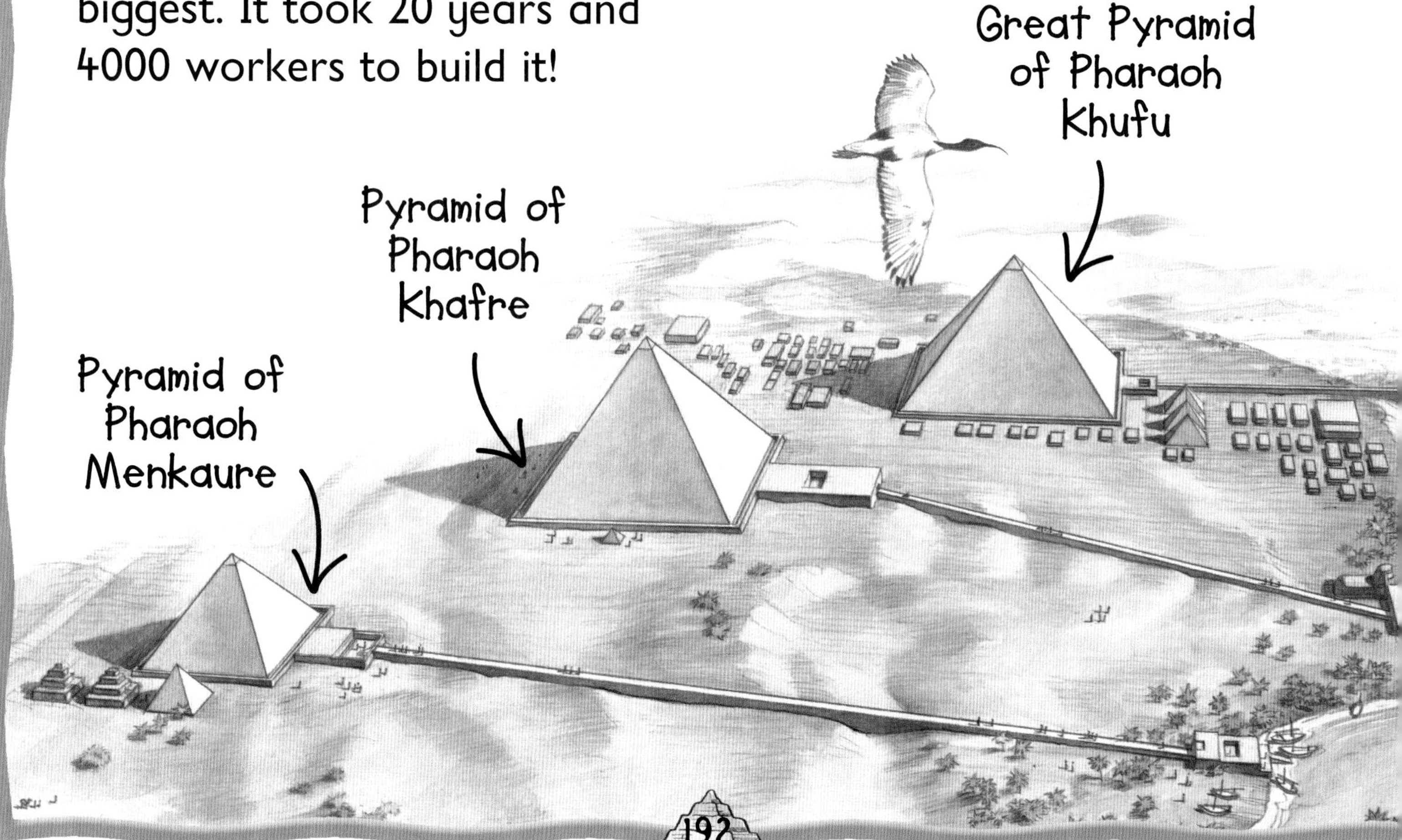

What guards the Great Pyramid?

The pyramids were full of treasures. A stone statue was built to guard the Great Pyramid at Giza. It was carved in the shape of a sphinx. A sphinx has the body of a lion and the head of a man. The sphinx at the Great Pyramid has the face of Pharaoh Khafre.

The sphinx

Tomb robbers!

'The Book of Buried Pearls' told robbers all about the treasures inside the tombs. It also showed them how to get past spirits that guarded the dead.

What was inside the Great Pyramid?

The Great Pyramid had two huge burial chambers. They were built for the pharaoh and his queen. A corridor called the Grand Gallery led to the pharaoh's chamber. The corridor's ceiling was 8 metres tall!

Map

Draw a plan of a pyramid. Include secret tunnels and hidden rooms to stop the robbers.

Who was the top god?

Ancient Egyptians worshipped more than 1000 gods. The most important was Ra, the Sun god. Every evening, Ra was swallowed by Nut, the sky goddess. At night, Ra travelled through the land of the dead. He was born again each morning. Later, Ra became Amun Ra, king of the gods.

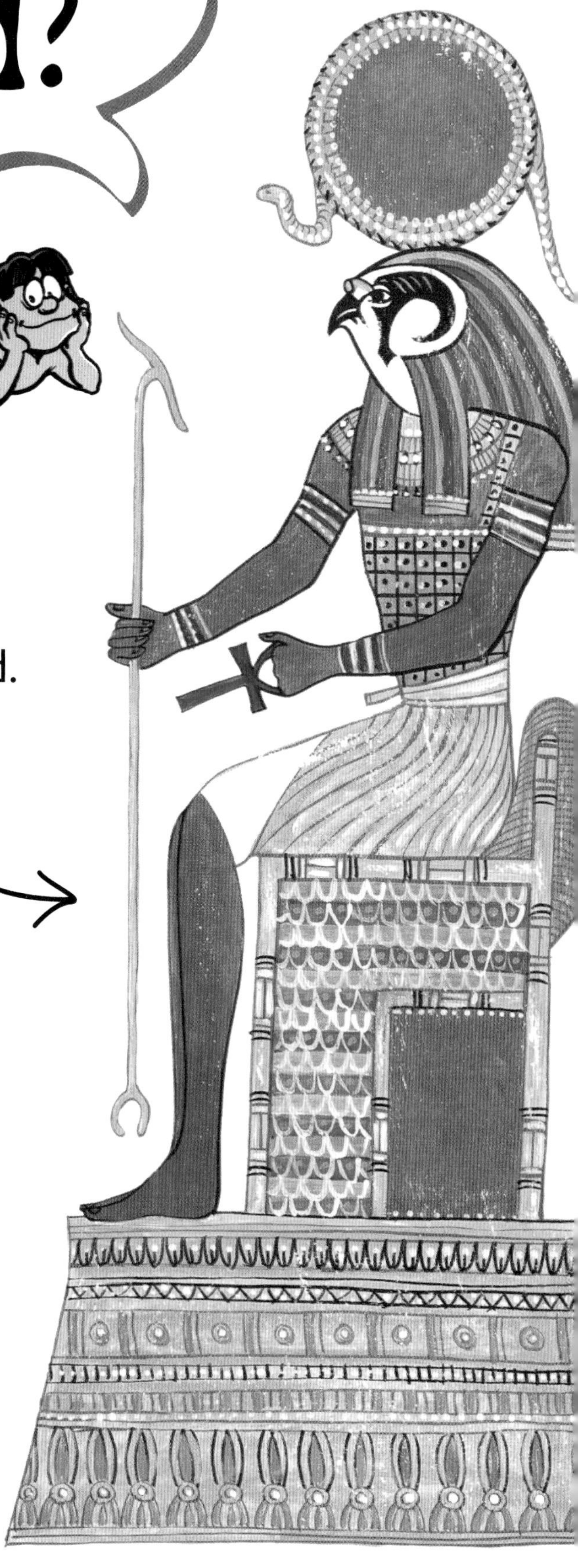

Ra

Dead body god!

Anubis was the god in charge of dead bodies. He looked like a jackal, a kind of dog. People who wrapped bodies for burial often wore Anubis masks!

Why were cats important?

Cats were sacred (holy) animals in ancient Egypt. The goddess for cats, musicians and dancers was called Bastet. When a pet cat died it was wrapped up carefully and placed in a special cat-shaped coffin. Then the cat was buried in a cat cemetery!

Who took care of the temples?

Fabulous temples were built for the gods. Many temples were built for Amun Ra, king of the gods. Priests looked after the temples, their riches and the lands around them. These massive statues of Pharaoh Ramses II guard the temple at Abu Simbel.

Draw

Draw a picture of Ra travelling through the night in the land of the dead. He travelled in a boat.

Temple at Abu Simbel

Which queen found a magical land?

Queen Hatshepsut sent explorers to look for Punt, a magical land she had heard about. Punt was said to be filled with treasure and animals. The explorers returned with gold, ivory, perfumes and special oils. In fact, Punt was probably part of present-day Somalia in Africa.

Shaving for the gods!

Ancient Egyptians could only visit temples for the gods if they shaved off their hair and eyebrows!

Who was the boy king?

Tutankhamun became king of Egypt when he was just nine years old. He was just 18 years old when he died. His tomb was discovered in 1922. Inside was a solid gold death mask of the king.

Death mask of Tutankhamun

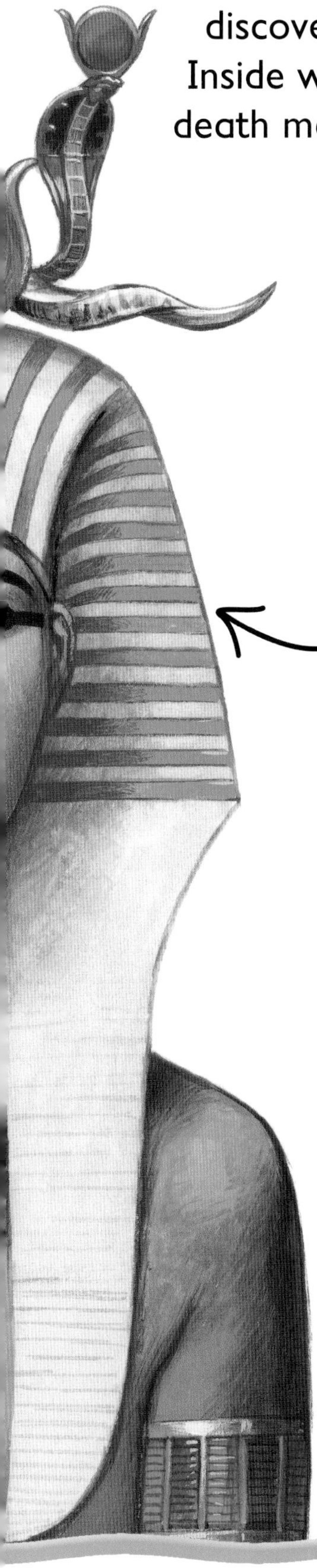

Queen Hatshepsut

Make

Find six boxes that fit inside each other. Decorate them with things a pharaoh might use in the next world.

What did tomb robbers find?

Ancient Egyptian kings were buried with all the things they might need in the world of the dead. These included gold, silver, jewels, furniture and even cooking pots.

Robbers stole the lot – even the bodies! But robbers did not find King Tutankhamun's tomb.

How do you make a mummy?

Ancient Egyptians mummified their dead. First, the inside parts such as the brain, but not the heart, were removed. Then the body was salted and dried. Cloth was stuffed inside the body to help it keep its shape. Then the body was oiled and wrapped in lots of bandages.

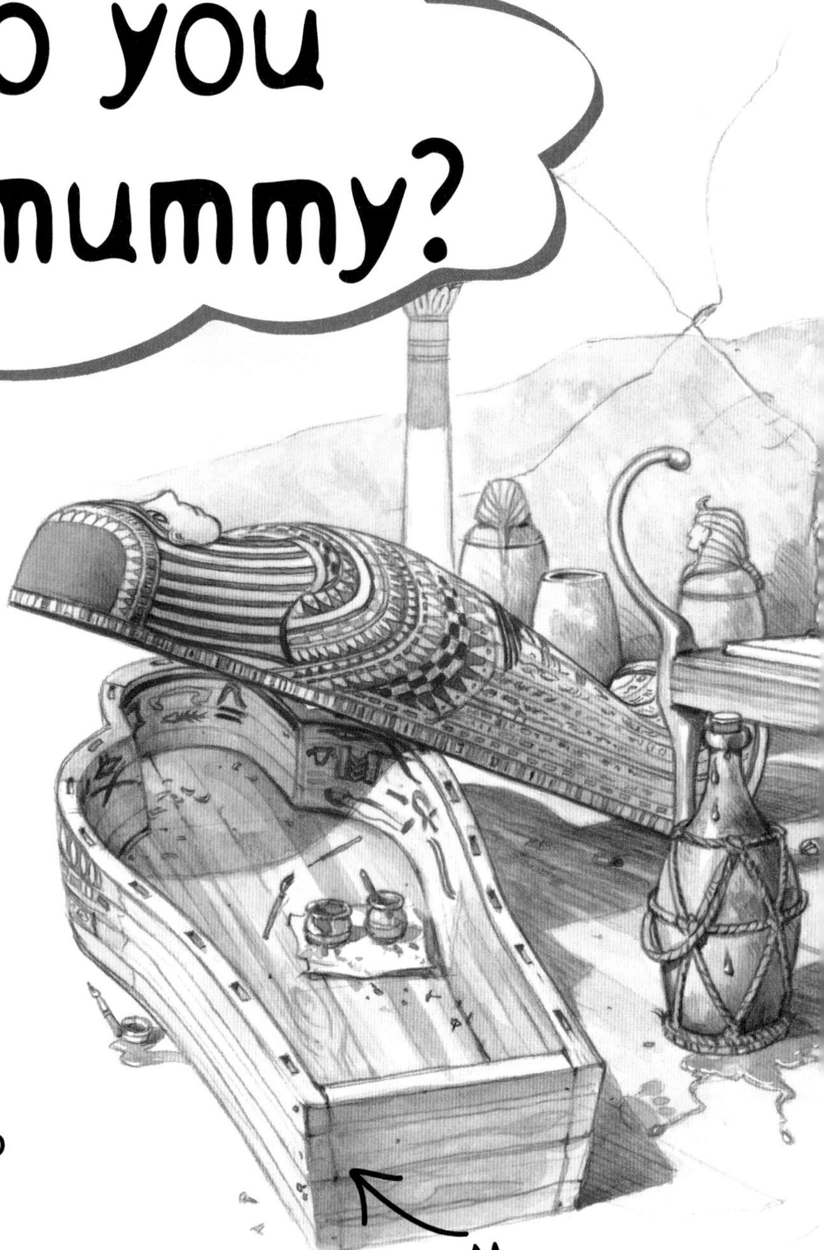

All wrapped up!

The mummy was wrapped in tight bandages. This helped to stop the body from rotting away.

Make

Cut out a mummy mask from card and paint it with a face. It could be the face of an animal.

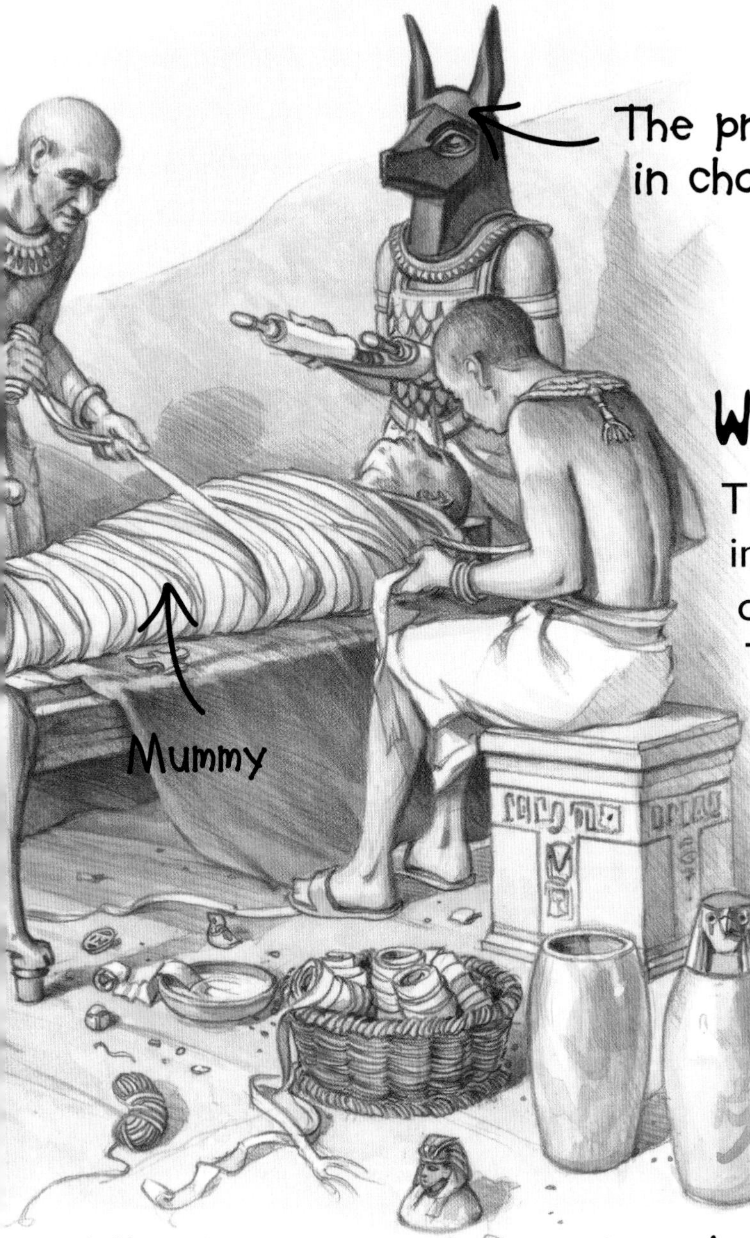

What did the priest do?

The priest sent the dead person's spirit into the next world. He touched parts of the body with special instruments. This was so that the body could move around in the world of the dead. The mouth could speak and eat in its new life after being touched!

What were mummies kept in?

The mummy was placed in a case. Some cases were just wooden boxes. Others were beautifully decorated. An important person, such as a pharaoh, was placed in a stone coffin called a sarcophagus (sarc-off-a-gus).

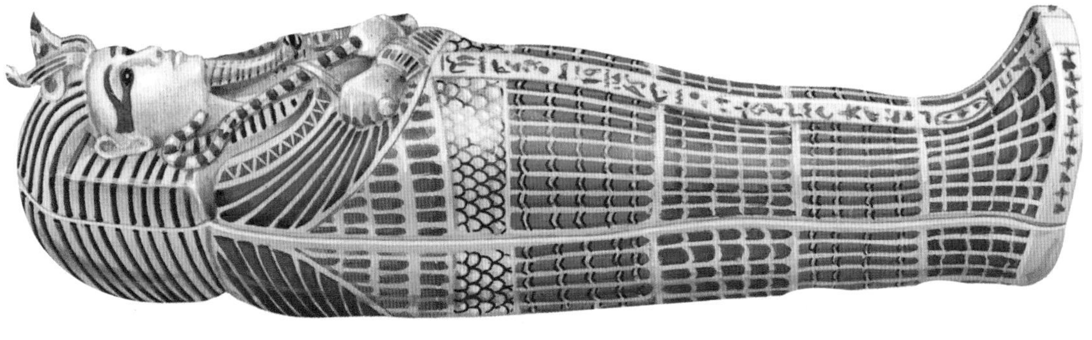

Did Egypt have an army?

Ancient Egypt had a powerful army that won many battles. About 3500 years ago, the Egyptians made a new weapon. It was a chariot pulled by two horses and driven by two soldiers. They drove very fast at the enemy and fired arrows at them.

Who defeated Egypt?

General Ptolemy defeated Egypt over 2300 years ago. The rulers who followed him were called the Ptolemies. They built a new city called Alexandria. It was guarded by a massive lighthouse. The city also had a museum and a huge library with thousands of books.

Buzz off!

Egyptian soldiers were given golden fly medals! Perhaps it's because the soldiers annoyed the enemy so much!

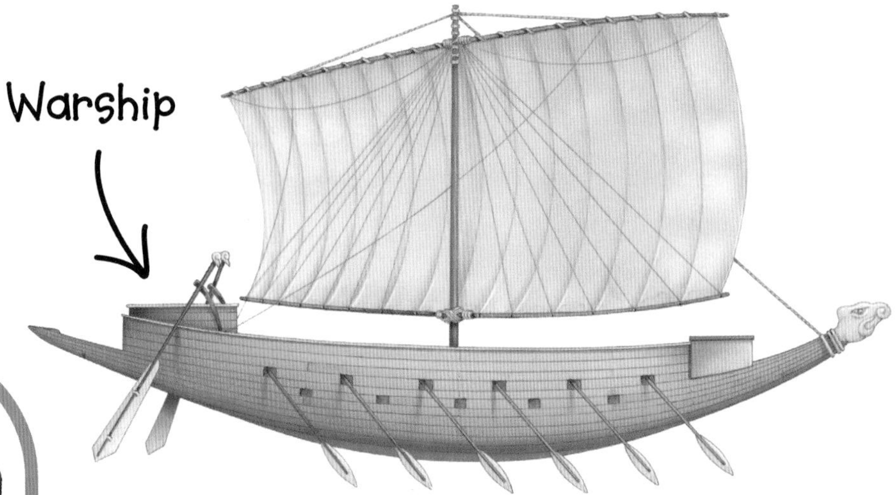

Who were the Sea People?

The Sea People attacked Egypt and tried to take over the country. Pharaoh Ramses III sent lots of warships to try to defeat them. The ships had sails and oars for travelling quickly at sea. The Sea People were beaten back by the Egyptians.

Read

Can you remember what new weapon the Egyptians made? Read the pages again to remind you.

Did food grow in the desert?

Most of Egypt was in the hot desert. However, every year in July, the great river Nile flooded the dry fields. The water brought rich, black soil with it. This soil spread in wide strips on each side of the river. Farmers sowed their seed in this good soil.

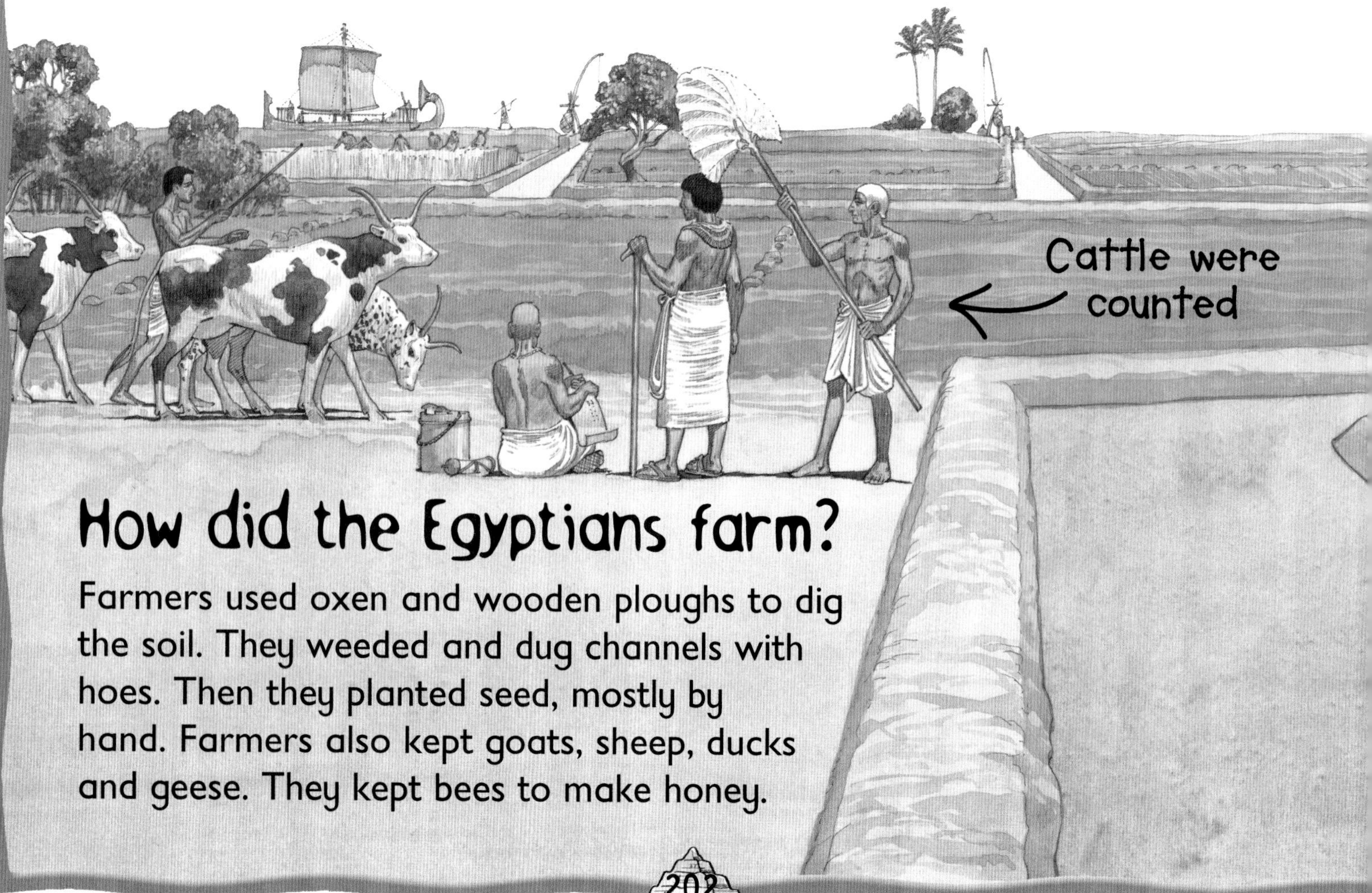

How did the Egyptians farm?

Farmers used oxen and wooden ploughs to dig the soil. They weeded and dug channels with hoes. Then they planted seed, mostly by hand. Farmers also kept goats, sheep, ducks and geese. They kept bees to make honey.

Get lost!

Young boys were paid to be scarecrows! They frightened birds with their slingshots and loud shouts!

What did farmers grow?

Farmers grew barley for beer and grapes for wine. Dates, figs, melons, cucumbers, onions, leeks and lettuces grew well in the rich soil. Wheat was also grown to make bread.

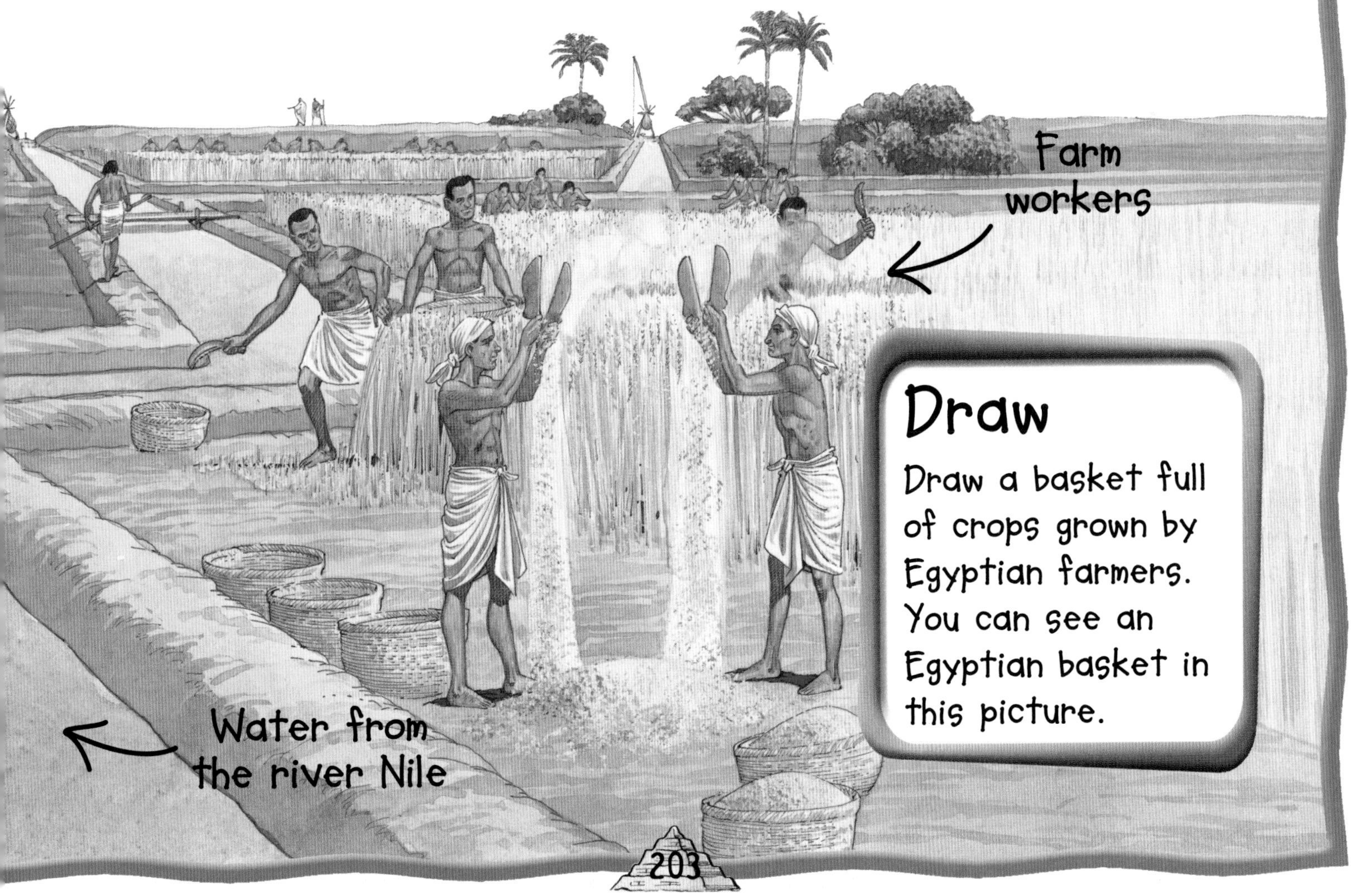

Draw

Draw a basket full of crops grown by Egyptian farmers. You can see an Egyptian basket in this picture.

Who had the best jobs?

Doctors, high priests or priestesses and government officers had the best jobs.

So did viziers. A vizier helped the pharaoh to rule the land. Next came the traders and craftsmen, such as carpenters and jewellers. Labourers and farmhands had the poorest jobs.

Who was head of the family?

In ancient Egypt the man was the head of the family. The eldest son was given all the land, property and riches when his father died. Women could also own land and property and get good jobs.

Little monkey!

Pet baboons were sometimes trained to climb fig trees and pick the ripe fruit!

Vizier checking grain

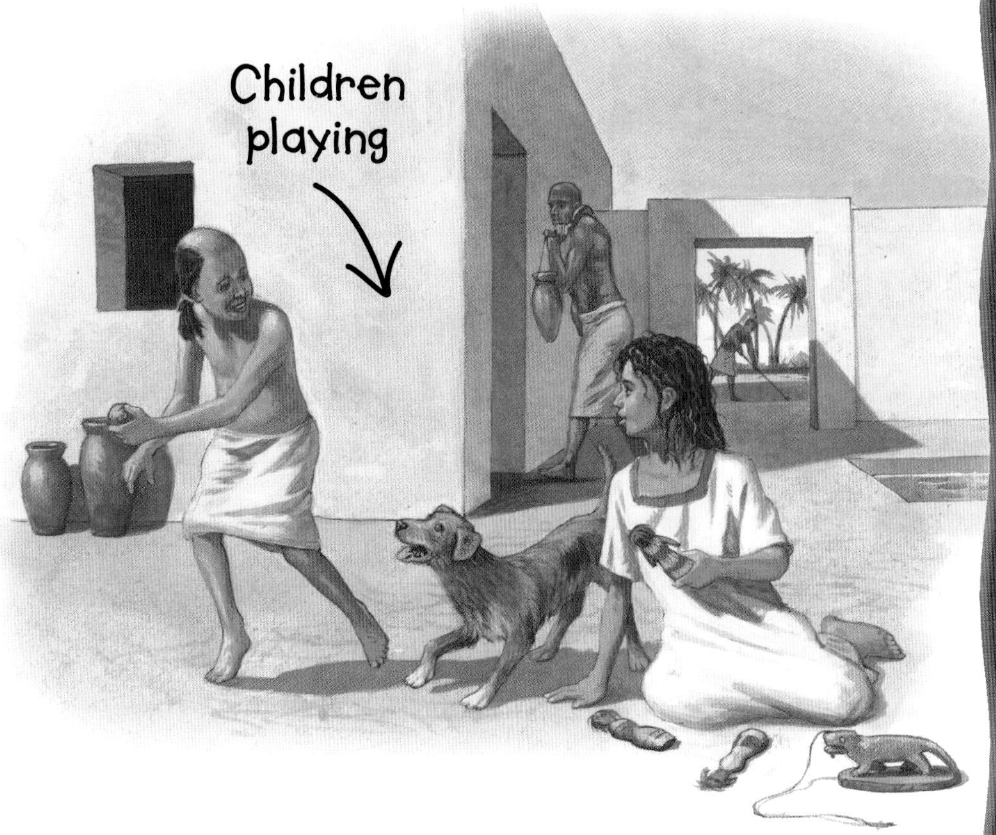

Children playing

What did children play with?

Children played with toys made from clay and wood. They had carved animals with legs and heads that could move. They also had spinning tops, clay balls, toy horses and dolls. Children played games such as leapfrog and tug-of-war, too.

Imagine

Imagine you are an Egyptian worker. Which job would you choose to do and why?

Who had the biggest houses?

Rich Egyptians lived in large country houses called villas.
Villas often had several storeys. Some had walled gardens with fruit orchards and a fish pond. Poor families often lived in one room. Many lived on crowded streets in the towns and cities.

How did the Egyptians cook?

Some ancient Egyptians cooked their food in a clay oven. Others cooked on an open fire. Clay ovens were made from baked clay bricks. Wood or charcoal were burned as fuel. Cooks used pottery saucepans with two handles.

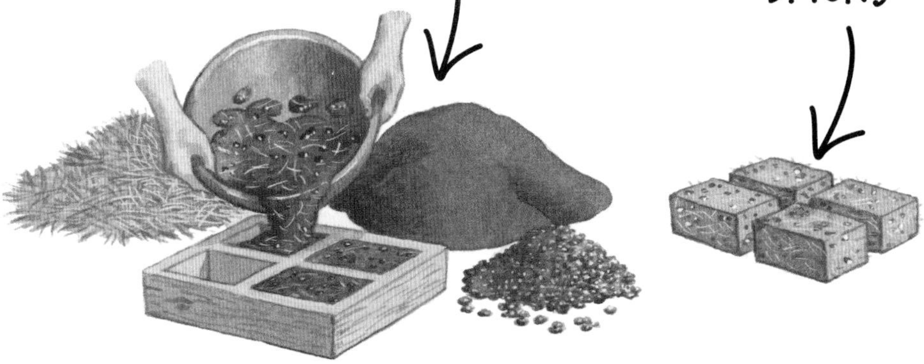

Were houses built with bricks?

Egyptian houses were built with bricks. Mud from the river Nile was mixed with straw and pebbles. The mixture was shaped into brick shapes and dried in the hot sun. Trunks from palm trees held up the flat roofs. Inside walls were plastered and painted.

Make

Mix clay with dried grass and pebbles. Put the mixture in an ice-cube tray. Let your bricks dry in the sun.

Sticky fingers!

Ancient Egyptians ate with their fingers. Rich people washed their hands between each dish. Their servants brought jugs of washing water for them.

Who shaved their hair off?

Both men and women shaved their hair off. They believed that this kept them clean. Men and women also wore make-up such as black kohl, which lined their eyes.

Fingernail paint and face powder were also used. Red colouring was worn on lips and cheeks.

Cosy toes!

Rich people wore shoes made with padded leather. Sandals were made of the grass-like papyrus plant. Poor people went barefoot.

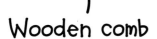

Did Egyptians ever wear wigs?

Rich Egyptians wore wigs made from human hair or sheep's wool. The wigs were kept in boxes held on stands. Egyptians also used hair dye. Girls plaited their hair into pigtails. Some boys wore a pigtail on one side.

Wigs

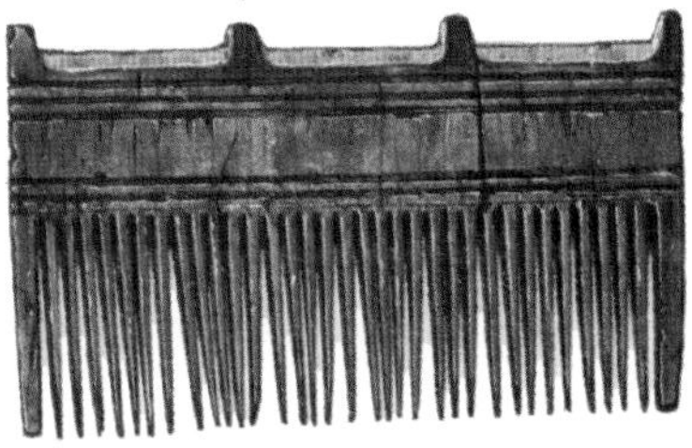

Wooden comb

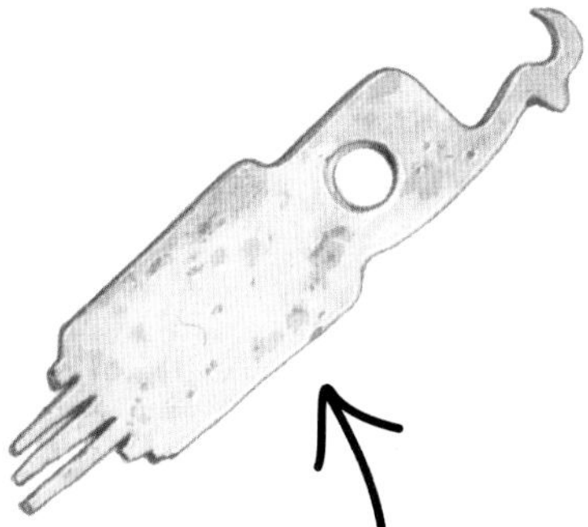

Ivory comb

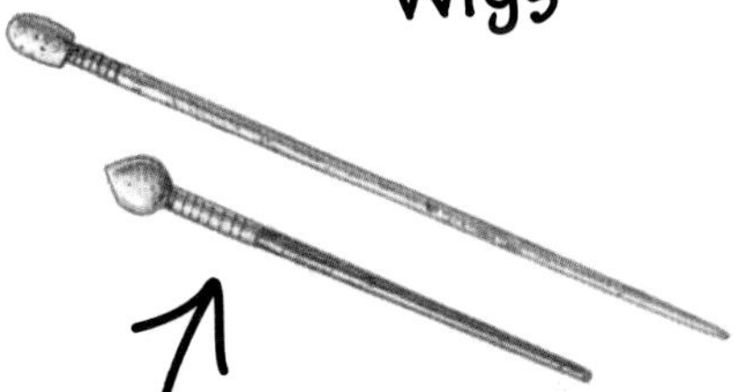

Hair pins

What was the fashion?

Rich women wore the best linen cloth with beads sewn onto it. The cloth was dyed in pale colours. It was made into long dresses and cloaks. Men wore long robes. They also wore cloths wrapped around the waist. These were tied in a knot.

Make

Draw an Egyptian wearing clothes and make-up. Use wool to make a wig. Glue this to the person's head.

Quiz time

Do you remember what you have read about Egypt?
These questions will test your memory. The pictures will help you. If you get stuck, read the pages again.

page 193

1. What guards the Great Pyramid?

page 195

2. Why were cats important?

3. Who was the boy king?

page 197

4. Which queen found a magical land?

page 196

5. What were mummies kept in?

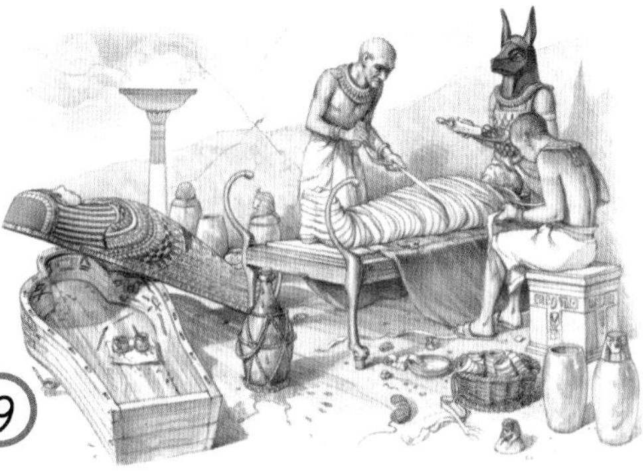

page 199

6. Who defeated Egypt?

page 200

7. What did farmers grow?

page 203

page 204

8. Who was head of the family?

page 205

9. What did children play with?

10. How did the Egyptians cook?

page 206

11. Who shaved their hair off?

page 208

12. What was the fashion?

page 209

13. Did Egyptians ever wear wigs?

page 209

Answers

1. The sphinx
2. Because they were holy
3. Tutankhamun
4. Hatshepsut
5. Mummy case or sarcophagus
6. General Ptolemy
7. Barley, grapes, dates, figs, melons, cucumbers, onions, leeks and lettuces
8. The man
9. Wooden or clay toys, spinning tops, clay balls, toy horses and dolls
10. With clay ovens or open fires
11. Men and women
12. Dresses, cloaks and long robes
13. Yes they did

Medieval questions about...

Knights and Castles

Why were castles built on hills?

People began building castles over 1000 years ago. They were built on a hill so that people could see the enemy better. The hill was made from a huge mound of mud and stones. It was called a motte.

Were all castles made from wood?

Early castles were made from wood. They were not very strong and they caught fire easily. People began to build stone castles. These were much stronger. They lasted longer and did not burn.

Stone castle

Slimy walls!

Builders often covered wooden castles with wet, slippery leather. This stopped them from burning so easily.

What was a moat?

Builders dug a big ditch around the castle. Then they filled it with water. This watery ditch was called a moat. Enemy soldiers got wet and cold if they attacked the castle from the moat. It was hard to fight from the bottom of it, too!

Think

Stone castles were a lot warmer in winter than wooden ones. Why do you think this was so?

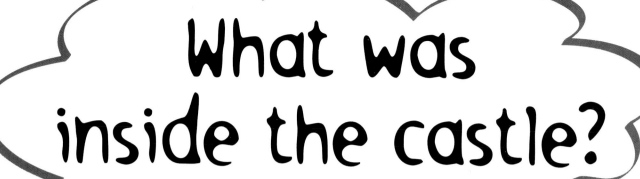

What was inside the castle?

A big courtyard was inside the castle. This was called a bailey. A thick wall was built all around it. Smaller buildings were put up inside the bailey. Sometimes there were gardens. There were often animals and chickens, too!

Where was the safest place?

The safest place in the castle was a tall, strong tower. This tower was called a keep. The lord of the castle lived there with his family. In later times they slept on the top floor. There were big rooms downstairs to hold feasts for visitors.

Thick walls!

The walls of the keep were at least 3.5 metres thick! This meant that building a castle took a long time. It was also a very expensive job.

How did people get bread and water?

A castle often had its own mill and bakery. Many castles got water from a well. The well was dug inside the bailey. A massive wheel drew water up into the castle. Later castles had piped water with taps.

Measure

The walls of the keep were 3.5 metres thick. Use a tape measure to see how thick this is.

What happened at knight school?

A knight had to train for 14 years! First, he went to a lord's house when he was seven years old. There, he was taught how to ride and to shoot with a bow. Then he became a squire and was taught how to fight with a sword.

Count

A nobleman's son went to knight school when he was seven. He studied for 14 years. How old was he when he became a knight?

Who had the best horses?

Rich knights owned three horses. The heaviest horse was used for fighting and in tournaments. The quickest was used for long journeys. The third carried the bags!

Dying for love!

Jaufre Rudel was a French knight. He sent love letters to the beautiful Countess of Tripoli, even though had never seen her! When he finally met her he fell into her arms and died!

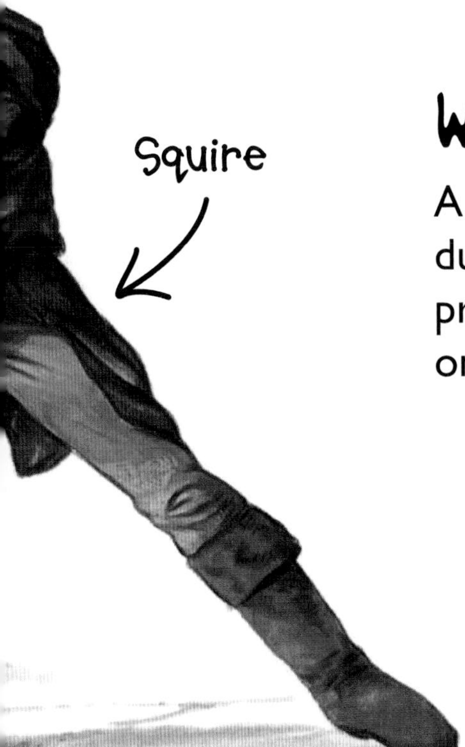
Squire

What was dubbing?

A new knight was given a special ceremony called a dubbing. First, he had to spend a whole night in church, praying on his knees. Then the new knight was tapped on the shoulder with a sword.

Did knights fight with a ball?

Knights hit the enemy with a spiked ball on a long chain. This was called a 'morning star'.

Knights used swords, too. Foot knights from Switzerland used a halberd. This was an axe with a hook on the back. It was good for getting a knight off his horse!

Get to the point!

Soldiers called 'retrievers' fetched all the fallen arrows. They had to run through the battle to get them!

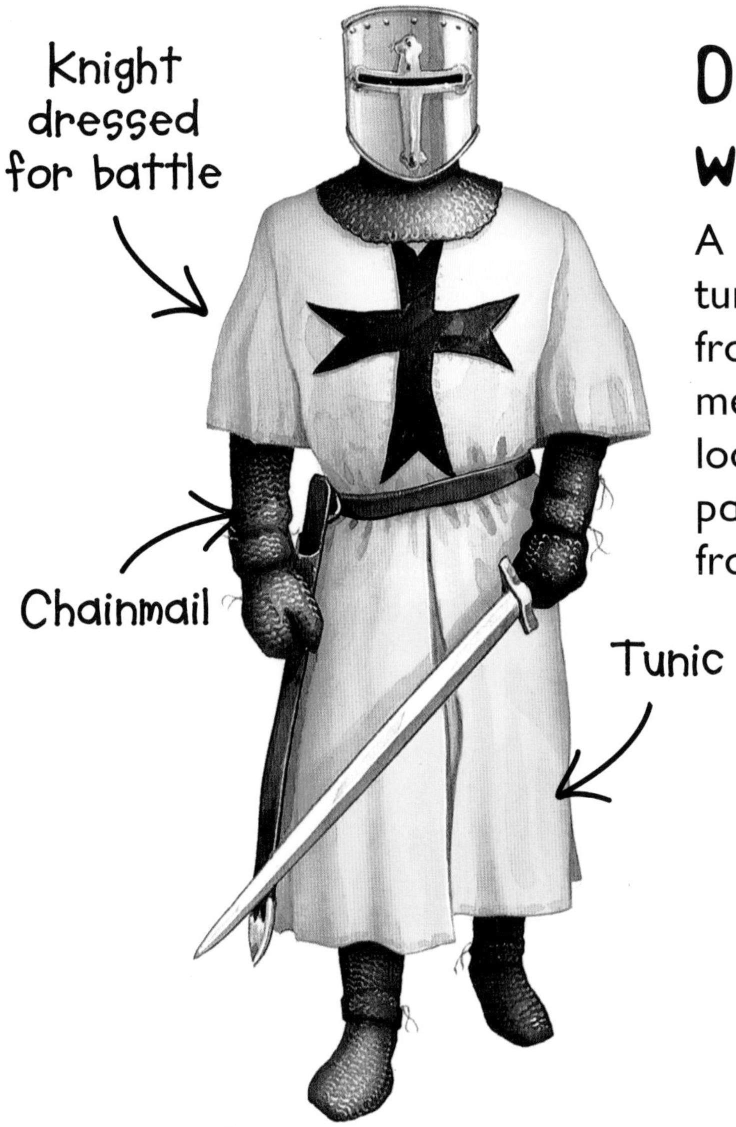

Did knights wear woolly jumpers?

A knight in early times wore a bright tunic with long sleeves. It was made from wool or linen. He also wore metal armour called chainmail. It looked and felt like knitted wire! A padded jacket stopped the chainmail from scratching the skin.

Design

In later times, knights wore steel armour. They even wore metal shoes! Design your own suit of armour to protect a knight.

How long was the Hundred Years War?

The Hundred Years War was fought between the English and the French. It actually lasted for 116 years, between 1337 and 1453. English and Welsh soldiers used longbows against the French. The bowmen could fire 12 arrows every minute!

How were knights told apart?

A knight wore a helmet that covered his head. Even his soldiers could not recognize him! Each knight put a special symbol on his shield and robes. The symbols and colours were called a 'coat of arms'.

Knight wearing coat of arms

Don't shoot the messenger!

Using a coat of arms was called 'heraldry'. This is because the lord's messenger was called a 'herald'. The herald wore his lord's coat of arms as he crossed the battlefield.

What was a herald?

A herald was a messenger. He carried messages for knights during battles. The herald had to be able recognize each knight by his coat of arms. The heralds were very good at recognizing coats of arms. This eventually came to be known as heraldry.

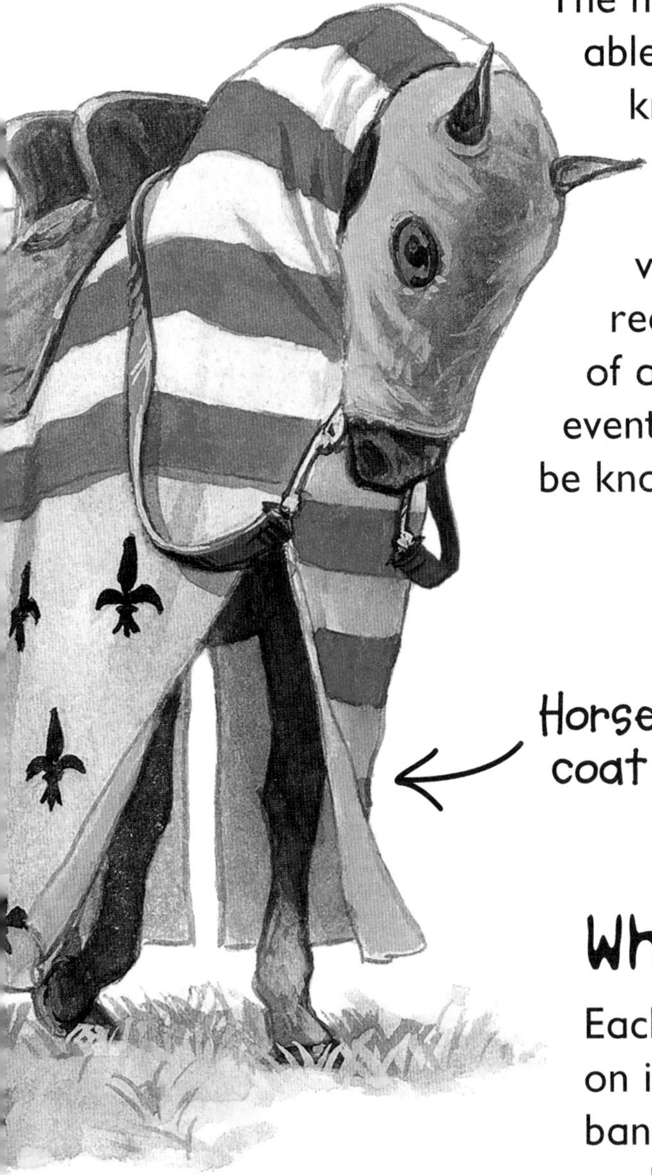

Herald

Horse wearing coat of arms

Where did soldiers meet?

Each lord had a banner with his coat of arms on it. Knights and soldiers gathered around the banner on the battlefield. The lord could then explain his battle plans. The winner of a battle often stole the enemy's banner from him.

Make

Draw and cut out a shield from cardboard. Paint your own symbol on it.

Did knights have fun?

Yes they did! Knights took part in competitions called tournaments. These helped them to improve their fighting. The knights formed two teams that fought each other in pretend battles.

Did knights only fight on horseback?

At a tournament, knights also fought on the ground. They wore heavy armour. Skill and speed were much more important than strength.

Make

Write and design a programme for a tournament. You can include fighting competitions and entertainment.

Rotten cheat!

Some knights tried to cheat in a jousting competition. They wore special armour that was fixed to the horse's saddle!

Knight taking part in a tournament

How did knights find a wife?

Ladies from the king's court went to tournaments. The knights showed off their bravery to their favourite lady. Each knight tried to push another knight off his horse with a long pole called a lance. This was called jousting.

Jousting knight

What was a siege?

People sometimes became trapped inside a castle if the enemy surrounded it. This was called a siege. The people inside could not get food supplies. So they had a terrible choice. They could either starve to death or surrender to the enemy.

Think

Try to think of ways to get into a castle without being seen. Look at the castle on page 216 to help you find a way in. Draw a map of your route.

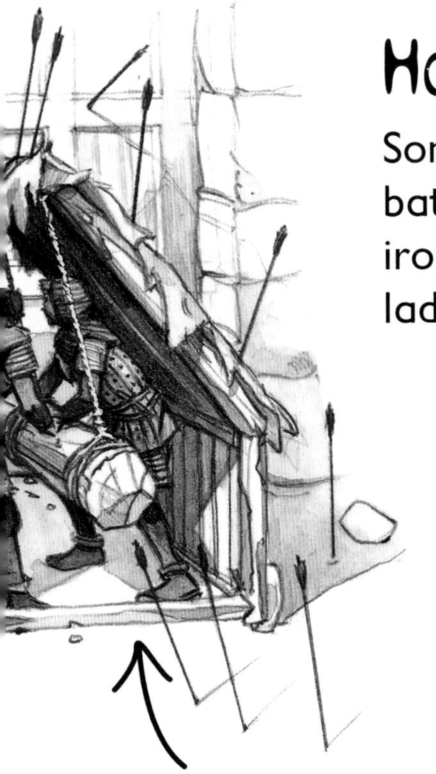

Battering ram

How did the castle crumble?

Sometimes the enemy bashed down the castle gates with battering rams. These were thick tree trunks capped with iron. The enemy also tried to climb the walls with giant ladders. Huge catapults hurled burning wood and stones.

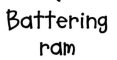

Hairy weapons!

Giant catapults were wound up with ropes made of human hair! The hair was made into plaits and was very strong.

Siege

How did enemies get inside a castle?

Sometimes enemy soldiers dug tunnels underneath the castle. They then popped up inside the castle walls. The enemy also pushed wooden towers against the castle walls. Soldiers hiding in the towers leapt out and climbed into the castle.

Quiz time

Do you remember what you have read about knights and castles? These questions will test your memory. The pictures will help you. If you get stuck, read the pages again.

1. Why were castles built on hills?

page 214

2. What was a moat?

page 215

3. Where was the safest place?

page 217

4. What happened at knight school?

page 218

5. What was dubbing?

page 219

6. Did knights fight with a ball?

page 220

7. Did knights wear woolly jumpers?

page 221

11. How did a knight find a wife?

page 225

8. How were knights told apart?

page 222

12. How did the castle crumble?

page 227

13. How did enemies get inside a castle?

page 227

9. What did people die from?

page 223

10. Did knights only fight on horseback?

page 224

Answers

1. So people could see the enemy
2. A watery ditch around a castle
3. The keep
4. Boys were trained to be knights
5. A special ceremony for a new knight
6. They fought with a spiked ball on a chain
7. No, they wore chainmail and tunics
8. By coats of arms
9. From disease, the Black Death
10. No, they also fought on the ground
11. When he was jousting
12. The walls were bashed with battering rams
13. They dug tunnels under the castle

Plundering questions about...

Pirates

What is a pirate?

A pirate attack

Pirates are people who steal from ships and ports. As soon as the first ships began to carry goods, pirates began to attack them. About 600 years ago, there were many pirates sailing on the seas and oceans around the world.

Hairy pirates!

'Barbarossa' was a nickname for two pirate brothers. 'Barbarossa' means 'Redbeard' – because they both had red beards!

Who was afraid of the Barbarossas?

Every sailor was afraid of the two Barbarossa brothers! They were pirates who attacked ships about 500 years ago. One of the brothers captured the town of Algiers in North Africa. The other attacked ships that belonged to the Pope, who was the leader of the Christian church.

Make

Make your own Barbarossa mask. Draw your pirate's face on card. Use red wool to make a big red beard.

Did all pirates want treasure?

Pirates from the Mediterranean were called corsairs. They didn't want treasure. Instead, they took people from ships and ports and sold them as slaves. Corsairs also captured rich people. They were paid a lot of money to release them.

Corsairs and their ships

Who stole the Spanish gold?

About 500 years ago, Spanish captains sailed to the Americas. There they found gold, silver and jewels. The Spanish stole it from the American people and took it back to Spain. Pirates often attacked the Spanish ships before they got home and took the treasure from them.

Act

Try to act out your own story about Spanish and English captains. One is trying to steal treasure from the other.

When were pirates not pirates?

English captains such as John Hawkins raided Spanish treasure ships. England and Spain were enemies at this time, so the English thought it was okay to steal from the Spanish. The captains wanted to be called 'privateers' instead of 'pirates'.

Pirate queen!

Queen Elizabeth I of England encouraged her sea captains to be privateers. However, the privateers were often robbed before they reached England!

Can you be a pirate with one leg?

Yes! Francois Le Clerc was a dangerous pirate with just one leg. In the 1550s, he raided Caribbean islands owned by Spain. He captured the port of Havana on the island of Cuba. No one would pay Le Clerc to give up the port, so he burned it to the ground.

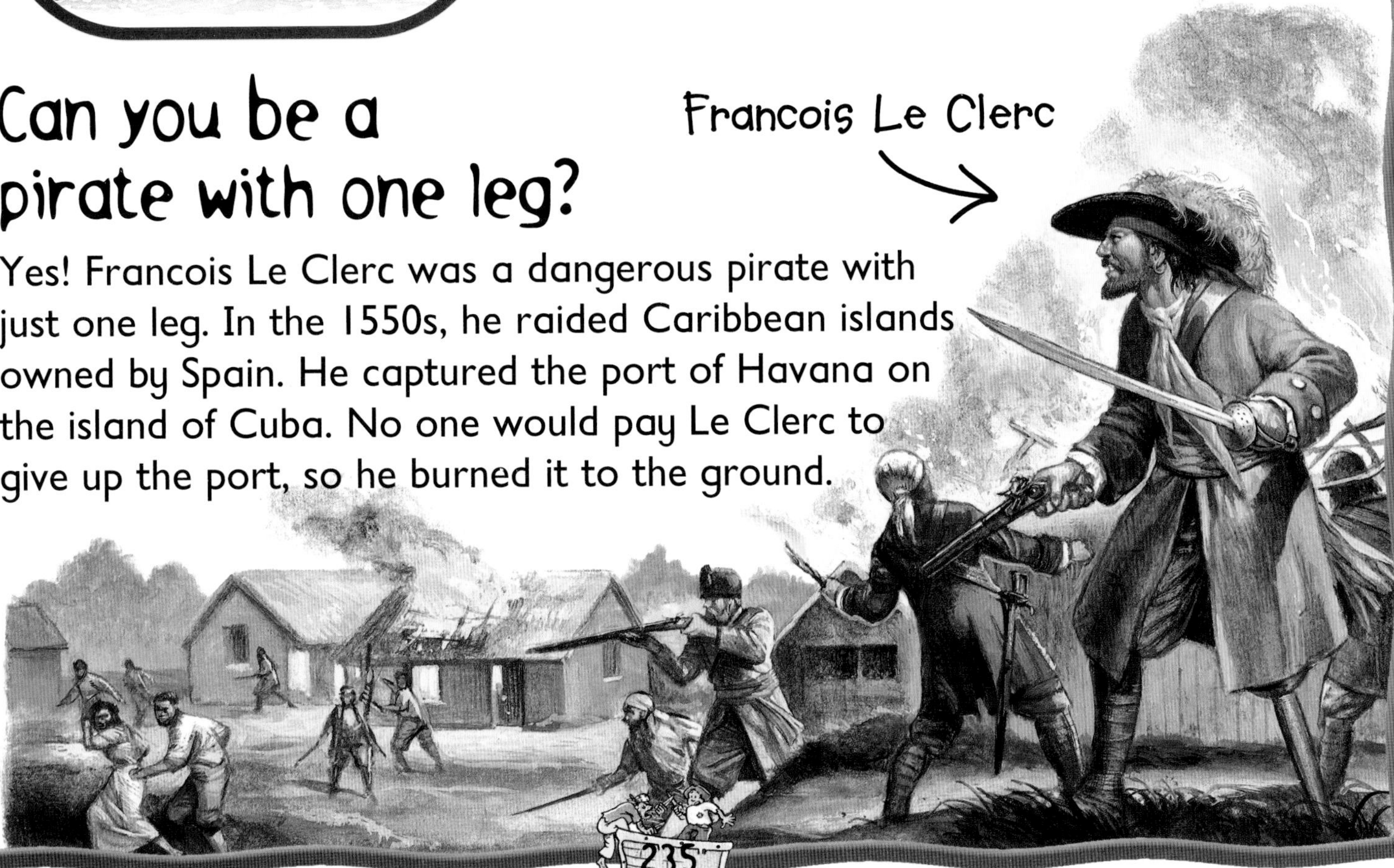

Did sailors fight the pirates?

Sailors fought hard against pirates when they were attacked. But they didn't try to fight Francis L'Ollonais in the 1660s. He was very cruel and tortured his prisoners. When Francis attacked a ship, the captain and sailors usually gave up without a fight.

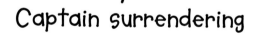

Captain surrendering

What did pirates do with their money?

Pirates sold their treasure to people at the docks. They usually made lots of money. Most of the money was spent in public houses!

Spend! Spend! Spend!

Pirates could spent 3000 pieces of silver in one night. That's about £45,000 in today's money!

Francis L'Ollonais

Where was there a pirate paradise?

Port Royal was a harbour on the island of Jamaica. A strong fort guarded the harbour. Pirates could even mend their ships in the docks. Jamaica was ruled by the English, who left the pirates alone.

Paint

Paint a pirate scene with ships and a port. There might be lots of ships, with the pirates carrying their treasure onto dry land.

Pirates in Port Royal

Could women be pirates?

Yes, they could! Mary Read dressed up as a man and became a sailor in the 1700s. Her ship was raided by pirates and Mary decided to join them. Her ship was raided by 'Calico Jack' and his wife, Anne Bonney. Mary made friends with Anne and they fought against the navy.

Mary Read and Anne Bonney

Make

Make a plate of food for a pirate's prisoner! Take a paper plate and stick on cut-out food – such as caterpillars!

Whose prisoners ate caterpillars?

Ching Shih was a Chinese pirate. In 1807, she controlled many ships that raided China's coast. Ching Shih was a great leader. She had very strict rules for her sailors. Her prisoners had to eat caterpillars in boiled rice!

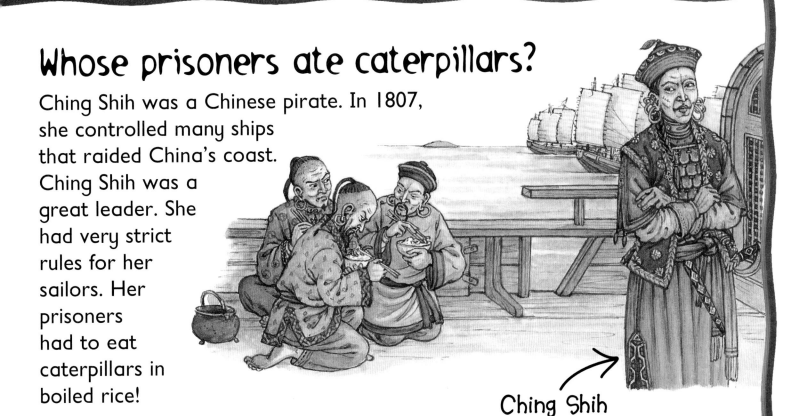

Ching Shih

Baldy!

Grace O'Malley shaved her head to look more like her sailors. She was given the nickname 'Baldy'!

Who said she was sorry?

Grace O'Malley went to sea when she was a young girl. She ended up controlling pirate ships off the coast of Ireland. Grace had 20 ships under her command. In 1593 Grace asked Queen Elizabeth I of England to forgive her for being a pirate.

What were the best ships?

Pirate ships had to be very fast! Many were small and easy to sail. Schooners were ships that had two masts. Corsairs sailed in galleys – ships that had oars as well as sails. The captain had a cabin in the stern (back of the ship). Treasure, gunpowder and food were stored in the hold, beneath the deck.

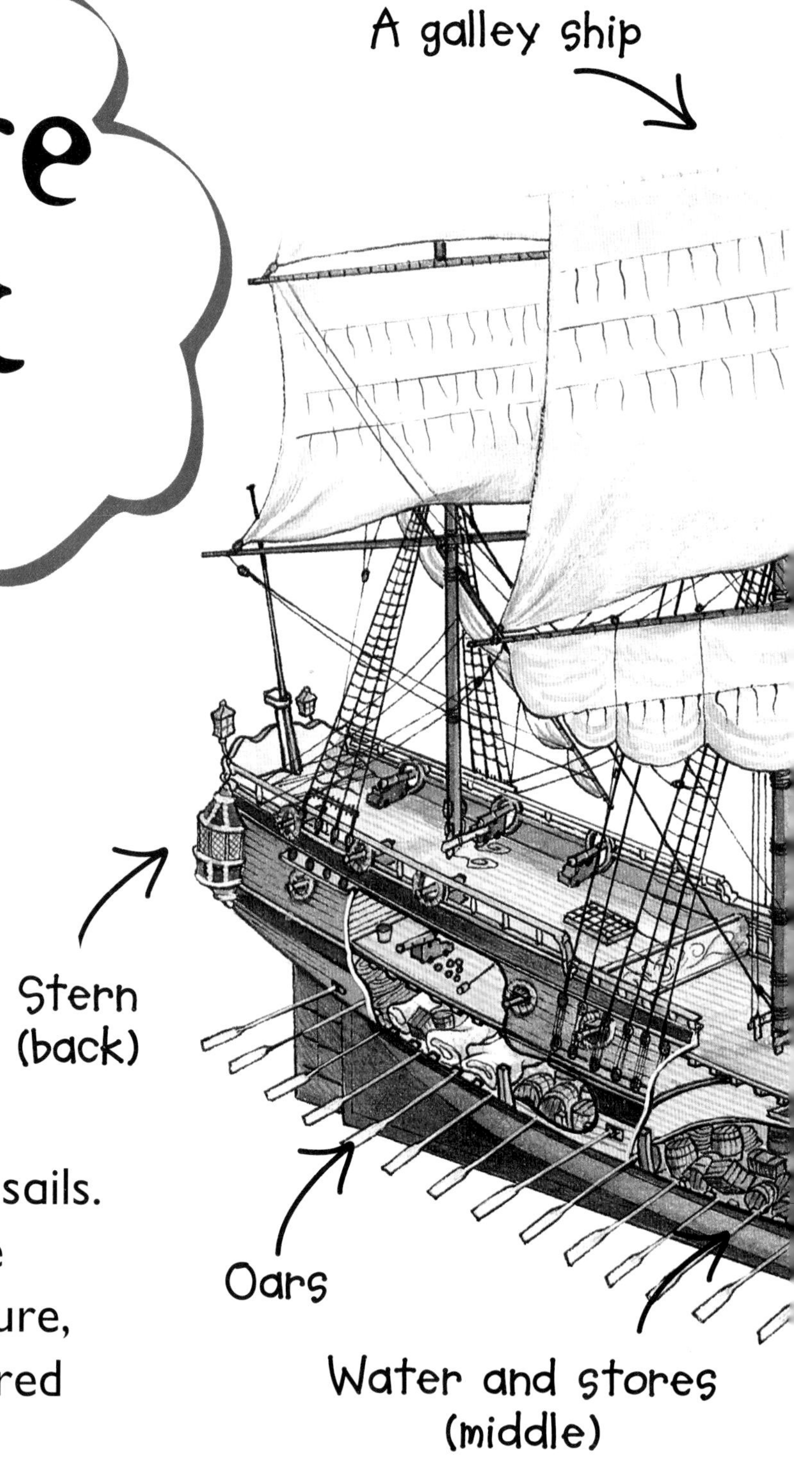

Where did pirates sleep?

Most pirates slept on the deck unless the weather was bad. Some put up hammocks below deck in the middle of the ship. It was cramped, smelly and noisy. This made some pirates ill. So did their food. They didn't eat enough fruit and vegetables!

Recycling!

Pirates even stole their prisoners' clothes! They usually sold them, but sometimes kept the best items for themselves.

Write

Look at the picture of the galley. Write a guided tour of the ship. Describe how the pirates lived on it, too.

What did pirates eat?

Pirates mostly ate dry biscuits and pickled meat when on board ship. They hunted for fresh meat when they landed on islands. They also collected fresh water and fruit. Pirate cooks often had only one arm or leg. They couldn't fight, so they cooked!

Who was afraid of a flag?

Merchant seamen were terrified when they saw the flag of a pirate ship. Early flags were bright red. By the 1700s, pirates flew black flags. Each pirate captain added his or her own symbol. Sometimes this was the famous white skull-and-crossbones.

Were buccaneers heroes?

Buccaneers were violent thieves. Some people thought they were heroes. Bartholomew Roberts was a buccaneer. His nickname was Black Bart. He was handsome and bold, yet he never drank anything stronger than tea! In the 1720s, he captured 400 ships.

Duck!

When pirates attacked a ship, they shot at sailors working on the sails. They also shot at the helm, the steering area of the ship.

Where was the treasure?

Sailors often hid their treasure. Pirates had to break down walls and doors to find it. They threatened their prisoners until they revealed the treasure. Pirates had frightening weapons such as knives, daggers and pistols.

Pirates looking for treasure

Design

Design your own pirate flag. Choose a bold colour. You could draw your own frightening symbol on it.

What was the best treasure?

Gold and silver was the best pirate treasure. It could be gold or silver coins, plain bars or made into fine ornaments. Silk cloth and hardwoods such as ebony were also valuable. So was ivory. But pirates were not so happy with cotton, coal or iron.

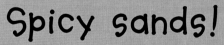

Pirates and their stolen treasure

Spicy sands!

Spices from India and Sri Lanka were very valuable, but they were difficult to sell. Pirates often dumped them overboard. These spices piled up on the beaches.

Was the treasure shared?

The captain was in charge of sharing out the treasure. Officers got more than ordinary sailors. The cook and the carpenter got less because they didn't fight. Captains tried to divide everything fairly. Unhappy pirates might attack the captain and take over the ship!

Make

Make a mini treasure chest. Take a small box and paint it to look like wood. Then fill it with painted cut-out jewels.

Where were all the jewels?

Pirates stole jewels from ships all over the world. Diamonds came from Africa. Red rubies and blue sapphires came from Burma. Green emeralds were mined in Colombia. Divers scooped up shiny pearls from the Persian Gulf.

Treasure chest

What were pirates scared of?

Shipwreck was a pirate's greatest fear. Terrible storms could blow up in the warm waters around the Caribbean, the Indian Ocean and the Far East. In 1712, a storm blasted Port Royal in Jamaica. Winds smashed ships to pieces.

Shipwreck

Telescope

Compass

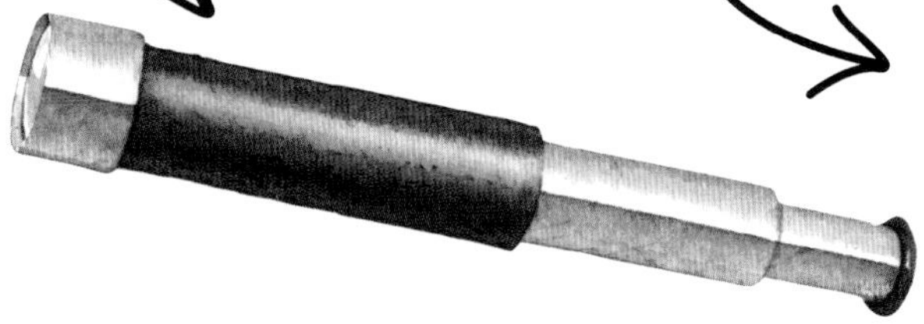

Map

How did pirates find their way?

Pirates used the position of the Sun and stars to guide them in the right direction. They also used a compass to help them. A telescope helped pirates to see landmarks and work out their position. Pirates used maps to find their way on land.

Write

Pretend you are captain of a pirate ship. Write down all the jobs that are carried out on board every day.

Round and round!

Captain William Dampier was a brilliant navigator. This means he knew where he was going! In the 1680s he sailed around the world three times.

How did pirates save a sinking ship?

Pirates tried to pump out water if the ship was leaking. Sometimes ships 'ran aground'. This means they got stuck in shallow water. The pirates had to throw out anything heavy. This helped the ship to refloat. Sometimes they threw out food barrels and cannons.

Who is Long John Silver?

Long John Silver is a one-legged pirate. But he isn't real! He appears in a book called *Treasure Island*. This adventure story is all about pirates and buried treasure. It was written by Robert Louis Stevenson in 1883.

Dancing pirates!

Blackbeard was a real and dangerous pirate. In 1798, his story was made into a ballet!

What ate Captain Hook's hand?

Captain Hook is a fierce pirate in a story called *Peter Pan*. It was written as a book and a play by J.M. Barrie in 1904. Peter Pan is the hero. He cut off Captain Hook's hand and fed it to a crocodile. That's why the Captain needed a hook.

Captain Hook

Did pirates sing?

Gilbert and Sullivan were famous songwriters. They wrote a musical about pirates in 1879, called *Pirates of Penzance*. But the pirates were softies! They wouldn't steal from orphans – children who had no parents – so everyone pretended to be an orphan!

Write

Write your own pirate story. Your pirates can be kind or cruel. They could be modern pirates. What would treasure be like today?

Quiz time

Do you remember what you have read about pirates?

These questions will test your memory. The pictures will help you. If you get stuck, read the pages again.

1. What is a pirate?

page 232

2. Who was afraid of the Barbarossas?

page 233

3. When were pirates not pirates?

page 235

4. Did sailors fight the pirates?

page 236

5. What did pirates do with their money?

page 236

6. Could women be pirates?

page 238

7. Whose prisoners ate caterpillars?

page 239

11. Where were all the jewels?

page 245

8. Where did pirates sleep?

page 240

12. How did pirates find their way?

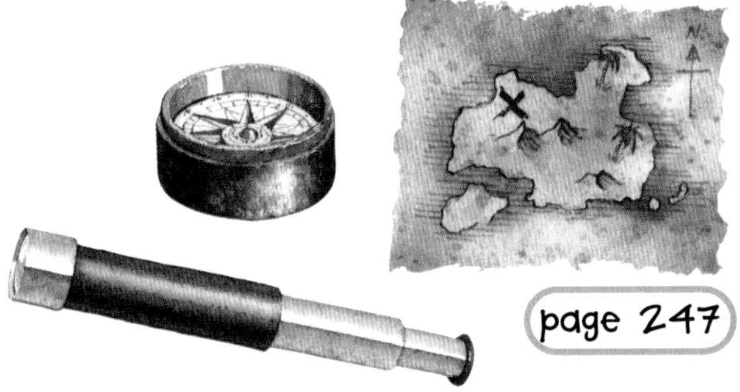

page 247

9. What did pirates eat?

page 241

13. What ate Captain Hook's hand?

page 249

page 242

10. Who was afraid of a flag?

Answers

1. A person who steals from ships and ports
2. All sailors
3. When they were privateers
4. Yes, sailors fought hard against pirates
5. They spent it in public houses
6. Yes, they could
7. Ching Shih's prisoners
8. On the deck, or below deck in hammocks
9. Dry biscuits and pickled meat
10. Merchant seamen
11. Jewels came from all over the world
12. With a compass, telescope and map
13. A crocodile

Index